The **UN**OFFICIAL X -Files COMPANION

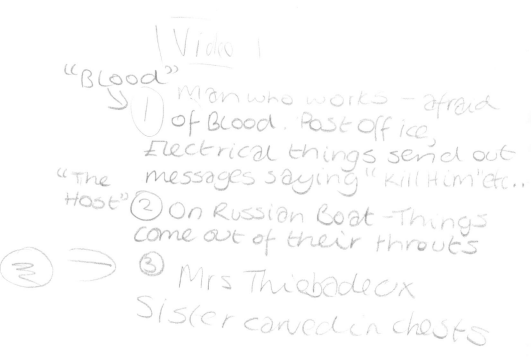

Video

"Blood" ① Man who works - afraid of Blood. Post office, Electrical things send out "The messages saying "Kill Him" etc..

Host" ② On Russian Boat - Things come out of their throats

③ → ③ Mrs Thiebadecx Sister carved in chests

The UNOFFICIAL X-Files COMPANION

An X-phile's Guide to the Mysteries,
Conspiracies, and Really Strange Truths
Behind the Series

BY N. E. GENGE

MACMILLAN

To J. H. Sainsbury,

*who believed in the value of
classical educations, curiosity,
and open minds. I miss you.*

First published 1995
by Crown Trade Paperbacks, New York

First published in Great Britain 1996 by Macmillan
an imprint of Macmillan General Books
25 Eccleston Place, London SW1W 9NF
and Basingstoke

Associated companies throughout the world

ISBN 0 333 65441 2

9 8 7 6 5 4 3 2 1

A CIP catalogue record for this book is available from
the British Library

Design by Lauren Dong

Printed and bound in Great Britain by
BPC Consumer Books Ltd
A member of
The British Printing Company Ltd

Contents

Season Two   BEYOND DEEP THROAT

SEPARATE MISSIONS

A PARTNERSHIP RENEWED

UNDER FIRE

Acknowledgments

A project like this requires the assistance of many wonderful people and I'm grateful for the opportunity to thank them publicly for the many things they've done privately.

For just the right reference at the right time, the generous people lurking among the stacks at the Queen Elizabeth II Library at Memorial University (St. John's), the medical library at the Health Science Center (St. John's), and the Raymond J. Condon Memorial Library and Resource Centre (Labrador City).

For help tracking down oddities across the Pond, the staff of the Victoria and Albert Museum and the British Library.

For good humor as well as much needed information, the Public Relations staff at the Federal Bureau of Investigation.

For help above and beyond duty's call, Ling Lucas and Ed Vesneske, Jr., good agents and even better people.

For all their help in bringing this odd collection together: Patty Eddy, Elke Villa, Adrienne Ingrum, Steve Weissman, Lauren Dong, Chris Pike, Laurie Stark, and my editor, Wendy Hubbert.

And, most importantly, for whatever sanity I have left, for unflagging support, for unconditional love, and for taking on the work of two parents and a housekeeper without having to be asked, Peter.

Introduction

Despite the indisputable success that has come to *The X-Files* —steadily rising ratings, a spate of cover stories from *TV Guide* to *People* to *Entertainment Weekly,* a flourishing grass-roots fandom—the show started out as a gamble. From the very beginning, it was a calculated risk that a program consistently creeping beyond comfortable stereotypes could make it past bean counters and focus groups to an audience that had yet to even ask for it.

"It is an action show, right?"
"Well, sometimes."
"And it's got aliens, right?"
"Uh . . . yes, sometimes."
"It does have a male and female lead?"
"Yes."
"Good, so it's not some ensemble male-bonding thing."
"Uh, no—"
"Sort of a Twilight Zone *meets* G-Man?"
"Sort of."

The X-Files had none of the instantly identifiable factors that create smashes. There was no well-known, craggy-jawed male lead, no leggy blond partner draped over his shoulder. And creator Chris Carter had no intention of providing them, of pandering to outdated formulas. He'd even fought the sci-fi and horror labels that draw in aficionados desperate for *anything* in their favorite genre. Despite his unsettlingly short list of previous credits, Carter had a clear, driving vision for this program, and it was solidly in place. It remained to be seen whether others would share that vision and whether the combination of a smart woman and a sensitive guy chasing giant parasites and little green men across the country would capture America's attention—if America was even *home* on Friday nights.

Early word, from publications like *Entertainment Weekly,* was "This one's a goner." Considering that "speculative fiction" programs like *Highlander, Forever Knight,* and the newly renovated *Star Trek* universe were already being pumped into homes every week, *The X-Files* in its first season was looking for a piece of a well-sliced pie. How many sci-fi/horror fans could there be, and, more importantly, how fickle was that audience? With the exception of *Star Trek: The Next Generation,* no modern speculative fiction program had broken the third-season barrier. And what the networks wanted was something with the staying power of *Murder, She Wrote.* A sort-of-horror/sort-of-science fiction/sort-of-drama just didn't fit the profile. In fact, if *The X-Files* followed the sci-fi pattern, its shelf life would be shorter than mayonnaise.

Still, Gallup polls claimed that better than 40 percent of Americans believed they were "not alone" in the universe, the viewing habits of the X generation were still a mystery to the industry, and Americans remained fascinated by anything vaguely New Age. Maybe it *was* worth a try.

For those watching *The X-Files* creep up the rating charts, the first season finale came a little too quickly. Despite steady growth, at the end of season one, the Neilsons dubbed *The X-Files* merely a "mid-range show." A core of loyal viewers tuned in weekly, but were they enough to carry it through a second season? According to those magic people called marketing specialists, the answer was "Yes!" By breaking the raw numbers down into demographics, they'd begun illuminating what made *The X-Files* and its fans different, and why a show that finished only 102 out of 118 rated programs should be continued.

True, *The X-Files* wasn't even nipping at the heels of classics like *Murder, She Wrote,* but while it had fewer supporters, those supporters had important qualities marketers couldn't ignore. X-Philes were bright, usually well-educated, white-collar workers who were still young enough to spend any loose change in their pockets. They were in an age group that was as difficult for advertisers to capture as it was for network programmers to understand. More importantly, those fans were *talking* about the show. They gathered almost religiously at office water coolers on Monday mornings, couples watched the show before starting the weekend's social rounds, VCRs whirred, and on-line groups sprang up on all major computer networks. Store owners were faced with consumers looking for nonexistent *X-Files*-related merchandise. Local television stations racked up an unprecedented number of calls asking if the show had been renewed. Buzz, that self-propelled groundswell of popularity, is advertising's Holy Grail, and *The X-Files* had it.

Now, could it last? Once again, the failure of so many other speculative fiction shows to maintain their momentum hung specterlike around *The X-Files* and eyes everywhere turned back to those all-important numbers.

Ratings for the summer season swiftly convinced any non-converts that something unusual was happening. A show airing nothing but reruns was gathering more fans, vocal fans as capable of discussing production technique and an episode's literary background as the admittedly tantalizing physical attributes of its lead actors. These self-declared X-Philes included the cream of our university populations, lawyers, technicians, scientists, celebrated artists, and, yes, even agents of the FBI. Perhaps for the first time in the history of television, fans identified with one another because they weren't couch potatoes!

The second season presented special challenges for cast and crew, not the least of which was the high expectations of its viewers: fans who now had even more viewing options. To carve out its own space in the line-up, *The X-Files* was up against a veritable explosion of otherworldly programs, including the very show that had been one of its influences. *Twilight Zone* was back, joined by newcomers *Star Trek: Voyager, SeaQuest DSV, Babylon 5,* and *Earth 2.* The sci-fi pie was starting to look like a tart.

At a time when *The X-Files* could have been forgiven for seeking any advantage to set itself above the competition, a curious thing happened. Instead of trying to attract viewers with grandstand acting or the latest twist in special effects, *The X-Files* built on its own strengths. Writers dug deeper into what terrifies and intrigues us, scripting claustrophobic stories that had fans hanging on the most subtle of clues and expressions before gasping through the commercials. In episodes like "Humbug," "Ascension," and "Irresistible," David Duchovny and Gillian Anderson would display an unmatched range of talent without ever, even once, sacrificing the integrity of the characters they'd created. Behind the cameras, directors and crew sought and found new ways to impress their images on the viewer's mind. The rules were being established. *The X-Files* would find its place, but not by tossing the leads in bed during Sweeps Week or appealing to some theoretical lowest common denominator among its audience.

With a theme like "The Truth Is Out There" and descriptions "ripped from the headlines," viewers may have hoped for snippets of real-life mystery, but little else on TV could prepare them for so meticulous a blending of fact and fiction that they lost sight of where the story left off and skillful research began. The seamless integration of writing, acting, and stylistic elements created so complete, so internally realistic a package that, regardless of how bizarre an episode's content, fans were left wondering . . . what if? It was during the second season, as *The X-Files* really hit its stride, that tour guides at the FBI's Washington Bureau began hearing "Can we see the X-Files?" from visiting students, that affiliate stations were swamped with mail, and journalists scrambled to get celebrity interviews.

When the second season closed, a Golden Globe proclaimed *The X-Files* to be the season's best drama. Of course, X-Philes already knew that. Somehow, the brainy woman and the flawed hero had captured our imaginations—along with various mutants and aliens. For forty-eight minutes a week, X-Philes sat glued to their sets; for much of the 10,032 minutes between installments, we played "what if" games. Before long, X-Philes were gathering as much media attention as *The X-Files.* Far from being the Elvis-spotters the press had suggested would form the show's following, X-Philes were gaining a reputation for curiosity, for discrimination, and for native intelligence—unusual qualifications for membership in the ranks of a television fandom.

Just as learning the difference between character and actor can heighten appreciation of a performance, so too can an understanding of all the pieces that must come together to make the finished whole more satisfying. To that end, in the pages that follow we will introduce you to the actors as they want to be known, nail down those tantalizing theories that fly so easily from our favorite agents, challenge you with trivia, and hope you'll chuckle with us on those occasions when, despite the best of intentions, something slipped past all those talented people. Enjoy!

Season One

THE DEEP
THROAT YEARS

Case #: X-1.01-091093

Monday 18th April

Code Name: "The X-Files: The Pilot"

CASE SUMMARY

Agent Dana Scully, newly assigned to a controversial division and given tacit instructions to evaluate the work of an older and more experienced agent, immediately finds herself involved in a case unlike anything she'd been prepared for in school. Dragged clear across the country to investigate what her new partner claims are alien abductions, she's given something to think about when an exhumed body has some unusual features. Whether a hoax or something more unworldly, this case is the first to test the new team.

DEEP BACKGROUND

Forty Seconds of Curiosity

Start with a bang. Whether your product is television, hair tonic, or the latest suspense novel, you've got to catch your audience before you can sell them anything. *The X-Files*, which packs more wallop into its forty-eight minutes of airtime than almost any other program, takes that advice to heart. Even the credits pull you in with a montage of images that seems to beg for an explanation.

In the approximately forty seconds it takes to scroll through the names of the creator, writer/producers, director, leads, and guest stars, *The X-Files* flashes no less than ten separate images at viewers—and only a few are of the leads. There's barely enough time for the first picture to strike the retina before the next demands your attention. While the curious pictures, along with the prerequisite spooky music, certainly pro-

EYEWITNESS STATEMENT

So, who did you tick off to get stuck with this detail, Scully?

—Mulder, "The X-Files: The Pilot"

vide an adequate backdrop for the credits, they also touch on the major themes explored by this unique program.

If you'd somehow managed to miss all the media attention, never seen an episode, and defied the statistics by belonging to a circle of friends that *didn't* include an X-Phile, the opening image, with its classic flying saucer and the "FBI Photo Interpretation" overlay nearly hidden in the corner, would tell you you'd stumbled onto something unusual. The FBI and UFOs—together?

Better not think on that too long though, not if you want to give yourself half a chance to decipher the pictures yet to come. Were those lei lines or some sort of peculiar radar scope glowing under the pointing hand? And what was that ball? "Government Denies Knowledge" Of what? Though opening credits are designed to provide information (while satisfying the Guild), *The X-Files'* montage seems intended to present more questions than answers.

Perhaps the image that lingers longest is the softly glowing blue hand with its single red bone. A stylized picture reminiscent of the Kirlian photography once hailed as proof of psychic auras, it's certainly representative of *The X-Files'* frequent excursions into areas as mysterious as UFOs but considerably more human. The falling white silhouette—another classic of the paranormal fields, indicative of the Near Death Experience—has, since the events of episodes like "One Breath," "End Game," and "Død Kalm," become more appropriate than was anticipated when the pilot was assembled.

The static ball, a smaller version of the ones that school kids use to treat themselves to really bad hair days at museums, is another striking image. As much fun for adults as children, they're still squarely within the field of science, an area Scully isn't about to abandon without more than Mulder's scattered theories.

Enjoyment of any episode of *The X-Files* demands the active engagement of the viewer's brain. While we can trust its creators to build on the promise of their credits, to drag us through the tangled web of federal politics, to scare us and intrigue us, there's only one question arising from the credits that we'll never have answered: Why *do* Mulder's and Scully's signatures look so very much alike?

The *X-Files'* Timeline

The X-Files, unlike most episodic series, doesn't have a show bible to keep track of all the backstory and character history dredged up from the minds of its creators each week. Concerned that the bible could stifle their creativity or limit how an "X-File" could be defined,

An electrostatic generator: the latest version of the lava lamp.

In this episode, Mulder asks Scully to perform an autopsy on Ray Soames's body. Oddly enough, Ray Soames's headstone appears in future episodes on the other side of the country. Watch for it!

the crew relies on their own memories, creator Chris Carter's guidance, and a lack of freelance writers to keep the program consistent on internal details from week to week.

Overall, that seems to have worked out just fine, but, as writers are more inclined to remember words than numbers, it's not surprising that the odd discrepancy has crept into *The X-Files'* internal timeline. Ever wonder how long Scully was missing after Duane Barry abducted her? Or how long it takes to wrap up a case? Ever find yourself wondering why two such interesting characters never seem to have private lives? Warm up your fingers and follow along with the timeline that would be in the show bible, if there was one.

Date	Key Events (in X-time)
October 11, 1960	Fox Mulder is born.
January 22, 1964	Samantha T. Mulder is born.
February 23, 1964	Dana Scully is born.
November 27, 1973	Samantha T. Mulder is abducted from her home. Though Mulder claimed to have been twelve at the time, he must have been thirteen. Oops.
October–December 1988	Mulder graduates from Quantico and is almost immediately assigned to the VCS (Violent Crimes Section) where he writes the profile leading to the capture of serial killer Monty Props.
September 16, 1989	John Irvin Barnett, the subject of Mulder's very first case, "dies" in prison.
March 7, 1992	Special Agent Dana Scully joins the FBI's X-Files division.
March 22, 1992	Scully and Mulder wrap up their first case, # X-1.01-091093, fifteen days later.
EXACT DATE UNKNOWN	Case # X-1.02-091793, "Deep Throat"
July 23, 1993	On concluding case # X-1.03-092493, "Squeeze," Mulder and Scully have Tooms remanded to a psychiatric institution.
August 9, 1993	Though "The Jersey Devil," case # X-1.05-100893, airs *after* "Conduit," it precedes that episode in internal X-Files time.
August 26, 1993	Case # X-1.04-100193, "Conduit"
September 26, 1993	The X-Files team is assigned to case # X-1.06-102293, "Shadows."

Date	Key Events (in X-time)
October 5, 1993	"Shadows" wraps up.
October 24, 1993	Mulder and Scully take on an alien of a different sort in "Ghost in the Machine," case # X-1.07-102993.
November 7, 1993	Case # X-1.08-110593, "Ice," opens.
November 11, 1993	"Ice" wraps up, but *after* Mulder and Scully are confined to a quarantine period.
EXACT DATE UNKNOWN	"Space," case # X-1.09-111293
EXACT DATE UNKNOWN	"Fallen Angel," case # X-1.10-111993
EXACT DATE UNKNOWN	"Eve," case # X-1.11-121093
EXACT DATE UNKNOWN	"Fire," case # X-1.12-121793-11214893
EXACT DATE UNKNOWN	"Beyond the Sea," case # X-1.13-010794
EXACT DATE UNKNOWN	"GenderBender," case # X-1.14-012194
EXACT DATE UNKNOWN	"Lazarus," case # X-1.15-020494
EXACT DATE UNKNOWN	"Young at Heart," case # X-1.16-021194
EXACT DATE UNKNOWN	"E.B.E.," case # X-1.17-021894
March 7, 1994	On the anniversary of Agent Scully's assignment to the X-Files, "Miracle Man," case # X-1.18-031894 opens.
EXACT DATE UNKNOWN	"Shapes," case # X-1.19-040194
EXACT DATE UNKNOWN	While no dates were given for case # X-1.20-041594, "Darkness Falls," it's difficult to believe that this case and four others could be completed between March 7 and March 27—considering Scully and Mulder were hospitalized for injuries incurred as a result of this case.
EXACT DATE UNKNOWN	"Tooms," case # X-1.21-042294
March 27, 1994	"Born Again," case # X-1.22-042994-40210 begins.
April 19, 1994	The final notes for "Born Again" are jotted into Mulder's field notes.
April 25, 1994	"Roland," case # X-1.23-050694
May 8, 1994	Case # X-1.24-051394, "The Erlenmeyer Flask"
May 11, 1994 (approx.)	The X-Files division is closed.
August 1994 (approx.)	Reopens three months later.
EXACT DATE UNKNOWN	"Little Green Men," case # X-2.01-091694
EXACT DATE UNKNOWN	"The Host," case # X-2.02-092394
EXACT DATE UNKNOWN	"Blood," case # X-2.03-093094

1. Spooky.
2. Medical doctor.
3. Sunflower seeds, a taste he shares with his father.
4. Fox.
5. Samantha.
6. Silk. See the pilot.
7. "The following story is inspired by actual documented cases." "Inspired" is the keyword here and was never meant to lead viewers to believe there was an X-File division in the basement of the J. Edgar Hoover Building. The X-Files is not a real FBI division, there are no real X-Files, and the incidents in each episode are only loosely based on anything approaching reality. The show is pure entertainment.
8. Monty Props.
9. "I Want To Believe."
10. "Einstein's Twin Paradox: A New Interpretation."

YOUR SCORE: 7

Fill in your trivia scores as you go, then check your total and compare it to the master score table at the end (p. 224) to see if you're FBI material.

Date	Key Events (in X-time)
EXACT DATE UNKNOWN	"Sleepless," case # X-2.04-100794
EXACT DATE UNKNOWN	"Duane Barry," case # X-2.05-101494
EXACT DATE UNKNOWN	"Ascension," case # X-2.06-102194
EXACT DATE UNKNOWN	"3," case # X-2.07-110494
EXACT DATE UNKNOWN	"One Breath," case # X-2.08-111194
November 11, 1994	"Firewalker," case # X-2.09-111894 opens.
November 13, 1994	As "Firewalker" is wrapped up, Mulder and Scully are supposedly confined for a thirty-day quarantine. How they managed to squeeze in *three* more cases before November 14 is something of an X-File in itself.
EXACT DATE UNKNOWN	"Red Museum," case # X-2.10-120994
EXACT DATE UNKNOWN	"Excelsis Dei," case # X-2.11-121694
EXACT DATE UNKNOWN	"Aubrey," case # X-2.12-010695
November 14, 1994	"Irresistible," case # X-2.13-011395, is opened —and solved—by two agents who won't get out of their "Firewalker" quarantine for another *twenty-nine* days!
EXACT DATE UNKNOWN	"Die Hand Die Verletzt," case # X-2.14-012795
EXACT DATE UNKNOWN	"Fresh Bones," case # X-2.15-020395
Jan. 16, 1995 (approx.)	"Colony," case # X-2.16-021095
February 3, 1995	"End Game," case # X-2.17-021795
EXACT DATE UNKNOWN	"Fearful Symmetry," case # X-2.18-022495
EXACT DATE UNKNOWN	"Død Kalm," case # X-2.19-031095
EXACT DATE UNKNOWN	"Humbug," case # X-2.20-033195
EXACT DATE UNKNOWN	"The Calusari," case # X-2.21-041495
EXACT DATE UNKNOWN	"F. Emasculata," case # X-2.22-042895
March 17, 1995	"Soft Light," case # X-2.23-050595 Banton's first victim is known to have died on March 17. If, as claimed by Mulder, the X-Files' team is brought in five weeks later, "Soft Light" officially started on April 21— *after* "Anasazi."
March 31, 1995	The third "Soft Light" victim dies.
EXACT DATE UNKNOWN	"Our Town," case # X-2.24-051295
April 10, 1995	"Anasazi," case # X-2.25-051995

Monday 25th April

Case #: X-1.02-091793

Code Name: "Deep Throat"

When a missing pilot's wife calls in the FBI, Mulder and Scully are pitted against the considerable resources of a restricted air base. Despite the warnings of a modern-day Deep Throat, Mulder remains determined to find out what (or who) is responsible for the strange lights inside the base's air space—and why a distinguished pilot can't remember how to fly! Caught during his first attempt at infiltration, Mulder's fate hangs on Scully's willingness to ignore the rule book.

Area 51—The Forbidden Country

Even on government-issue maps, there's a curiously featureless section simply labeled "Area 51." According to these maps, all creeks stop at its borders, no roads exist inside it, and the topography is uniformly flat. A little investigation would reveal Area 51's true status as a remote section of the high-security facility Nellis Air Force Base.

Like the fictional research facility called Ellens Air Force Base in this episode, Area 51 is an awfully well-protected piece of worthless real estate. However, Area 51 and Nellis AFB are *real*. It's here that many believe we'll find the remains of a UFO that crashed in Roswell, New Mexico.

Area 51 is both the best and worst kept secret of the past few decades. Everyone knows it's there. With prominent security signs warning visitors to keep off, and further injunctions to keep all cameras and videotape

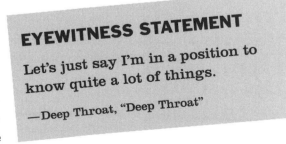

EYEWITNESS STATEMENT

Let's just say I'm in a position to know quite a lot of things.

—Deep Throat, "Deep Throat"

7

recorders pointed away from what's behind the extensive fencing, it would be hard to deny that there's *something* in there.

Area 51, Dreamland, Skunk Works, The Ranch, whatever you choose to call it, isn't much to look at, at least not from the few vantage points that haven't been gobbled up by its expanding borders. A few buildings, a three-mile runway, and a lot of telecommunication dishes are all that's visible. Yet this is the place where the U-2 was developed and tested, the same place where the SR-71 spy plane that would fly over Cuba in the 1960s was quietly brought into existence. It's also the home of the Stealth bomber, a project the government was still vigorously denying months *after* photos of the new plane were distributed.

Despite Area 51's history of covert aeronautical research, and the fact that everyone knows just where to look, it's difficult to confirm any reports of bizarre lights in the sky, strange noises emanating from the test site, or the few blatant claims that UFOs regularly fly over it. Area 51 is but a tiny piece of the sprawling New Mexico test site, no part of which is accessible by the public. Groom Mountain provides an imposing physical barrier to one side and the remaining approaches require hours of travel over open desert terrain.

When something is so openly hidden, people get curious. When, as happened in 1984, someone turns up a document claiming that a Project Aquarius, run by an organization known as Majestic 12 (aka MJ-12), recovered alien technology flying across the New Mexico sky as early as 1972, people get downright determined to discover what's going on. However, as has always been the case at Area 51, no one would talk.

The National Security Agency (NSA) was quick to acknowledge the existence of a Project Aquarius, and was just as swift in its denial that it was, in any way, related to UFOs. What exactly Project Aquarius is remains something of a mystery, and mysteries breed even more questions to stir up the love/hate relationship the public already had with a facility whose expanding borders often meant land grabs.

With many public queries and no official answers forthcoming, the sudden appearance of a Mr. Bob Lazar caused quite a stir among the many people actively trying to discover what was happening in Dreamland. Here was a man who not only claimed to have worked at the secret installation, but who seemed eager to describe everything he'd seen and heard for the public and on the record. On a New

Mexico news program, Lazar claimed to have worked in S-4, just outside Area 51, and to have examined no less than nine extraterrestrial spacecraft. Top Hats, the Standard Floor Model, and the Sports Coupe were just a few of the names Lazar gave to the crafts he'd seen.

His descriptions, matching those of observers in such widely scattered areas as Germany and Argentina, rocked both skeptics and believers. Skeptics were impressed by Lazar's gall in claiming not only to have seen extraterrestrial craft, but to have *touched* them. Believers began flooding back to the few available lookouts near

Area 51

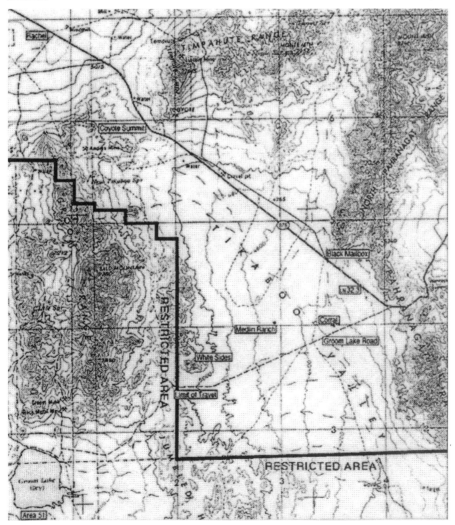

The X-Files is seen in over sixty countries, sometimes in its original English version, but often dubbed into the local language.

In Taipei, Taiwan, and the Republic of China, it airs as *X-Dang An*. "The Uncanny Files of the FBI," *Akte X-Die Unheimlichen Faelle des FBI*, airs in Germany, Austria, and neighboring Switzerland. Of course, Switzerland also airs the French version, *Aux Frontières du Réel*, "At the Borders of Reality." In Sweden, 'Philes watch *Arkiv X* while, across the border, the Finns crowd around the tube to await *Salaiset Kansiot*, "The Secret Files."

Area 51. They hung on Lazar's every word. If he was legitimate, here was the first positive sign that all the speculation, all the hours spent peering across the desert from Freedom Ridge, all the effort expended on a paper-trail search through thousands of documents under the Freedom of Information Act, had been more than the work of "delusional minds."

If Lazar was legitimate.

Years later, it's still in question.

Lazar claims to have degrees from several universities; they claim he's never attended or graduated from any of their programs. He claims to have worked at another high-security facility, Los Alamos; they categorically deny his story. Even the hospital where he was born seems unable to prove a Bob Lazar ever existed. That's been enough for those anxious to yell "Hoax!" and move on; for those that can't quite put the images Lazar had painted out of their minds, it's been yet another beginning, another search for the truth.

Careful digging has brought up information that refused to fit the official declaration that Bob Lazar was a liar. In the Los Alamos Test Facility's in-house phone directory of 1982, Lazar's name sits right where he claimed it would, among those of other scientists and technicians. Yet the administration of Los Alamos remains firm in its stand that no Lazar *ever* worked there. An interview from the same year, from a Los Alamos newspaper, clearly lists Lazar as a resident of the area, a physicist at Los Alamos, and an aficionado of jet cars. It's not much, but enough to keep researchers listening.

If Lazar is telling the truth, this is the first crack in a silence that has lasted half a century. Perhaps the watchers on Freedom Ridge won't have to go to the mountain after all. Maybe what's in there will come to them.

The Original Deep Throat

By threading unresolved but real events from American history through its stories, *The X-Files* has managed to add a second, more subtle, layer of reality to its fictional world. Unlike UFO sightings or the mutants decorating tabloid covers, regular reports of real-life government coverups and misconduct are difficult for even the least credulous viewer to completely shrug off. When *The X-Files* dubbed its anonymous source "Deep Throat," it deliberately connected the show's fictional FBI to the Watergate scandal, a move that couldn't fail to evoke tales of interagency rivalry, murky allegiances, and "terminal prejudice." Without a single line of dialogue, this new

Deep Throat lent mystery, danger, and even an odd sort of authenticity to the events unfolding on screen.

For those old enough to remember the events of 1972, the opportunity to discover the identity of even a fictional Deep Throat was irresistible. Images of reel-to-reel tapes, secret signals, and shadowy meetings in bizarre locations were tantalizing reminders that at least part of what they were seeing had once been well within the realms of possibility. For those too young to remember the paranoia that had seeped outward from the nation's capital, they were about to discover one of America's most enduring mysteries.

Sometime in May or June of 1972, G. Gordon Liddy, a former FBI agent, along with James McCord and E. Howard Hunt, both "retired" CIA officers, arranged the installation of wiretaps in the Watergate offices of President Richard Nixon's opposition in the Democratic National Committee: Chairman Lawrence O'Brien and then-party official Spence Oliver.

Just as Mulder would later sit listening to sexually charged discussions in the episode "Little Green Men," a real FBI agent, Alfred C. Baldwin III, had listened to literally hours of wiretapped phone conversations through Oliver's line. Unknown to Baldwin at the time, he probably wasn't even listening to official calls of the DNC offices. Instead, the calls he monitored so carefully appeared to have been from a high-class call-girl operation catering to the upper echelons of political circles, including congressmen and senators. For some reason, O'Brien's tap, which should have been providing corroborating material, never seemed to work properly.

On June 16, in the process of repairing the bugs and copying files, McCord and his hired helpers were caught. Their plan, conceived in the office of then-Attorney General John Mitchell, funded by political contributions, and carried out by government agents at President Nixon's request, had blown up in their faces.

Into the middle of this stepped Deep Throat, a mysteriously well-informed source who is now credited for providing the essential information that allowed *Washington Post* reporters Bob Woodward and Carl Bernstein to crack the Watergate coverup. Despite the reliability of his information, however, Deep Throat's anonymity cast a sinister air over his involvement, leaving the door open to further questions.

In many post-Watergate books, Deep Throat is portrayed as a high-ranking member of the intelligence community, probably CIA, a man with a military background, a man who'd learned the fine art of political diversion. Instead of a "friend" of *The Post* and Woodward, this Deep Throat is a savvy political animal who, knowing *The Post*'s open hatred of Nixon's administration, used that paper to steer attention toward the White House and away from CIA involvement in a prostitution ring that could itself be a part of an intricate intelligence operation. It's a ploy that *The X-Files'* own Deep Throat could applaud and, if correct, one that's withstood two decades of concentrated investigation.

The similarities between the real and fictional man include minute details as well as broad strokes. In their book, *All The President's Men,* Bernstein and Woodward outline some of the intricate signaling procedures used to contact their "precariously placed" source, procedures instantly recognizable by any X-Phile. Bernstein and Woodward shifted flower pots about, turned yellow garbage cans upside-down on fire escapes, and considered the notion of using drapes as signaling devices. Fox Mulder shone blue lights from his windows or taped Xs on the glass. Like the real Deep Throat, Mulder's source liked to leave messages in newspapers. Through means that even Woodward never discovered, the real Deep Throat would intercept Woodward's *New York Times* and leave contact times inside. Luckily for Mulder, who received cassette tapes as well as notes within the pages of his papers, no one seemed as interested in his newspaper as Woodward's neighbors were in his copy of the *Times.*

Even after the disappearance of *The X-Files'* Deep Throat, the character's influence continues. *The X-Files* no longer needs complex set-up scenes or long verbal diatribes to establish that hidden forces are at work. Deep Throat's death proved that beyond a doubt.

Case #: X-1.03-092493

Code Name: "Squeeze"

CASE SUMMARY

While tracking Eugene Victor Tooms, a mutant serial killer with a knack for squeezing up drains and down chimneys, Scully is caught in a tight professional position between two other determined agents. On one side is Tom Colton, classmate and FBI mainliner who shares her preference for earthly explanations; on the other is Fox Mulder with his compelling, if impossible, evidence, and his acceptance of a basement-office career path. Will a successful conclusion to this case require her to abandon her beliefs?

Fingerprints: Nature's ID Codes

DEEP BACKGROUND

If serial killer Eugene Victor Tooms had crawled out of his nest more often—or read the newspaper before shredding it—he'd have known how far criminology had come since the days when fingerprints had to be *physically* brought to the lab.

STRANGER THAN FICTION

Like most new and emerging technologies, fingerprinting was neither automatically nor enthusiastically embraced by the judicial system. Judges, law enforcement officers, and prison personnel couldn't believe the swirls and ridges were unique, that *everyone* was naturally coded. It seemed too good to be true.

Once the distinctive nature of fingerprints was proven, inevitable resistance came from a public that suddenly realized their anonymity could be forever lost and their lives

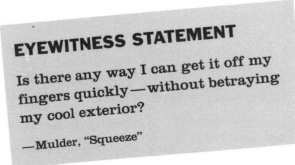

EYEWITNESS STATEMENT

Is there any way I can get it off my fingers quickly—without betraying my cool exterior?

—Mulder, "Squeeze"

If you'd actually like to hear Doug Hutchison (Tooms) speak a full sentence, you might check out some of his other work:

The Lawnmower Man (1992)
The Chocolate War (1988)
Fresh Horses (1988)

Doug Hutchison, who played cannibalistic Eugene Victor Tooms, is a real-life vegetarian. He sent Chris Carter a nice big cow's liver after his performance.

To date, Tooms's is the only case Mulder and Scully have had to tackle twice.

irrevocably tied to a few ink blots. A full decade passed before restrictions on how fingerprint collections could be used finally satisfied both law enforcement agencies and civil libertarians. Even if Tooms had been caught back then, his fingerprints—all ten inches of them—would likely have ended up in some hobbyist's collection instead of a police file. They were legal, but few people knew how to properly record them, and the public retained their suspicions.

In a case of life imitating art, it was through a fictional piece by the popular Mark Twain that fingerprinting first caught the average American's imagination. *Pudd'nhead Wilson* was written in 1894 and is probably the first North American literary example of the criminalist's new tool at work. The title character, Wilson, a man of no spectacular ability or intellect, kept glass slides of his guests' fingerprints simply because he found them curious. No one was more surprised than he when his bizarre collection became the center of attention during a police investigation. Twain's widely read story is often credited with being a better PR piece than anything the police could have conceived. Without a doubt, it educated an entire generation of criminals to the value of gloves. Too bad Eugene was napping at the time.

Across the Atlantic, Scotland Yard established its original fingerprint lab in 1901, and the fledgling division eagerly awaited its chance to gain fame by providing the instrument to catch some notorious criminal. Alas, such was not to be. In 1902, one year before Tooms killed his upstairs neighbor, Harry Jackson gained his fifteen minutes of fame as one of the first criminals ever convicted on the basis of fingerprint evidence. His crime? He'd stolen a set of ivory billiard balls.

However, glory would eventually come to Scotland Yard's avid young technicians, both in the courts and in dozens of stories and novels, all turning on the smudge of a single finger. Of course, even if Tooms had been real, he'd have been snoring it off beneath Exeter Street before any of those books made their way to the United States.

ENTER THE FBI

Two important events in law enforcement history occurred in 1911 and, though no one knew it then, together they'd alter the face of criminal prosecutions in the United States forever. In September 1911, while still in high school, Cadet John E. Hoover entered ROTC Company B and decided *not* to become a minister. That same year, fingerprint evidence was upheld in a United States courtroom for the first time. The two events, seemingly separate, came together in 1924 when the young man who'd been Cadet Hoover became Director J. Edgar Hoover of the newly formed Federal Bureau of Investigation.

Though the technology came to be accepted in the intervening years, without a central agency where *all* fingerprint records could be made available to police officers in every state, the information was useless. Whatever else Hoover may or may not have been, he understood the value of information and fought hard to gain control of the vast network of criminal information attached to the Fingerprint Files.

Prior to being housed at the FBI, American fingerprints came under the auspices of Correctional Facilities. Inmates, naturally less than committed to law and order, were forced to maintain a fingerprint card index as part of their repayment to society. Needless to say, many cards were conveniently lost. Even after the records were put in the hands of people somewhat more dedicated to the identification and arrest of criminals, it wasn't easy. Hundreds of man-hours were required to match a single crime scene print to a record.

Unfortunately for Tooms, by 1933, when he next crawled out of his cocoon, fingerprint records were under the control of an agency that could not only gather them from across the country, but redistribute them just as quickly, thanks to the Yard's Henry Battley, who created the ideal file system in 1930. Even though the science was still new, it was a fashionable sort of newness and Tooms's print would have been retrieved with near-religious dedication.

Tooms must have gone back to sleep early in 1963. Otherwise, he couldn't have failed to see headlines announcing the arrest of Reverend Martin Luther King's assassin. Though Hoover, still director of the FBI, had distrusted King the reformist, the Bureau's Fingerprint Files had been thrown open to identify the partial print found on his killer's rifle.

While the mutant hibernated, the FBI instituted the Automated Identification Division System, which would spawn associated systems across the country and inspire NCIC, the central system connecting all the rest. By 1986, 178 million prints were on file at the FBI, and the fingerprint section was beginning to specialize in retrieving prints from a multitude of surfaces. Visible prints — formed by dirt or blood, for example — or three-dimensional prints, formed from soft surfaces, could now be photographed directly. Latent fingerprints, not ordinarily visible, could be brought out by dusting techniques when the surface is hard, and by chemical techniques when the surface is porous.

Today's fingerprints are identified on the basis of agreements in a significant number of individualities, commonly known as "points." These are the bifurcations, ending ridges, and dots in the fingerprint pattern. If sufficient points are found with spatial relationship to other points, a basis exists for identifying a fingerprint. It was formerly considered necessary to have twelve points to identify a fingerprint, but in current practice, with better collection processes, a lesser number is often used. Even palm, foot, and partial prints can be presented in court.

Fingerprints have been lifted from human skin, the interior of chemically treated pools, and even more difficult surfaces like rock and brick. Future advances will bring up older prints, provide more portable laser and ultraviolet lights to make sure no prints are missed, and, with the growing number of children being printed, provide a wider pool of raw data. If our fictional mutant had managed to elude Mulder and Scully in the present, when he next emerged, in 2023, he'd likely have found out that even gloves were no assurance against identification.

Just a small snack . . .

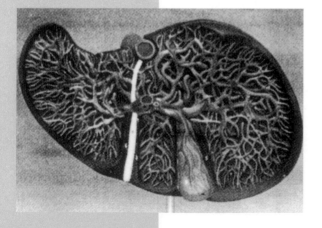

Case #: X-1.04-100193

Code Name: "Conduit"

CASE SUMMARY

When Ruby Morris disappears from the family's campsite and her mother claims she was abducted by aliens, no one but Mulder is listening—until her young son's doodles perk up the collective ear of the National Security Administration. Mulder, thoughts of his own missing sister prodding him, is convinced that Kevin is the key to recovering one, if not both, of the missing girls. He isn't about to let even Kevin's suddenly wary mother stand between him and the truth.

DEEP BACKGROUND

Abduction!

Without physical evidence, the case for UFOs, abductions, and alien visitations depends heavily on the veracity of eyewitnesses and precise reporting. In thousands of communities worldwide, dedicated watchers await a phone call, news flash, or, more frequently now, e-mail reporting a sighting in their area. Their equipment, be it Geiger counter or tape recorder, is always ready. Their cars, backed in to save precious seconds, are never low on gas and many watchers can beat firefighters into the meticulously arranged clothes by their bedsides.

While such intense preparedness appears to border on the obsessive, UFO watchers have little choice. They've realized that regardless of the sheer mass of testimonials they collect, or how reliable their witnesses, those reports will never reach some mysterious critical mass whereby the thousands of reports already on hand suddenly coalesce

EYEWITNESS STATEMENT

I knew that if I screamed loud and long enough that someone would listen. But I never expected the FBI.

—Darlene Morris, "Conduit"

17

into respectability. Even the most famous UFO cases, involving ordinary people with nothing to gain by wild fantasies, present difficulties when viewed objectively.

BETTY AND BARNEY HILL

In September 1961, a very ordinary couple, Betty and Barney Hill, were driving back through New Hampshire after a relaxing holiday. A rapidly moving light overhead caught their attention. They stopped to train a pair of binoculars on the odd object, but it streaked out of sight. With nothing more than a glimpse of light, which could have been anything, the two shrugged off the incident and continued.

Betty and Barney Hill

They'd gone only a short distance when the light returned, dogging their progress until they stopped. A circular craft hovered above them. Figures moved behind blue-tinted windows. Intrigued, Barney left the car and moved closer, wary but unafraid—until wings abruptly snapped out to either side. Though nothing alarming appeared, no high-pitched humming threatened an imminent laser blast, Barney found himself, panic-stricken, racing back to the car almost before he was aware of moving. When he looked back, the craft was gone.

Though they wasted no time getting home, and their brief stops had taken only minutes, the Hills arrived two hours later than they should have.

Over the next few days, Betty's dreams were haunted by bizarre images of abduction scenes. Those two missing hours loomed larger. Finally, desperate and afraid, she sought out the assistance of a hypnotist to fill in the lost time, and took her husband with her.

Like Mulder, the therapist the Hills eventually found was a believer in the value of hypnotic regression who quickly arranged for both separate and joint sessions. Dr. Benjamin Simon was the recorder of their incredible tale. Their matching stories revealed a dramatically different version of events than that accepted by their conscious memories.

The Hills didn't stop their car on sighting the UFO the second time. The car stalled. The craft, which had hovered above them, settled to the ground and that's when the aliens appeared. They eased the couple from their car, across the road, and up a ramp into the UFO.

Inside, they were separated and, in a scene familiar to anyone who watched Mulder re-create Scully's abduction or Duane Barry relive his memories, were subjected to what's best described as "sampling." Before they were permitted to leave, Betty Hill was shown a shimmering, three-dimensional star map. At the aliens' urging, she studied it carefully and, under hypnosis, was later able to replicate it. The Hills were released shortly thereafter and Betty was already back in the car when Barney suddenly awoke and found himself running.

Peculiar as this all sounds, the Hills' separate stories were, when compared, internally consistent on detail.

The map, the only "tangible" from their encounter, was turned over to an amateur astronomer who thought perhaps she could find a match between this configuration and the configurations known to humans. Five years later, she did. She concluded that, according to the map, the Hills had encountered natives of the Zeta Reticuli system and either 1) the aliens were going to Zeta Reticuli or 2) humanity would one day go to that system.

The story was released to the public several years later when *Look* magazine serialized the events and John Fuller's popular *Interrupted Journey* hit bookshelves. The book was eventually adapted into a film titled *The UFO Incident* and, in 1975, a "fictionalized but based on fact" version of the lives of an ordinary postal employee and his equally ordinary wife, a social worker, was beamed into homes all over America.

The Hills' story made for great television, but how seriously should the UFO community take it? Without making any moral judgments, and strictly on the basis of an even standard for all scientific investigations, the Hill case leaves something to be desired. Simply put, its credibility was based on some gross assumptions.

ASSUMPTION 1: HYPNOTIZED PEOPLE ARE INCAPABLE OF LYING.

False. While the majority of hypnotized people don't lie, the majority of *non*hypnotized people don't lie either. People under the influence of hypnosis can lie and have done so. Some have even devised wild schemes like tacks in their shoes to fool the machines. They can and have recalled a memory of a memory instead of the original incident, and they have been completely unresponsive to control items when the examiner *knew* the subject knew the correct response. *If* the Hills had been attempting to perpetrate a hoax,

TRIVIA BUSTER 4

Easy Stuff: Give yourself 1 point for each correct answer.

1. What two numbers did Kevin use to create his pictures?
2. What did the bartender have tattooed on his arm?
3. What was it about Darlene Morris's camper trailer that caught Mulder's eye?
4. What was the name of Darlene Morris's missing daughter?
5. To what department did Mulder send Kevin's pictures?

Getting Tougher: Give yourself 2 points for each correct answer.

6. What is Samantha Mulder's date of birth?
7. What was the address of the Mulder family residence at the time of Samantha Mulder's abduction?
8. Name the lake Mulder described as a UFO hotspot.
9. What was the number of the Morrises' campsite?
10. What is Samantha Mulder's middle initial?

they'd given themselves plenty of time to get their stories straight. Only one of them drew a map.

ASSUMPTION 2: THE THERAPIST BELIEVED WHAT HE WAS HEARING.

False. Though professional ethics kept him silent until the case had been publicized and his own reputation was brought into question, Dr. Benjamin Simon did record his own opinion *after* the film was released. Betty Hill, who'd been terrified by stories read to her by her sister, had abduction nightmares *prior* to the "encounter" in New Hampshire. On awakening from those nightmares, she'd turned to the nearest person, her husband, and, in the darkness of their room, built for him images of her terrifying dreams. In Dr. Simon's opinion, Barney was merely regurgitating the words of a particularly eloquent wife. A respected member of the medical community, Dr. Simon spent hundreds of hours with the couple before rendering his personal judgment that, like thousands of other people, Mrs. Hill was expressing a frightening fantasy within a safe environment.

ASSUMPTION 3: THE MAP REALLY WAS A MAP.

Although an astronomer had spent years on the project, she was, in fact, a school teacher for whom astronomy was a hobby, an amusement. Even she quickly admitted that the match in her analysis of Mrs. Hill's map and Zeta Reticuli was one of many possibilities. Another astronomer, Donald Menzel, actually proved statistically that *any* set of circles and lines reduced to a two-dimensional image could match *something* out there.

If the Hill case won't bring UFOlogy into the respectable sciences, within it can be seen common story threads recognizable to even the most casual followers of UFO history. These threads are used to great effect in fictional accounts like this and other episodes of *The X-Files*.

So accepted into popular culture have the details of alien abduction scenarios become that even viewers with no interest in UFOlogy can't fail to recognize them. The bright lights, the floating figures of Duane Barry and Samantha T. Mulder, the paralyzation of a younger Fox Mulder, and the pseudo-memories that even an adult Mulder with a psychology degree can't sort out—all hark back to the classic abduction case. It was a series of bright, moving lights that first attracted the Hills' attention. Both Betty and Barney reported weightlessness as they were loaded onto and released from the flying saucer. Their muscles seemingly being frozen was the first sensation they reported under hypnosis.

The X-Files, which makes no bones about the fictional quality of its work, has freely incorporated whatever elements of the body of abduction literature that could push their stories forward. But for serious students of paranormal phenomenon, incidents like the Hill case present a chicken-and-the-egg dilemma: Are all abduction stories similar because they're *all* the result of media hype and fiction that recycles the old stories? Or, as abductees claim, are there similarities in fiction because of the reality of alien abductions?

Though we've yet to assemble a full address, Scully's apartment number is 402. Her building number, 1419, is the model number for IBM's early zebra code reader.

Personnel Dossier
#121-627-161

Name:	**Dana Katherine Scully**
Position:	Special Agent, DOJ,
	Federal Bureau of Investigation
Currently Assigned:	The X-Files
FBI ID #:	2317-616
Contact #'s:	(Home) 202-555-6431
	(Cellular) 202-555-3564

Personal Information

DOB:	February 23, 1964
Height:	5'2" Hair: Red Eyes: Blue/Green/Hazel
Marital Status:	Single/Never Married/No Dependents
Parents:	Father—Captain Jim Scully (deceased)
	Mother—Margaret Scully
Siblings:	Two brothers (one older, one younger) are both unremarkable. Older sister, Melissa, known to entertain certain "New Age" philosophies.
In Case of Emergency:	Notify—Margaret Scully (mother)
	Religious Affiliation—Roman Catholic (N.B.: A Living Will is on file.)

Educational Information

Agent Scully completed an undergraduate degree in physics from the University of Maryland before completing a medical degree.

ASTROLOGICALLY SPEAKING . . .

Scully is a Pisces—a sign supposedly prone to fantasy, dreaming, and a firm belief in all things paranormal. How ironic.

PISCES

QUALITY: **Mutable.**
ELEMENT: **Water.**
KEY PHRASE: **I believe.**

DESCRIPTION:
The Piscean has a truly open mind; the capacity to believe and understand a wide range of human experiences.

POSITIVE CHARACTERISTICS:
Compassionate, sympathetic, emotional, sacrificing, intuitive, introspective, musical/artistic.

NEGATIVE CHARACTERISTICS:
Procrastinating, talkative, melancholy, pessimistic, emotionally inhibited, timid, impractical, indolent.

Graduated FBI Training, Quantico, in 1992.
(N.B. Maintained open relationship with Instructor Jack Willis during training.)

Work History (chronological)

Completed Medical Residency
Assigned Quantico Training Facility, Instructor
Assigned X-Files, Field Agent (March 6, 1992)
Reassigned Quantico Training Facility, Instructor
Reassigned X-Files, Field Agent

Supervisory Notes (chronological)

1. It is the hope of this department that Agent Scully, coming from, and to all appearances more dedicated to, a more "traditional" scientific approach, will be able to properly assess the quantitative value of Agent Mulder's work, while observing that agent's general deportment and state of mind.

2. During a recent interview, our debriefing agent had cause to believe that assigning Agent Scully to the X-Files may not have been as well advised as originally thought. While this agent continues, in general, to adhere to the criminal investigation techniques outlined as optimal by this office, a tendency to "open-mindedness" has been observed.

3. Following a job-related abduction by Duane Barry (a known psychotic who we suspect to have been working with an accomplice), Agent Scully received treatment for her injuries and was encouraged to discuss the incident with the Bureau's in-house psychiatric staff. As such appointments are covered by doctor-patient confidentiality, no information regarding those sessions is available at this time. Reports of her field capability continue to support her decision to return to her previous duties but constant reviews of her case files will be continued for the present time.

(N.B. Until such time as Agent Scully is able to compile a description of the events of her abduction, X-File #73317 must remain open.)

22

Case #: X-1.05-100893

Code Name: "The Jersey Devil"

CASE SUMMARY

When Mulder claims Bigfoot is hunting Atlantic City's back alleys, even Scully thinks he's gone beyond the realm of extreme possibility. However, putting Mulder and his theories out of her mind in favor of some well-deserved personal time isn't as easy as she'd anticipated. Lucky for Mulder.

The Many Incarnations of the Jersey Devil

DEEP BACKGROUND

Chris Carter didn't create the Jersey Devil out of thin air for this episode, nor was he just tapping into the Bigfoot legend. The Jersey Devil has stalked New Jersey since at least 1780 and may trace its roots in folklore a full fifty years before that. Its history, however, takes researchers on a circuitous route through manifestations and motivations so diverse that only the name could possibly connect them.

The earliest version is the Leeds Devil, a name still used in certain areas. Sometime in 1735, a story circulated that when a Mrs. Leeds delivered her thirteenth child, she could only watch in horror as the "devil child" flew away from her and up the chimney. Tedious hours spent poring over local records revealed nothing specific to support or deny the story. Many families named Leeds, or distinguished as being So-and-So "of Leeds," pepper par-ish and civil records, and certainly large families were in vogue at the time, but there's a dearth of direct, contemporaneous records to support the idea that a thirteenth child in a family named Leeds disappeared.

EYEWITNESS STATEMENT

This thing chewed somebody's arm off! That's not exactly a *DEFENSIVE* posture!

—Scully, "The Jersey Devil"

23

However, proof has seldom been a requirement in order to continue a perfectly good legend and, real or not, the Leeds Devil had several characteristics that tend to encourage its mythic survival. The "devil" image provided a reference point vague enough to include almost anything, yet because of an early association with a single geographic location, the Devil, like the Loch Ness monster, could be adopted by locals. With an emotional investment in the creature, there was a subtle pressure to sustain its existence.

For the remainder of the century, witnesses appeared content to build on the original tale, allowing the creature to age off-stage and grow into an adult-sized monster instead of something small enough to whisk down their own chimneys. Most sightings describe it as a winged creature, usually with a ram's or bull's head consistent with the devil image of the period when "horned devils" frequently displayed the head of some animal instead of a human head.

The changes to come over the next two centuries reflected the amazing ability of the legend to expand and adapt. When a rash of deaths among livestock swept the area between 1830 and 1840, and no clear cause was found, the Jersey Devil developed the ability to become invisible and stalk even animals under close supervision.

It regained its solid form about thirty years later, but it would undergo so many physical changes between then and modern times that it could put to shame even *The X-Files'* ability to morph its characters. Keeping the ram's head image and acquiring a bird's body to go with its wings, the Jersey Devil became a bizarre creature, but one capable of explaining some odd footprints found in new snow. From there it became a flying lion, an indeterminate but swift, feathered creature with four legs, an even vaguer "monster" by 1928, a "half-man, half-beast" by 1932, and then a traditional devil with pointed ears and tail.

As an example of a legend's ability to remain current, consider the 1948 version of the Jersey Devil, just one year after the nation was swept up in UFOs and the Roswell crash. Lost for the moment were any of its "devil" or "animal" aspects. Instead it was most frequently described as a "green, clearly male, upright monster." Even Mulder could be forgiven for calling that a fair representation of the aliens sweeping across sci-fi covers and movie posters.

However, when the Jersey Devil next arose, it had reverted to its animalistic nature. Perhaps influenced by the Bigfoot tales, it slowly evolved into something more like a cross between a Tasmanian devil and a human being.

While Carter's version of the Jersey Devil bears little resemblance to the child who flew up a chimney, it remains within the creature's historical bounds. And on a purely practical level, it was probably easier to film the haunting figure of Claire Stansfield, who played Carter's Devil, than either a winged lion or a ram-headed ostrich.

Victor: Wolfboy of France

According to creator Chris Carter, inspiration for episodes comes from news articles that tickle the writers' fancies, nightmares that send them fumbling for light switches, and the numerous reference books that have slowly accumulated in a particular bungalow in a corner of the Fox lot.

In "The Jersey Devil," Mulder and Scully, aided by a New Jersey park ranger and an anthropologist from Scully's alma mater, search desperately for a wild woman they suspect has added human beings to her diet. As even the show's characters admit, stories of Bigfoot and other beastmen have been circulating since we first squatted around a campfire.

And at least one of those stories was real. In the early 1800s, a boy, rooted out of a wolves' lair near Aveyron, France, was delivered up to the National Deaf Mute Institute in Paris. The child, estimated to be twelve years old, lapped water, refused all food except raw meat (preferably warm from a fresh kill), bit anyone who came too close or carelessly turned his or her back on him, and spent his nights growling, his days grunting inarticulate sounds and shrill wails. It took Jean Marc Itard, who became the boy's lifelong teacher, nearly a month to get close enough to the boy to discover a three-inch-wide, six-inch-long scar covering the front of the child's throat over his larynx.

Despite the lack of treatment standards for special patients, the boy, a bit of a celebrity, was reasonably well treated. Itard, convinced that a human being existed somewhere inside this snarling, pock-marked figure, named him Victor and developed a program of studies he hoped would bring the child back into society.

Progress was slow and some interesting behaviors led to setback after setback: The day Victor began burrowing in the gardens ended his outdoor privileges for many months. How could the child sit, staring into nothing, without even flinching, as a pistol was fired not ten feet away? And why would the same child react immediately, often violently, to the cracking of a walnut shell behind him? Convinced Victor's senses were intact, but "societally dulled," Itard began to adjust the boy's routine, including activities he hoped would stimulate Victor's senses and create a bridge into his too-often distant mind.

Every day for a full decade, Victor was tickled, bathed in hot and cold water, and massaged. Slowly, some sort of communication developed, though even Itard was hard-pressed to describe it.

> *He no longer bites at me when angered. Instead, he will gnaw on his own hands until his environment is altered to his new tastes. He wraps his arms around me when he is once again happy. The bites he drops on my neck and face are mere nips. I think he means them affectionately as he only does this when he is particularly relaxed. If only I could look into his eyes and see something of a man in there.*

It would be another five years before Victor could be trusted in a normalized environment. Finally capable of eating a regular diet with something other than his hands, of dressing himself, and of controlling his most violent outbursts, Victor was permitted to join the regular population of the Institute. However, what hopes Itard had held that exposure to a new environment, new people, and new freedoms would help Victor regain his humanity were quickly dashed. Although the violent episodes of his childhood didn't recur, Victor, now close to thirty years old, whimpered and cried when separated from his mentor. His meager language skills faded and he spent his days in self-imposed isolation, staring at walls, rocking on his haunches, and avoiding eye contact. Returning him to his garret apartment didn't help.

Itard, confused and frustrated, now resorted to an aggressive version of the sensory program he'd begun with Victor when the boy had first arrived. The tickling was replaced with the newly developed shock therapies. The hot and cold baths became steam treatments and ice immersions. Nothing seemed to help.

> *I find myself doubting so many things . . . that I ever saw a glimmer of humanity, that we should ever have brought him here, that anything I do benefits him! Almost, I could wish for the early rages. At least in rage I could identify with him.*

Victor, in all his years at the Institute, never indicated any interest in human women, treated human children much the way a socialized person treats a puppy, and didn't at any time try to escape.

He died at the age of forty, still distanced from people, still a mystery to the man who'd spent nearly thirty years with him. Behind his back, many of Itard's colleagues referred to Victor as the dog Itard had never had as a child; suggested the man had spent a lifetime disproving Rousseau's already mostly ignored theory of the "Noble Savage"; and believed that Itard should have recognized from the beginning that the "boy had not become an idiot for being abandoned in the woods, but, rather that he'd been abandoned in the woods *because* he was an idiot."

Itard, however, was not as naive as his peers thought. He'd long since made the connection between the slash across Victor's throat and the likelihood that the boy had survived a murder attempt by someone unwilling to support an "idiot." Some years after Victor's death Itard remarked, "I regret not a moment of those years, no. My only regret, if indeed regret it is, is that I have not, in my own mind, yet been able to convince myself that Victor would not have been better off where he was found. I would not have added to his misery, not knowingly."

Whether Itard should be held accountable for employing techniques a modern medical community would term barbaric is a matter of some debate still. What is beyond doubt is that Itard's work with Victor also forms the basis of the touch-therapy technique (which, to date, is one of the very few treatments that appears to help autistic children and adults); Itard's care protected Victor during a period in history when he could as easily have become a circus exhibit; and Itard was perhaps the first to methodically record his treatment of a mentally impaired patient and allow those records to be reviewed by an outside agent. If Itard's actions can be criticized today, it's due in large part to his willingness to be criticized in his own time.

Perhaps Itard is one of the very few people who would have been capable of understanding both Mulder's desperate rush to keep his beastwoman out of harsh and uncaring hands and his willingness to endure the "millstone of humiliation" in his search for truth.

The wendigo, mistakenly called Bigfoot, is a Canadian entity that is well known around *The X-Files* location in Vancouver. Half-phantom, half-beast, it lives in the forests and preys on human beings, particularly children. The belief in this horror dates back to the earliest Indian legends, and it is said that the wendigo will eat the flesh of its victims. According to R. S. Lambert in *Exploring the Supernatural*, "Wendigos (who might be women as well as men) were believed to have entered into a pact with evil spirits, lurking in the forest, who helped them kill their victims." In W. T. Cox's *Fearsome Creatures of the Lumber Woods* (1951), a number of other Canadian "wood horrors" are listed: hodags, whimpis, hoop-snakes, celofays, and filamaloos.

Case #: X-1.06-102293

Code Name: "Shadows"

CASE SUMMARY

When an ATM security photo implicates a secretary named Lauren Kyte and a shadowy unidentified man in the unusual deaths of two thieves, Mulder and Scully can't decide if Kyte is a suspect or a victim. A car driving off on its own, three more deaths, and the involvement of Kyte's company in an arms conspiracy all seem tame compared to the ghostly events that begin to occur. Whether the cause or the target of this activity, Lauren Kyte is the only key.

DEEP BACKGROUND

A Haunting Experience

The X-Files' knack of twisting folklore into new forms has kept viewers pinned to their seats week after week, watching episodes like "The Jersey Devil" and "Firewalker," which retold old stories to a new or a broader audience. It's no surprise, then, that the show would eventually tackle the traditional ghost story. In "Shadows," the crew continued the evolving history of what is perhaps the oldest of all stories.

For a show that has to pack an awful lot into its time slot, beginning with a recognized narrative form is actually an advantage. Because every-

Gillian Anderson, during an interview on CBS's "Midday," revealed that she herself had once felt an unusual presence in her new home in Vancouver. Taking the advice of a friend, she had the house cleansed by a Native American shaman and the sensation disappeared.

EYEWITNESS STATEMENT

I would never lie. I willfully participated in a campaign of misinformation.

—Agent Mulder, "Shadows"

one knows the basics of a ghost story, the writers could be reasonably confident they could hop in, midstory, without totally losing their viewers. Then once they had viewers hooked, the story could go anywhere.

THE TRADITIONAL GHOST

Regardless of ethnicity, ghosts universally belong in the realm of the dead—usually the troubled dead. All traditional ghost stories begin with a restless spirit with some unfulfilled driving purpose still disturbing its rest. As often as not, these shades' connection to the material world is a particular person or location important to them in life, which may make it impossible for them to complete their task without assistance from the living.

The Tower of London's bloody history made it a natural repository for disgruntled spirits. The dozens of ghosts that have roamed its damp rooms over the centuries have all contributed to the classic form of the ghost story. Two young princes, murdered there in 1483, were seen wandering up and down stairwells, through walls, and past windows for almost two centuries. In 1674, their bones were found and buried in a proper ceremony, after which they were never seen again.

The most famous ghost in the Tower is Anne Boleyn, wife of Henry VIII until he had her beheaded in 1536. Unlike the little princes who seemed to wander aimlessly, Anne may even still be on the lookout for her unfaithful husband. Shrill screeches in the middle of the night, cold touches about a visitor's face and neck, even a push down a long flight of steps have been attributed to Anne. So common had the ghost's outlandish tricks become by 1992 that visitors were told to "Mind the rail on your way upstairs. Wouldn't do for Anne to give you a nudge." As Henry is long dead, Anne may continue to haunt the Tower for eternity in search of vengeance.

ENTER THE POLTERGEIST AND THE MODERN URBAN LEGEND

In more recent times, however, people became less inclined to believe a ghost is nothing more than a ghost. There arose a need to explain not only traditional ghostly sightings but also odd occurrences with no visible manifestations.

Sometime around the 1950s, the idea of the German poltergeist arrived in the United States and was incorporated into both new and existing stories. The poltergeist, usually conceived of as a free-roaming, energetic, but bodiless knot of pure will, replaced the old ghosts. With the rise of New Age theories, which frequently include neutral, but powerful forces that permeate the fabric of time and space, this new poltergeist hung around for several decades.

During this time, urban legends—tales that depended on neither supernatural nor ghostly influences for their horror—began to circulate. These stories, like that of the woman who discovered a burglar in her house after her veterinarian found the thief's fingers in her dog's throat, rely on pure horror of a basic human variety.

THE PARANORMAL VISITATION

In the early 1980s, the ghost story underwent its next incarnation. A swelling interest in things like psychokinesis and telepathy suggested that *people* were causing the bumps, bangs, moans, and even visual effects that had long been attributed to entities beyond the material world. Any and all of these things could be encompassed by parapsychology; there was nothing that couldn't be explained by one or another of its various disciplines.

So, when *The X-Files* took on its ghost story in this episode, there were at least three different available outcomes. Was Lauren haunted by her boss, Graves, an unsettled spirit attempting to avenge his murder? Was the distraught Lauren the focal point of a poltergeist-like energy force capable of keeping a car's headlights running long after the engine was turned off? Or was she herself the source of the mysterious events? Perhaps Lauren's own subconscious knowledge of the events in her office and her fear of the FBI led to the flying objects.

E.T., THE LAW, AND YOU

In an attempt to be prepared for all contingencies—and no doubt in response to the paranoia of the McCarthy era—the United States once had a law making it illegal for any U.S. citizen to "approach, communicate, or enter into any agreements with extraterrestrial citizens." Breaches of the law could result in "fines up to $5,000, imprisonment, or both."

Case #: X-1.07-102993

Code Name: "Ghost in the Machine"

CASE SUMMARY

A new kind of alien intelligence is awakening in the depths of the EURISKO building—an artificial intelligence that's determined to survive at all costs. When Mulder's old partner becomes the next victim of a building that's about to be the first architectural serial killer, the two agents find themselves up against electrocution, decapitation by garage door, shredding by recirculation fans—and the American government, which wants to keep the monstrosity for its own use.

Artificial Intelligence: Augmenting the Mind

DEEP BACKGROUND

For Fox Mulder, "Ghost in the Machine" must have been a nightmare case. Here was an agent who preferred to jot notes on yellow legal pads and let his shiny new computer terminal collect dust. Artificial intelligence, machines that tapped phones, sucked your partner down ventilating shafts, and committed murder, just weren't in his scheme of things.

But computer technology has always taken queer and unexpected turns and in creating this episode's sentient computer, *The X-Files* played with our love-hate relationship for contraptions whose full capabilities we mightn't completely understand.

In computing's infancy, science promised us robots to tackle our mundane tasks, machines to eliminate our heavy labors, and databases

EYEWITNESS STATEMENT

It's a puzzle, Miss Scully, and scruffy minds like me like puzzles. We enjoy walking down unpredictable avenues of thought, turning new corners, but, as a general rule, scruffy minds don't commit murder.

—Brad Wilczek, "Ghost in the Machine"

so expansive that technological progress could be taken for granted. Those promises have, more or less, been fulfilled, if not in ways we'd immediately recognize.

For example, few people would say they have housekeeping robots at home. Yet most of us do. Instead of a *Jetsons*-type robot whisking about, science has provided us with dedicated machines to wash dishes, pluck the lint from our rugs, and scrub clothes. These appliances perform tasks for us but, unlike *Star Trek*'s Data, they don't match our mental image of a robot. They have no character, nothing to separate one from the other.

The same is true of the many computers being dragged home from electronics stores across the country. Even if they can calculate pi to the *n*th degree, no PC has ever been called intelligent. (Quite the contrary in many cases!) However, that was the original dream, to create a machine that reflected our thinking style, our creativity, even our personalities; to create an extension of our minds as levers had extended the ability of our bodies. It's a goal that even a cursory survey of our literature proves has been with us a long time. Had Gepetto lived in these times, he'd have been an AI specialist.

In its most simple form, Artificial Intelligence is any system that mimics human thinking. In "Ghost in the Machine," Deep Throat mentions a chess program capable of beating a grandmaster. There are literally hundreds of similar programs on the market, for backgammon, Othello, canasta, and poker, as well as chess, all capable of playing competitively against a human opponent. What makes LESTER unique is that it cheats!

CRAY mainframe: the big brother of COS.

Most game programs follow a set of rules. In the case of chess, the program makes every conceivable legal move and then chooses the most advantageous. LESTER went a step further. As it played, it *learned* that some moves were never played even though they were completely legal. By observing a line-by-line assessment of its logic path, programmers could be sure that it wasn't failing to compute those possibilities, it was ignoring them. Like its human opponent, the program began to concentrate on only the pertinent moves, not *all* moves. Over time, it began to use a pattern of play almost indistinguishable from a human's.

Even more incredible, it learned to recognize its opponents and to adapt its "style" of play to each one. It had learned that some of its opponents made consistent choices given the same situation repeatedly, that others had favorite attacks, and that some were particularly likely to miss a hole in their defenses. When an opponent typed in his name, the program immediately adjusted its priorities, changing its behavior in response to its environment.

The ultimate challenge, of course, would be to create a situation where the program worked outside the rules, thinking independently. After a few inconclusive attempts to create such a scenario, the research team literally fell into the perfect setup when a subroutine that notified the human player if he or she made an illegal move was removed. Most of the human opponents were high-ranked players, unlikely to make silly errors, and the code was deemed unnecessary. Within a week, a grandmaster was complaining loudly that they'd disturbed an essential part of the programming because LESTER was making illegal moves.

Concerned that they'd accidentally corrupted their data, that all the games that had been played to bring LESTER to this point were wasted, the programmers lost no time checking their code. The investigations showed that LESTER wasn't malfunctioning, it was doing exactly what they'd hoped it would do, expanding its parameters. At some point after the subroutine was removed, the grandmaster had indeed made an illegal move. LESTER, faced with a situation where no legal move would allow it to win, made exactly the same illegal move. While not a true personality, LESTER was obviously different from any other piece of game code—and that's only the beginning.

Memory, decision-making, prioritization, and other forms of thought can't be dissected, they can't be directly observed, yet they're the essence of what it means to be human. With the conditional success of traditional AI systems, it became theoretically possible to create a "silicon brain" where scientists could watch not one but thousands of signals operate in tandem. These complex systems, like the Central Operating System at work in the EURISKO building, are the next generation of Artificial Intelligence.

While the COS may never become manifest reality, the issues raised in "Ghost in the Machine" are immediate concerns for computer scientists, neurobiologists, psychologists, physicists, philosophers, and even theologians. Just as their colleagues in molecular biology struggle with the ethical implications of creating new life-forms through genetic engineering, all those involved in the AI field are wondering how to define life. Would the COS qualify as a life-

The setting for this episode, Crystal City, Virginia, doesn't exist. It's an allusion to Silicon Valley.

form? According to every definition of life we have, including those used to make the declaration of legal death, the COS was alive. Was an attempt to destroy it murder?

The Computer Boneyard

Computers are an endangered species on *The X-Files*. In the very first episode, Scully's motel room and her cherished notebook computer go up in flames. In "Ghost in the Machine," her personal desktop model happily gives up its electronically stored data to the first machine with a higher-speed processor to call it up. Since then, a dozen different machines have passed through the hands of both agents, a rate that's put a different model on their individual desks almost every week!

For fans, this stream of technology has provided more than one humorous moment, and the oddest of the lot occurred in this episode. Viewers who play along with the extreme possibility of alien abductions and werewolves wouldn't have much difficulty believing a sophisticated machine could pluck Scully's name from a tape recording. They'd even agree it was then possible to match that name to a phone number in some database, and they'd definitely agree that COS could then call Scully's machine via modem. But what would have them rolling on the floor, clutching their sides, and wiping tears from their eyes, is the notion that COS could have actually *gotten* anything out of a machine that wasn't even turned on. Anyone who owns a coffeemaker could tell you that no matter how sophisticated the machine, it won't make coffee if it's unplugged.

A similar, if tongue-in-cheek, disregard for the rules of computing has given sharp-eyed fans even more laughs. If you've ever tried to run a DOS program on anything other than an IBM-compatible machine, you know all the beeps and error messages a computer can throw at its user. Operating systems that perform wonders on one machine can't be used on a competitor's terminal. Well, *The X-Files* did what an untold number of computer users wish they could do in the real world: create a bizarre hybrid of the most popular operating systems. In custom screen shots, a Mac's .bin and .hex files sit happily beside DOS-based conventions like autoexec.bat and config.sys. And, just in case that doesn't solve whatever compatibility problems might arise from mixing operating systems, the crew created a brand new operating system and tossed in a few files of their own, like AUTOEXEC.BAT.SYS.

Finally, in the world of *The X-Files,* you don't even have to use your own machine to get the answers you need. In "End Game," for example, Scully gets her electronic mail from Mulder's machine. Hundreds of people on the Internet would *love* to be able to pull off that trick.

With seemingly no logical restriction on what these miraculous machines can accomplish, it's no wonder the X-Files division wants to try out as many as they can.

The Outside eXperts

Considering the morbidity rate of specialists within Mulder and Scully's circle of acquaintances and the scarcity of informants that they can still trust, it would be surprising if they weren't building a private contact list to circumvent the strict chain of command and information within the Bureau. It would certainly explain why, for example, when Scully suspected a case of Munchausen Syndrome by Proxy in "The Calusari," she chose the same social worker who'd listened to her so attentively in "Irresistible." If we could peek into the personal notes of Mulder and Scully, this is what we might find:

BERUBE, TERRENCE ALLEN (DR.)
CASE #: X-1.01-091093
Genetics specialist
Murdered

BRAUN, SHEILA (DR.)
CASE #: X-1.22-042994-40210
Pediatric psychologist
Unlikely to render aid, closed to the possibilities.

BRIGGS, FRANK (DET.)
CASE #: X-1.03-092493–
X-1.21-042294
Detective, retired
Note: Special knowledge of Eugene Victor Tooms, and a demonstrated willingness to assist in the solution of this case.

CARPENTER, ANNE (DR.)
CASE #: X-1.24-051394
Pathologist
Killed under mysterious circumstances while assisting on an investigation.

DASILVA, NANCY (DR.)
CASE #: X-1.08-110593
Toxicologist
Performed well in the field under difficult circumstances. May be amenable to future assistance.

DIAMOND (DR.)
CASE #: X-1.05-100893
Professor, Dept. of Anthropology
Note: Dr. Diamond proved himself both an expert in his area of study and a steady presence in the field. May be willing to render further assistance at a future date.

GENEROO, MICHELLE
CASE #: X-1.09-111293
Communications specialist, NASA
Note: Ms. Generoo's expertise, in combination with her knowledge of NASA's programs, may prove useful in separating information from disinformation in the event of further official "weather balloon" and "satellite" explanations for unresolved observations.

GERRARDI, FRANCIS (DR.)
CASE #: X-2.04-100794
Sleep specialist
Degree of openness or willingness to assist is unknown at this time.

GREEN, PHOEBE (INSPECTOR)
CASE #: X-1.12-121793-11214893
Contact: Scotland Yard
Ms. Green is an experienced local operative in the London area.

GRISSOM, SAUL (DR.)
CASE #: X-2.04-100794
Sleep specialist
Deceased

HAKKIE, DEL (DR.)
CASE #: X-2.05-101494
Psychiatrist
Supervising physician of Duane Barry, inadvertently involved in hostage situation. Unlikely to volunteer his assistance.

HODGE (DR.)
CASE #: X-1.08-110593
Medical doctor
Unlikely to become involved in inquiries tangential to his own projects.

KEATS (DR.)
CASE #: X-1.23-050694
Aeronautics/propulsion engineer
Unlikely to provide assistance.

KENDRICK, SALLY (DR.)
CASE #: X-1.11-121093
Eugenics specialist
Note: Whereabouts of Dr. Sally Kendrick are unknown; possibly deceased.

LONE GUNMEN, THE
PERSONAL CONTACT
Proven reliable and available for further assistance.
(Known members: Frohike, Langly, Byers, The Thinker)

MURPHY, DENNY (DR.)
CASE #: X-1.08-110593
Geologist, specialty—ice flow
Note: Deceased

NEMMAN, JAY (DR.)
CASE #: X-1.01-091093
Coroner, general practitioner, Oregon
Note: After falsifying autopsy reports, Dr. Nemman's value as a local resource is questionable.

NOLLETTE, FRANK (DR.)
CASE #: X-1.23-050694
Aeronautics/propulsion engineer

PIERCE, ADAM (DR.)
CASE #: X-2.09-111894
Volcanologist
Note: Deceased

RIDLEY, JOE (DR.)
CASE #: X-1.16-021194
Transgenics, aging specialist
Note: Dr. Ridley's ethical history makes him an unreliable source. Likely deceased.

SECARE, WILLIAM (DR.)
CASE #: X-1.24-051394
Specialty unknown
Murdered

SPITZ (DR.)
CASE #: X-1.22-042994-40210
Psychologist, specialist in hypnotic regression
Has participated in previous regression sessions. Shows willingness to continue. Open to possibilities.

SURNOW, RONALD (DR.)
CASE #: X-1.23-050694
Aeronautics/propulsion engineer

TREPKOS, DANIEL (DR.)
CASE #: X-2.09-111894
Volcanologist
Team leader of the Firewalker project. Undoubted expert in his field; however, whereabouts ought to remain unknown.

WILCZEK, BRAD
CASE #: X-1.07-102993
Computer scientist/developer/programmer
Note: Though Brad Wilczek's expertise in the area of artificial intelligence and neural networks would undoubtedly make him a noteworthy resource, his whereabouts remain unknown.

AN UNEASY PARTNERSHIP

Case #: X-1.08-110593

Code Name: "Ice"

CASE SUMMARY

When what should have been a happy group of scientists, still high from their record-beating drill into the Arctic ice, start slaughtering one another, Scully and Mulder, along with a research team, make a swift trip north. It quickly becomes apparent that the first thing to have died was trust. With a pathogen loose among the scientists that is capable of inducing a killing frenzy, all the agents have to depend on is one another—*if* they are who they think they are.

DEEP BACKGROUND

The Real Arctic Ice Core Projects: Digging Up a Frozen Past

Though the real ice drilling projects haven't turned up any parasites with a taste for human adrenaline, the ice fields do have life, more life than was ever thought possible. In the Antarctic, in oxygen-starved lakes right in the ice sheet, microbial organisms flourish. Algae have been found in both hemispheres, growing *through* the ice, invading every crack and crevice. The green and brown stains indicate algal strands miles long and capable of creating high-oxygen environments within ice.

Nor is life restricted to the microscopic. In large numbers, a pack of ice-borers can be terrifying. They were first discovered by Aprile Pazzo, who was observing penguins along the Ross Sea. As she was about to head back to camp, the penguins suddenly screamed and stampeded past her, clearly terrified. Looking around for a large predator and finding none, Ms. Pazzo attempted to retrieve the only

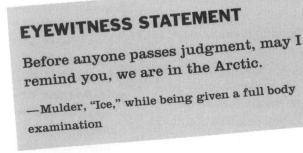

EYEWITNESS STATEMENT

Before anyone passes judgment, may I remind you, we are in the Arctic.

—Mulder, "Ice," while being given a full body examination

penguin of the flock who hadn't fled. Startled doesn't quite describe her reaction on discovering the bird had sunk into a circle of slush. Slush just doesn't exist in the Antarctic at that time of year. But heat was actually *rising* from around the floundering bird.

Grabbing the bird to keep it from sinking further, she heaved until it came free—and discovered a new animal. Clinging to the bird were a dozen hairless creatures with their teeth sunk deep into its flesh. Almost as soon as they were tugged free of the ice they released their grip, and it was all Pazzo could do to capture one of the savage 6-inch-long creatures that she described as "Repulsive!" The rest tunneled down through the slush.

Since that surprising first encounter, Aprile Pazzo has made it her business to observe the creatures she dubbed "hotheaded hairless ice-borers." Full-grown specimens don't seem to exceed 6 inches in length and even the largest weighs only a few ounces. Size alone wouldn't make them any more dangerous than a particularly nasty mouse, but the ice-borers, while related to rodents, have some pretty unique adaptations that make them perfectly comfortable in their Antarctic ice burrows.

With an incredibly high metabolic rate, the ice-borer's normal body temperature is 110 degrees Fahrenheit. Much of that heat is apparently released through a bony plate on the forehead that is suffused with so many blood vessels that it shines a brilliant red. This natural hotplate not only accounts for the slush pit that suddenly opened under the penguin, but also for the ice-borer's speed. Over a period of several months, Pazzo discovered that the molelike creatures could tunnel faster than a penguin could waddle and nearly as fast as a human in cold weather gear could jog.

Once underneath a colony of penguins, the ice-borers congregate on a single victim and surge up through the ice and snow. Suddenly finding itself in a puddle, the penguin is trapped and begins sinking. The ice-borers, who seem to be 90 percent teeth, slice through the unlucky bird in a matter of moments. Pazzo has seen them leave nothing behind but webbed feet and beak, and they've been known to attack even the 4-foot-tall emperor penguin.

Creatures like the ice-borer, now suspected of having been responsible for the disappearance of explorer Philippe Poisson, remind us that truth can be stranger than, and as terrifying as, fiction. Luckily for those working and living in the high Arctic on projects like the Greenland Ice Sheet Project (GISP), the ice-borer seems confined to the southern hemisphere. High atop the world, they're discovering some amazing things about our own history buried in the ice.

Easy Stuff: Give yourself 1 point for each correct answer.

1. What does A.I.C.P mean?
2. What was the name of the pilot who was unfortunate enough to be the parasite's first victim?
3. What unusual geographic feature had the original ice team drilled into?
4. How was the pilot infected?
5. How was the dog cured?

Getting Tougher: Give yourself 2 points for each correct answer.

6. How far north of the Arctic Circle was "Ice" set?
7. The character of Dr. Denny Murphy and his creators, writers Glen Morgan and Jim Wong, share a passion for a certain football team. Which one?
8. In what liquid did the parasites prefer to live? (It was found in the blood of their victims.)
9. To which part of the body did the parasite attach?
10. What was the name of the closest airfield?

Some bacteria can live in water as hot as 80 degrees Celsius; others are equally happy in supercooled water at temperatures as low as −20 degrees Celsius.

The dog in "Ice" is the real-life father of David Duchovny's dog, Blue.

Funded by the National Science Foundation, GISP recently struck bedrock in Greenland, creating the longest continuous ice core to be retrieved in the north.

The ice sheet "archive" in Greenland was created as snow fell year after year, trapping the gases, chemicals, and dust of the atmosphere, and eventually being compressed into ice. The GISP2 core, along with a complementary core drilled by the European Greenland Ice Core Project (GRIP), spans more than 100,000 years of history.

While the core studies have implications for fields as varied as agriculture and astronomy, one of the most curious theories supported by the core study is the Meteorite Footprint Theory. In 1908, an asteroid plummeted into the atmosphere over Siberia's Tunguska River region, exploding with an estimated energy of 15 megatons, flattening trees for hundreds of square miles. Preliminary studies of two shallow ice cores by Robert Sherrell of Rutgers University, Edward Boyle of the Massachusetts Institute of Technology, and Robert Rocchia, Centre des Faibles Radioactivités, France, have shown four- to twenty-fold jumps in the iridium concentration in Greenland ice since 1908. Iridium deposits can indicate a meteorite impact, because extraterrestrial material is much richer in the element than is the Earth's crust. If confirmed, this will be the first demonstration of a meteorite impact recorded in ice—the very event the X-crew played off in creating "Ice."

The challenge for the Greenland study group was to separate a meteorite's signature from that of a volcanic eruption. The researchers found an eighteen-fold iridium enrichment in Greenland ice corresponding with a sharp increase in sulfate produced by the 1783 volcanic eruption at Lakigigar, Iceland. They saw no such volcanic fingerprint in the 1908 ice, however, bolstering the Tanguska source hypothesis.

With the meteoric theory appearing solid, the teams could turn to the long-term effects of the impact. In the short term, the results were deadly; over time, however, the minerals in the meteorite might actually have seeded the area with elements that enabled the growth of new plants. Of no small consideration was the energy generated by the impact: energy that didn't just dissipate into thin air. Across the Siberian site are pockets of verdant growth, a condition scientists are ready to attribute to the force of a rock slamming into an ice sheet. Perhaps the notion of new life arising in the midst of freezing cold isn't so farfetched after all.

Case #: X-1.09-111293

Code Name: "Space"

When a communication specialist from NASA points out a history of sabotage that could well result in the deaths of more astronauts, Mulder gets to satisfy a boyhood dream—to visit Mission Control. Unfortunately, not everyone shares his love for the program. With Scully keeping his feet firmly on the ground, they both get past Mulder's hero-worship of former astronaut Colonel Aurelius Bolt to a solution that's not entirely earthly.

Armstrong's Angels and Other Encounters

In combining NASA history, astronauts, aliens, and Martian features for this episode, Chris Carter was drawing both on some of the most beloved theories of UFOlogists and what was, in many ways, the start of science fiction. Over the years, various parties have claimed to have proof that NASA knows more about UFOs than it lets on, that NASA astronauts have seen the objects up close with their own eyes, and that photographic evidence exists to support UFO claims that NASA won't release to the public.

The fact is that astronauts are individuals, some of whom may personally believe we aren't alone, and this has somewhat muddled the record when personal opinion has been taken as NASA's official

EYEWITNESS STATEMENT

The valve is made of ferrocarbon titanium. To score that material would take extreme temperatures, *launchpad* temperatures. If anyone in NASA were to take a look at that analysis, they would say it would be *impossible* for anyone to do that type of damage undetected.

—Michelle Generoo, "Space"

statements. Some accounts are difficult to discount, as the astronauts themselves have repeated their statements publicly.

MAJ. GORDON COOPER

A *Mercury* astronaut and the last American to venture into space alone, Cooper began his twenty-two orbits of Earth on May 15, 1963. According to some, in his last orbit, he contacted the Muchea tracking station near Perth, Australia, to report a glowing green object approaching his capsule—an object that was recorded by the Muchea radar system. Major Cooper had also, according to reports, seen a saucer-type UFO while piloting an F-86 Sabrejet over West Germany in 1951.

In a taped interview, Major Cooper said: "For many years I have lived with a secret, in a secrecy imposed on all specialists in astronautics. I can now reveal that every day, in the USA, our radar instruments capture objects of form and composition unknown to us. And there are thousands of witness reports and a quantity of documents to prove this, but nobody wants to make them public.

"Why? Because authority is afraid that people may think of God knows what kind of horrible invaders. So the password still is: We have to avoid panic by all means."

ED WHITE AND JAMES MCDIVITT

In June 1965, astronauts Ed White (the first American to walk in space) and James McDivitt were passing over Hawaii in a *Gemini* spacecraft when they saw a weird-looking metallic object with "arms" sticking out in all directions. Some claim McDivitt used a cine-camera to take pictures that were never released.

JAMES LOVELL AND FRANK BORMAN

In December 1965, *Gemini* astronauts James Lovell and Frank Borman reportedly saw a UFO during the second orbit of a fourteen-day flight. Gemini Control, at Cape Kennedy, told them that they were seeing the final stage of their own Titan booster rocket. Borman confirmed that he could see the booster rocket all right, but that he could also see something completely different. Though television broadcast of the communication between *Gemini 7* and Earth was scratchy and subject to misinterpretation, some viewers claim to have heard Lovell say, "We have several actual sightings."

MAJ. ROBERT WHITE

On July 17, 1962, Major Robert White reported a UFO during his fifty-eight-mile-high flight of an X-15. Major White reported: "I have no idea what it could be. It was grayish in color and about thirty to forty feet away." Then, according to *Time* magazine, Major White exclaimed over the radio: "There *are* things out there! There absolutely is!"

COMDR. EUGENE CERNAN

Apollo 17 commander Eugene Cernan, in a 1973 *Los Angeles Times* article about UFOs, said: "I've been asked [about UFOs] and I've said publicly I thought they [UFOs] were somebody else, some other civilization."

Of course, for Chris Carter's purposes, it hardly matters if the astronauts have or haven't been contacted by aliens, if NASA is or isn't hiding knowledge, or if the whole attempt to connect astronauts to the UFO phenomena is nothing more than an acknowledgment of NASA's towering reputation, a reputation that could only help bring UFOlogy into the research mainstream. There is one anecdote, however, that's been told over and over again without any contradiction. It concerns Neil Armstrong, perhaps the best known American astronaut. During an early mission, Armstrong was startled by a rainbowlike effect that could be temporarily seen extending over a considerable area. What has since been referred to as Armstrong's Angels was actually the waste ejected from the capsule.

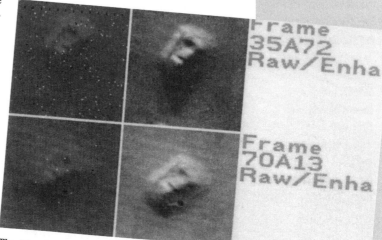

The Martian "face" from Colonel Bolt's nightmares.

Case #: X-1.10-111993

Code Name: "Fallen Angel"

CASE SUMMARY

When Mulder is caught sneaking into a secured area that he claims is a UFO crash site, Scully finds herself in the uncomfortable position of being sent to retrieve him. Barred from the scene but undaunted by the possibility of official sanction, Mulder's attention turns to Max Fenig, a UFO-chaser who apparently arrived *before* the crash. Who's chasing who becomes unclear when the military, the FBI, Fenig, and a dangerous unknown entity finally meet.

DEEP BACKGROUND

Chasing the Light

In an attempt to centralize, compare, organize, and analyze the more than 1,200 UFO sightings reported annually, a number of organizations have arisen. Watchers in literally every state and country scan the skies and wait for the next call. Far from being crackpots who phone into late-night talk shows claiming to have seen Elvis at Denny's, members of these groups are more likely to be engineers, military personnel, lawyers, doctors, and accountants. Their individual experiences differ, but these "normal" people have all found something in the collected reports that has led them to invest their time and risk their reputations in what many call a wild goose chase.

> **EYEWITNESS STATEMENT**
>
> Well, sir, the meteor seems to be hovering over a small town in eastern Wisconsin.
>
> —Chief Koretz, Project Falcon, "Fallen Angel"

BORDERLAND SCIENCES RESEARCH
FOUNDATION (BSRF)
Garberville, CA
Founded in 1945, the BSRF is a non-profit organization that collates information on UFOs, dowsing, hypnosis, Fortean phenomena, and related material.

THE FUND FOR UFO RESEARCH, INC.
Mt. Rainier, MD
A nonprofit, tax-exempt organization based in Washington, D.C., whose mission is to provide grants for scientific research and public education projects dealing with the UFO phenomenon.

INTERNATIONAL FORTEAN
ORGANIZATION (INFO)
Arlington, VA
A nonprofit corporation established for the educational and scientific study of Fortean phenomena. INFO investigates the strange and unreasonable events that happen in this world, including UFOs, lost civilizations, physical anomalies, Atlantis, Bigfoot, vanished civilizations, etc.

ISLAND SKYWATCH
Queens, NY
A tax-exempt organization whose goal is the scientific and objective study of the UFO phenomenon. A UFO Abductee Support Group is available.

J. ALLEN HYNEK CENTER FOR UFO
STUDIES (CUFOS)
Chicago, IL
A nonprofit organization whose goal is to promote serious research into the UFO phenomenon through the expertise of an international group of scientists, academians, and volunteers. CUFOS maintains the world's

largest repository of data about UFO phenomenon, second only to the U.S. government.

MULTINATIONAL INVESTIGATIONS
COOPERATIVE ON AERIAL
PHENOMENA (MICAP)
Wheat Ridge, CO
MICAP is an international membership group dedicated to the scientific exploration of the UFO phenomenon.

MUTUAL UFO NETWORK, INC.
(MUFON)
Seguin, TX
MUFON is a nonprofit, international scientific organization devoted to studying and researching the UFO phenomenon. MUFON members believe that a concentrated scientific study by dedicated investigators and researchers will provide the ultimate answer to the UFO enigma.

THE NATIONAL SIGHTING RESEARCH
CENTER (NSRC)
Emerson, NJ
A nonprofit organization that acts as an information-gathering organization that compiles massive amounts of data in order to provide the professional UFO investigator or researcher with a computerized, highly graphical database summary of all reported sightings of anomalous aerial phenomena within the United States.

THE SOCIETY FOR THE INVESTIGA-
TION OF THE UNEXPLAINED (SITU)
Little Silver, NJ
A nonprofit, tax-exempt organization that collects data on unexplained events, promotes proper investigation of both individual reports and general subjects, and reports significant data to its members.

Easy Stuff: Give yourself 1 point for each correct answer.

1. What did the code words "Fallen Angel" refer to?
2. Which organization does Max Fenig work for?
3. The first time Scully meets Max, he's halfway out a window. Where was the window?
4. Under an alias, Mulder wrote an article on the Gulf Breeze UFO sightings for what prestigious real-life magazine?
5. Where on Max's body was the scar that caught Mulder's attention?

Getting Tougher: Give yourself 2 points for each correct answer.

6. What name was given to the recovery operation?
7. Under what alias did Mulder write the magazine article?
8. From what two medical conditions did Max appear to suffer?
9. How many days did it take to "resolve" this case?
10. What was the "official" explanation for the cleanup?

UFO INFORMATION RETRIEVAL CENTER (UFOIRC)
Phoenix, AZ
A nonmembership organization that collects, analyzes, publishes, and disseminates information about UFOs.

UFOLOGY INVESTIGATORS LEAGUE
New Brunswick, NJ
A new organization designed to expand an international network of investigators who wish to document UFO cases in their areas.

UFOLOGY RESEARCH OF MANITOBA (UFOROM)
Winnipeg, Manitoba
Canada

UFOROM is a private, nonprofit, and volunteer organization that is involved in rational discourse, investigation, and research on UFOs and related phenomena, including traces, crash-retrievals, abductions, and cattle mutilations.

VICTORIAN UFO RESEARCH SOCIETY INC. (VUFORS)
Moorabbin
Victoria, Australia
VUFORS is the largest UFO society in the southern hemisphere and has been in existence since the 1950s.

Are We Alone Out Here?

In trying to answer the question of whether or not we're alone in the universe, Dr. Frank Drake, an American astronomer, president of the SETI project, and employee of the National Radio Astronomy Observatory in Green Bank, West Virginia, apparently became sick of the standard response that "it's a big universe."

Instead, in 1961, he created an equation that has as many answers as there are stars. In fact, the number of stars is one of the factors of his equation.

$$N = N^* f_p n_e f_1 f_i f_c f_L$$

To figure out the number of advanced civilizations, N, simply multiply

N^* the number of stars in the Milky Way galaxy, times
f_p the fraction of those stars with planets, times
n_e the number of planets capable of supporting life, times
f_1 the fraction of planets capable of supporting life on which life actually does arise, times
f_i the fraction of planets where intelligent life evolves, times
f_c the fraction of planets with intelligent life that develops a technologically advanced civilization, times
f_L the fraction of time that a technical civilization lasts.

Often described as the "glass of water" equation, the results of these computations vary depending on how optimistic or pessimistic the mathematician happens to be. While no one seems to agree on precise values for these variables, even the most conservative estimates indicate we are *not* alone.

However, if there are planets out there teeming with life, the distances involved in space travel make it appear unlikely we'll ever meet an extraterrestrial. The closest stars to Earth, other than the sun of our own system, is the triple star system Alpha Centauri, a mere 4.3 light years away. To convert that to miles, multiply 4.3 by 5,870 billion. Whether in light years, miles, astronomical units (AUs), or parsecs, a casual visit to Alpha Centauri is hard to imagine.

If you watch carefully, you'll see Max Fenig's cap, with NICAP stitched across it. Look for it on coat racks in future episodes.

FLASHBACK: SECTION CHIEF JOSEPH McGRATH

Section Chief Joseph McGrath, head of the Office of Professional Responsibility, is possibly the most dangerous man Mulder and Scully will ever come to face.

McGrath probably won't shoot them, inject them with alien DNA, or send them off to investigate deadly quarantines without a face mask. He doesn't operate in the murky areas the Smoking Man and Mr. X favor. Yet with Deep Throat dead, he's potentially more dangerous than even the most deranged criminal.

The Office of Professional Responsibility, parallel in function to the Internal Affairs department of larger police forces, is the sole arbitrator of an FBI agent's propriety in the field. Though the audience recognizes the greater good of Mulder's goals, the "unofficial" barricades thrown in his way, and the need to throw away the book from time to time, McGrath hasn't witnessed anything tangible and it was only through Deep Throat's intervention that he was prevented from eliminating the too-curious agents.

McGrath's goals and motives are nebulous at times, but in a real world, Mulder and Scully would have already provided him with enough ammunition to ensure their dismissal—with records to keep them in unemployment lines indefinitely. Mulder's little jaunt to Puerto Rico, for example, violated half a dozen sections of the criminal code (breaking and entering, theft, failure to report a murder), and, on a professional level, the prohibition against using your office to advance your personal agenda has been entrenched since Hoover. As Scully has frequently told him, Mulder is his own worst enemy: He continually puts his personal agenda ahead of his job. Ignoring regulations, instigating unauthorized investigations, flaunting his FBI authority, using his position to procure equipment, breaking into secured areas, and co-opting the assistance of other agents in his illegal activities must, sooner or later, pit Mulder against even the most liberal elements of the FBI.

Case #: X-1.11-121093

Code Name: "Eve"

CASE SUMMARY

When two young girls living on opposite sides of the country lose their fathers in identical murders, Mulder and Scully wonder if there's a connection between the two cases. Their investigation only brings up more questions. How could two completely unrelated children be genetically identical? And why would they *both* murder their fathers?

DEEP BACKGROUND

The Genetic Criminal—XXX/Y

A father arrives home, sees the sitter off, traps his two tiny children in the kitchen, and chops them into nineteen pieces. In the midst of that bloody carnage, he wipes the blood drops from his favorite cup and starts afternoon tea. Less than thirty days later his lawyer will stand in a New York court and suggest his client was "genetically predisposed" to violence, incapable of being anything other than the person programmed into his genes. Across the country, stunned viewers of the evening news ask "How could he. . . . Could I? Could it happen to me?"

It happens. It happens in white-picket-fence neighborhoods, and in the best of families. The savagery of such crimes, our incomprehension of the criminals, both revolts and fascinates us, prompting movies-of-the-week, gavel-to-gavel coverage of criminal trials, and yet another spate of scientific inquiry into the "genetic killers."

Little surprise, then, that the murky area behind such a killer's eyes should

EYEWITNESS STATEMENT

No, he remembers this kid. She told him he should use chlorine to eradicate the dinoflagellates in the swimming pool. That sound like someone you know?

—Mulder, "Eve"

attract the attention of *X-Files* writers Kenneth Biller and Chris Brancato. Not content to simply ask *what* hides back there, they challenged every stereotype that might have allowed viewers some reprieve from the shock quality of their script. To do that, though, they had to know the "genetic killer" inside out. That's no easy task. Biologists and psychologists are still arguing the nature versus nurture question while geneticists grope slowly toward some understanding of what we can and can't inherit.

On one side, naturists point to children from disadvantaged backgrounds who've risen to the heights of their chosen fields as examples of individuals who, though denied a supportive environment, still excel. "Good genes," these people say, "will always win out." On the other side, nurturists question what those individuals might have accomplished aided by even the most primitive resources and enough leisure moments to put them to use.

Obviously, an individual can't live his life twice for science's convenience, so the question of whether natural-born killers walk among us is largely moot. Even in rare cases of identical twins separated at birth, there is support for both sides. The Jim twins, Jim Lewis and Jim Springer, both married and divorced women named Linda to marry women named Betty. One had a son named James Alan, the other a son named James Allan. Both had dogs named Toy, chain-smoked the same brand of cigarette, served as sheriff's deputies, drove Chevrolets, raced stock cars, and had basement workshops. Both men built round white benches around trees in their front yard. Both men chewed their nails fanatically. Both preferred to sport mustaches but not beards.

Their medical histories were also strikingly similar. Both had gained and lost weight at the same age, both suffered what was mistakenly believed to be heart attacks, and both began having late-afternoon headaches at age eighteen. After a battery of standard personality tests, four psychologists, with better than two decades of experience each, were unable to say which test results belonged to which brother. If the Jim twins were typical of other separated twin pairs, the naturists had important evidence of an unalterable, inherent personality.

However, while the Jim brothers displayed a high degree of correlation in every testable area, they were the only pair in hundreds to do so. Statistically, the Jims remained nothing more than an interesting anomaly—until another set of curious statistics arose.

When genetics came into its own in the 1950s, the two sides thought they'd finally found the means to settle the issue. "Show us

ex·san·gui·na·tion *n.* [L. *exsanguinatus* drained of blood, fr. ex- + sanguin-, sanguis blood] (ca. 1909): the action or process of draining or losing blood.

49

SCIENCE NOTE:
Digitalis, the drug,
comes from foxglove,
the plant, not the
other way around,
as depicted in this
episode.

a crime gene," said the nurturists. Well, science seldom moves as fast as portrayed in film or on television. With minimal indications of which of the hundreds of thousands of genes might be the one they were seeking, the naturists began their search with a rather simplistic examination of the genetic history of criminals. One of the most easily observed traits was the number of chromosomes, or groups of genes, present.

In most of us, there are twenty-three pairs of chromosomes, with the twenty-third pair being the X or Y chromosome that determines our gender. A person with two X chromosomes, XX, is female; a person with an X and Y chromosome, XY, is male. An easily observable oddity here is the occasional presence of extra chromosomes. Regardless of how many X chromosomes a person has, the presence of even one Y will make a person male. Anyone with the XXY combination is male, as is anyone with the XXXY combination, or, rarer still, XYY.

In early studies among prison inmates, it was found that some several thousand prisoners had the easily observable XYY combination. As these individuals were typically bigger, taller, and more aggressive, they were quickly dubbed "supermales," but the question of whether this was the crime gene still remained. What was the distribution of this extra chromosome in the general population? After all, the only criminals available for study were those in prison — those who'd been caught.

In Denmark, in 1976, a much broader study was conducted on almost every male born in Copenhagen between 1944 and 1947. Of more than 30,000 men, twelve were discovered to have the XYY combination and, of those twelve, five *had* been convicted of one or more criminal offenses. In a general population with a crime rate of less than 2 percent, the XYY males had a rate of nearly 50 percent. It was starting to seem as though the "genetic criminal" did indeed exist. The discovery of XXX and XXXX females within the female prison population was also beginning to support the theory.

A further breakdown of the numbers, however, revealed some telling data for the other side. Yes, five men had criminal records, but not *violent* records. In many cases, the men were guilty of simple theft. One man stole his neighbor's lawnmower, hardly a crime on the scale of the tea-sipping murderer.

The next telling blow in the naturists' case was the almost uniformly low intelligence scores found in the XYY group. As with Down's syndrome, another condition resulting from extra chromosomes, the "supermales" and "superfemales" of the prison population scored significantly below average on IQ tests. Was the higher percentage of XYY men in jails a result of being too stupid to scheme or premeditate, much less plan a near-perfect crime? Was the truly frightening killer the genetically normal XY male? Without further results to support the model for a genetic killer, funding for the studies fell off and the issue was largely ignored.

Which is where writers Biller and Brancato picked up the tale. They chose women as their villains, a startling idea even today when women's prisons are filling fast. Shucking yet another layer from the stereotypic serial killer, they made their murderers children. The element they maintained, the still unresolved issue, was whether it was possible to genetically program a killer. Enter the Eves, with a genetic structure of nearly twice the normal number of chromosomes, intelligence scores that bent to the extremely high end of the scale instead of the low end, and the well-recorded characteristics of increased strength and a lowered tolerance for imposed morality. With criminals easily the equal of our favorite agents, the story was ready to be played out.

Meanwhile, fact met fiction deep in the labs of the real FBI. At about the same time Biller and Brancato set the Eves in motion for our entertainment, the FBI began a serious attempt to catalog the thousands of blood samples that have passed through their labs. Envisioning a DNA-print file as extensive and effective as the fingerprint files they've maintained for the past fifty years, the FBI hopes to be able to answer questions like those posed in "Eve."

Mind Wars: The Final Battlefield

In this episode, as Deep Throat carefully outlined the Litchfield experiment and its goal to create the perfect soldier through eugenics, he mentioned the strength and intelligence of the Eves but not one word explaining how they "just knew" how to independently orchestrate identical murders. For that, the audience has to slip back to the days of the Cold War and remember the paranoia that swept two continents: McCarthyism in the United States and gulags filled with political prisoners in the Soviet Union. During the Cold War period, both superpowers desperately sought some advantage, some weapon that couldn't be topped by the other side simply making the same thing but bigger.

Whether the Soviet Union or the United States was the first is

ANSWERS

1. Adam.
2. By phone. A series of clicks formed a code.
3. Give yourself full points for any three of: heightened strength, heightened intelligence, genetically identical, physically identical, or psychotic.
4. They overdosed her with digitalis.
5. Cattle mutilations.
6. They were exsanguinated. (Give yourself an extra point if you can spell it!)
7. A bunny.
8. The Litchfield experiment (or the Litchfield project).
9. She bit a guard's eyeball.
10. 56 total, extras at 4, 5, 12, 16, and 22.

YOUR SCORE: 12

hard to determine half a century later, but, without doubt, both sides diverted some small portion of their defense dollars into long shots like psychogenic weapons. Under project descriptions that carefully avoided the use of words like "psychic" or "paranormal," preferring instead "novel biological information transfer system," the CIA spent $100,000 in 1978 in an attempt to determine the level of Soviet advances. The Navy denies their involvement in a study of psychic submarine-finders between 1976 and 1978, but readily admits to "an investigation of the ability of certain individuals to perceive remote faint electromagnetic stimuli at a noncognitive level of awareness." Seven years after the end of the Maimonides remote viewing experiments (a study of how accurately psychics could envision unseen locations), Maimonides director Stanley Krippner discovered that the "private sponsors" who'd funded the work were, in fact, the CIA.

In the meantime, the Soviet Union was working on its own projects even more covertly than the United States. Russke Kroyke, the designation for the experimental work carried out in various centers around the USSR at that time, involved the following:

• A Moscow computer class was given an assignment to see if it was possible for a human, by will alone, to interfere with the delicate electronic pulses required by, for example, a hand calculator.
• Drawing on the theory that plants were capable of empathic responses, several Soviet commune workers were encouraged to "think hard about the growing seeds" while planting crops.
• Combining parapsychology with the traditions of their eastern neighbors, Soviet soldiers in the Leningrad area were enrolled in an "advanced" hand-to-hand combat course that actually involved little more than staring at your opponent until you *mentally* overcame him.

While many of these endeavors seem silly now, both the Soviet and American research teams were deadly serious about determining once and for all if mental warfare was a possibility. The notion that a thought might "distract" the sensitive guidance system of, for example, a wireless missile, was every bit as terrifying as the threat of full-scale nuclear war. The consensus appeared to have been that it was better to look silly in the short term than be dead in the long term, especially as these experiments were some of the cheapest ever made on either side's budget.

Personnel Dossier
#J-27061965-0105-2

Subject Name:	Unknown
Known Aliases:	**Deep Throat**
DOB: Unknown	Nationality: American
Address: Unknown	Contact #: Unknown

Supervisory Notes (chronological)

1. The subject known as Deep Throat operated in the Vietnam arena during the American conflict with that country. Though he has, in recent months, aligned himself with various factions within the Justice Department, specifically a minor subdivision of the Federal Bureau of Investigation, the subject was previously a known member of the Central Intelligence Agency.

2. The subject's security clearance at this time is unknown; however, surveillance teams have reported his easy movement through a number of high-security areas. While this is highly suggestive of a ranking security clearance, the extent of his actual penetration of these facilities remains unknown.

3. This subject is aware of the International Extraterrestrial Biological Entity Directive and has participated in the execution of this directive on as many as two occasions. As one of this subject's few known contacts was observed to actively attempt the prevention of the International EBE Directive, it appears that Deep Throat's activities are, at least in part, unknown to his contacts.

4. Contact between this subject and his "operatives" is on a covert level. Direct observation suggests Deep Throat is contacted by the simple expedient of a blue lightbulb directed at a window. The subject's response has been determined to be limited to brief calls consisting of nothing but clicks. Despite continuous surveillance, there is no apparent correlation between the clicks and the meeting destination. This suggests a complex, rotating signal system.

Contact is kept ... clicks formed a code. 5 means death

5. Determining the organizational affiliation of the subject known as Deep Throat is made more difficult by the existence of a "black budget," unreported funds, which could easily hide his presence on CIA payrolls or within the discretionary budgets of the section heads of a variety of other groups.

6. Discreet observation of the homes of various of Deep Throat contacts reveals that this operant has, on at least two occasions, passed documents of a sensitive nature to outside agents. Subject will require closer observation to confirm.

7. Regardless of the subject's formal affiliation, his access patterns have consistently shown that he has a more than passing acquaintance with a variety of military organizations. This may present a problem in future penetrations.

8. There do seem to be some areas where the subject's influence appears negligible. Notable among these is the High Security Facility where certain cryogenically preserved materials are currently stored. It is possible that these areas may provide opportunity for the distribution of disinformation at some later date.

9. This source has been subjected to extreme prejudice. File closed.

(N.B. As this source continues to elude standard intelligence operations, no standard format for information storage is available at this time. It is highly recommended that anyone with reason to access this file use associative rather than linear search methods.)

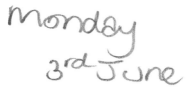

Monday 3rd June

Code Name: "Fire"

CASE SUMMARY

Sparks fly on several fronts when an old flame of Mulder's arrives on American soil to arrange the protection of a British diplomat under threat from a pyromaniac. As Mulder attempts to resolve both his stormy relationship with the vivacious Inspector Phoebe Green and a lingering childhood fear of fire, Scully's more prosaic investigations reveal the danger in their midst.

DEEP BACKGROUND

No Smoking Please!—Spontaneous Human Combustion

While Mulder's fear of fire is one many of us share, how much *more* frightening must it be to have a firsthand run-in with spontaneous human combustion, a phenomenon suggesting that people can burst into flames for no apparent reason.

Few known cases of spontaneous human combustion have been carefully recorded. Aside from satisfying the more macabre side of human nature, there's an understandable desire to comprehend and prevent such events. If one person can suddenly burst into flames without cause, why not another? Why not you, or me?

Though there are only a handful of documented cases, consistent circumstances link them easily. The most notable features of SHC are the lack of a fire source; the almost total combustion of flesh and bone that leaves only extremities undamaged; localized burning limited to the victim and his/her chair, sometimes leaving

EYEWITNESS STATEMENT

This is classic Phoebe Green, Mind Game Player Extraordinaire. Ten years it's taken me to forget about this woman and she shows up in my life with a case like this!

—Mulder, "Fire"

clothing undamaged. The concentration of occurrences usually indoors or in cars suggests that the phenomenon may be, in some way, related to enclosed spaces, but it has also happened outdoors.

CASES

The most famous case is, unfortunately for researchers, only famous because of the media attention devoted to it, not because it's the best example of SHC.

Mrs. Mary Reese, a Floridian, was last seen alive at about nine in the evening after crawling into her pajamas and her favorite house-coat and curling up in an easy chair. When her landlady left, Mrs. Reese was enjoying a before-bed cigarette.

The following morning, eleven hours later, the landlady returned to deliver a telegram—and maybe share a cup of tea—only to find the doorknob hot. Alarmed, she called to two nearby painters and, with them, entered the apartment. A wooden beam had caught fire, but there was no sign of the tenant.

Firemen were called to deal with the beam and, in the process, discovered a pile of ash, a foot in a slipper, a charred liver attached to a piece of vertebra, and a shrunken skull as small and hard as a baseball. Mrs. Reese's cozy chair and everything else in a well-demarcated circle, four feet in diameter, was gone. Plastic items in the proximity had melted, but fabrics equally close hadn't burned. A pile of newspapers at the edge of the circle wasn't even singed.

On entering the apartment, even experienced firefighters had failed to catch the faintest wisp of burned flesh, a near-impossible odor to get rid of in an open area, much less in a closed apartment. No trace of combustible chemicals was ever found and investigators had difficulty believing such destruction could arise from a single cigarette. Media organizations had a hard time believing it too, and were soon airing stories about the latest case of spontaneous human combustion.

The media, however, are seldom the final arbitrator of truth and two forensic investigators continued delving into the case. Though they disagreed on minor points, the analysts declared the death both accidental and explainable. They determined that Mrs. Reese, drowsy after her usual nightly sedative, dropped her cigarette, ignited her rayon housecoat, and was overcome before she could react. As the fire took hold, her body fat melted and helped fuel the flames—the candle effect. A film of grease covered the floor around the few remains of the body.

The main point left to be addressed, which might determine if this were a SHC case or a particularly unfortunate series of events, was whether a cigarette fire, even one driven by rayon and body fat, could account for the complete charring of the body. One doctor, who'd observed bodies in crematoriums at over 2,000 degrees Fahrenheit, had seen recognizable bones eight hours later. Others confirmed that bones left at lower temperatures for the eleven hours specified in this case could indeed be reduced to ash. Mrs. Reese's case, after investigation, was relegated to the "unfortunate, but not unusual" file.

It did, however, serve to alert the public to SHC and resulted in other unusual cases being investigated as they were reported. A truly bizarre case is that of Billy Thomas Peterson, who was apparently *dead* when he caught fire. Peterson had earlier gone out to his garage, closed the door, turned on the engine, and quietly committed suicide. When found, Peterson's body was badly burned, a religious statue attached to the car's dashboard had melted, but nothing else was affected. His clothes, even his underwear, were completely undamaged. His body hair, unsinged, protruded through the crisped skin and his bangs hung across a cracked forehead.

While other objects have been said to spontaneously combust, and are being investigated along with the cases of SHC, our devotion to the macabre makes it unlikely those object-related cases will supplant SHC in the minds of the media or of average people.

In the Name of International Cooperation: Scotland Yard

Scotland Yard—actually named New Scotland Yard, but even its own officers forget that—is the headquarters of what is essentially a municipal police force, the London Metropolitan Police. Perhaps for brevity, perhaps to accommodate local custom, or perhaps because of Scotland Yard's considerable reputation in both fact and fiction, the LMP has been "the Yard" almost since its inception back in 1829.

Created by Sir Robert Peel to replace a paid police force comparable to modern-day rent-a-cops, the Bow Street Police, the first HQ of the Yard was at 4 Whitehall Place, which opened onto Great Scotland Yard. The huge space, one of the easiest to turn a hansom around in, had been named after the "town castle" of visiting Scottish royalty which had originally been built on the site.

Despite a fixed address in a ritzy neighborhood, something their Bow Street predecessors could barely dream of, Scotland Yard ran

The hair stylist who turned Gillian Anderson's long, blond hair into its present smooth titian bob was acknowledged on-screen when the British MP was given his name: Malcolm Marsden.

[handwritten note: ah! The person who does her hair is Malcom! I never got it before!!!]

57

into the same difficulties as the force they were replacing. Making the police civil servants hadn't changed their image and, at first, Scotland Yard's officers may even have received worse treatment from the public. The first agency to use plainclothes officers, Scotland Yard was, in 1842, considered little more than a spy organization operating on domestic soil. As the FBI would later discover, the public didn't want to be spied on. Perhaps because of the vocal outcry against its officers, Scotland Yard laid down strict guidelines for them that would prevent many of the growing pains other forces of the time suffered. By 1878, when the Yard set up its Criminal Investigation Department (CID), it actually enjoyed considerable public support.

A small force at first, the CID was responsible for the gathering of information on criminal activities. That information, passed back to the main force for immediate action, was the first serious attempt to *prevent* crime instead of simply responding to it after the fact. With a mounting record of successful cases, the CID gained the personnel and financial awards necessary for the division's growth. The technologically advanced force now employs more than 1,000 detectives and enjoys a respect that would flabbergast the Bow Street Police, who often had to go to elaborate lengths to keep citizens from attacking their homes.

Around the turn of the century, the London police headquarters at Scotland Yard became badly overcrowded. In 1890, a new headquarters building was erected on the Thames Embankment and named New Scotland Yard. It too would soon be outgrown and, in 1967, the current headquarters were established in a spanking new building on Broadway. The name, New Scotland Yard, was kept.

Nowadays, under the direction of its commissioner, the Yard carries out a mandate little different from its original mission. Foremost among its goals are the detection and prevention of criminal activities, the protection of public order, and civil defense should a state of emergency be declared. In addition to those duties, its officers also ensure that cars are properly licensed and that crosswalks are safe for children running home to lunch from school. Though its reputation has become international, the Yard is still very much a local force and its internal divisions reflect that dual nature. Under the supervision of four assistant commissioners are the Yard's main departments: administration, traffic and transport, criminal investigation (the CID), and police recruitment and training.

The CID handles all aspects of criminal investigation including the criminal record office, fingerprint and photography sections, the company fraud squad, a highly mobile police unit known as the flying squad, the metropolitan police laboratory, and the detective-training school. In this sense there's a strong parallel between the functions and activities of the CID in Britain and the FBI in the United States. In fact, during the 1967 move, Scotland Yard was jokingly referred to as a Hooverian organization because of the tons of paper trucked from the Thames address to Broadway.

But there is one important activity undertaken by the Yard that isn't handled by their American cousins. In America, it's the Secret Service that is primarily responsible for the protection of domestic politicians and visiting dignitaries. However, as correctly evidenced by the appearance of Inspector Phoebe Green with the Marsden family, Scotland Yard fulfills that function across the pond. As Scotland Yard is also responsible for maintaining links between British law-enforcement agencies and Interpol, Phoebe's contact with local U.S. authorities would likely have been well within her scope at home.

Although Scotland Yard's responsibility is limited to metropolitan London, its "flavor" is decidedly international. Like the FBI, its assistance is often sought by police in other parts of the world, as well as in connection with unusually difficult or bizarre cases within England.

Gillian Anderson

DOB	August 9, 1968
Place of Birth:	Chicago, Illinois
Height: 5' 2"	Hair: Blond, colored auburn Eyes: Hazel
Marital status:	Married, Errol Clyde Klotz, 01/01/94
Dependents:	Piper, daughter, b. September 25, 1994 *(Through creative filming, Anderson's pregnancy was not included in the ongoing plotline. She worked until two days before the cesarean birth, and was back at work after missing only a single episode.)*
Parents:	Rosemary and Edward
Siblings:	2

Other residences: As a young woman, Gillian Anderson was widely traveled, following her father, also an actor, from Puerto Rico to London to Grand Rapids and Chicago. She has since lived in New York City and Los Angeles and currently makes her home in North Vancouver, British Columbia, Canada.

TRIVIA BUSTER 12

Easy Stuff: Give yourself 1 point for each correct answer.

1. How does Cecil L'Ively kill his victims?
2. What did Phoebe leave in Mulder's car?
3. What was L'Ively known to send to the wives of his victims?
4. Who rescues the Marsden children from the hotel fire?
5. Where did the Marsdens rent a house for their vacation?

Getting Tougher: Give yourself 2 points for each correct answer.

6. How did L'Ively kill the driver?
7. What alias did L'Ively assume on reaching the States?
8. Name the Marsden children.
9. Where did Mulder and Phoebe share a "certain youthful indiscretion"?
10. What chemical did L'Ively use to increase the damage caused by his fires?

Educational Information

Attended Fountain Elementary, Grand Rapids, Michigan.
Graduated from City High, Grand Rapids, Michigan, 1986.
Attended DePaul University's prestigious Goodman Theater School, graduating with a Bachelor of Fine Arts.
Studied at the National Theater of Great Britain at Cornell University, Ithaca, N.Y.

HA HA   Theatre Colour

Professional Information

Anderson's acting ambitions began back in Grand Rapids, where she became involved in community theater. While at DePaul University, she earned a role in *The Turning* but moved east—not west—at graduation, choosing to pursue a career in theater instead of film. Three years later she'd appeared in *The Philanthropist* at the Long Wharf Theater and won a Theater World Award for her performance in a production of Alan Ayckbourne's *Absent Friends*.

A dip into television with *Home Fires Burning*, a talking book version of *Exit to Eden*, and an episode of *Class of '96* later, she was willing to consider taking an episodic role. The character of Dana Scully, a bright woman who'd sacrificed nothing of her femininity to a demanding career, had an irresistible appeal.

Chris Carter had already decided Anderson was made for the role and, despite some "questions" from the network (which was flying in actresses for further auditions), Gillian Anderson was cast as Scully. The rest is *X-Files* history.

Gillian Anderson was married to Clyde Klotz on a Hawaiian golf course (seventeenth hole) by a Buddhist priest, shortly after meeting him when he worked as a visual artist on the set of *The X-Files.*

Case #: X-1.13-010794

Code Name: "Beyond the Sea"

CASE SUMMARY

Scully, on returning to work immediately after the unexpected death of her father, is particularly vulnerable to serial killer Luther Lee Boggs's tantalizing glimpse into the world beyond. When Mulder is shot and she's left to continue the case alone, she must reconcile herself to her father's death before she can put Boggs out of her mind and save the lives of two innocent teens.

From Séance to Channeling: Opening a Door

DEEP BACKGROUND

Though the episode "Beyond the Sea" was one of the most popular among X-Philes—especially those who'd been waiting for a Scully-centered episode—it was also one of the most frustrating. X-Philes can argue the likelihood of artificial intelligence going mad and even the possibility of aliens visiting our solar system with considerably more authority than they can debate whether Scully or Luther Lee Boggs was the ultimate source of the visions and premonitions throughout this episode.

Though some remain convinced that Scully should have just taken a few more days off, others aren't so sure something odd wasn't at work here. After all, people have been trying to glimpse whatever lies beyond death for a long time. Before the Greek Renaissance, when necromancy (divination by communicating with the dead) became part of orga-

EYEWITNESS STATEMENT

At the age of six, Luther Boggs slaughtered every pet animal in his housing project. When he was thirty, he strangled five family members over Thanksgiving dinner and then sat down to watch the fourth quarter of the Detroit–Green Bay game.

—Mulder, "Beyond the Sea"

61

*I already
knew that to
to Rob.*

nized religious observances, early oracles and mediums cast bones or gazed deep into animal innards. Though crystal-gazing and tea-leaf reading have lost their connection with the dead, they too were once among the means by which departed spirits could contact the living.

In the mid-1700s, the séance arose as a form of contact that, though modern, was as ritualistic and deliberate as any Greek invocation. Channeling, which some have described as a séance for one, was the talent Boggs claimed to possess and is, despite its New Age connotation, actually a reversion to one of the earliest types of mediumship. Both channeling and séances are now enjoying a revival period.

During channeling, the medium actually *becomes* the spirit sought. Voice, posture, patterns of speech, even the general appearance of the medium's face may change, taking on that of the person being contacted. During a séance, however, the medium's role is slightly more removed. Most mediums working within groups contact a familiar spirit who acts as a guide, a messenger between other spirits and the medium. Evidence of contact is less likely to be directly connected to the medium. While voices can become evident, they are often disembodied, and if music is heard, it will come from the air, not the agent. Instead of actually assuming the guise of the spirit, a ghostly apparition composed of a mysterious substance called ectoplasm seems to settle around the medium.

Automatic writing is another means by which mediums may establish a connection with spirits. Perhaps because it requires the use of hands that are otherwise occupied in a séance, or because it assumes that the medium has become inseparable from the spirit, automatic writing is generally limited to channelers. While under the influence of a spirit, a channeler's hand scrolls across the paper. In some cases, the purpose is merely to assure the seeker that they've reached the correct soul by replicating the spirit's handwriting; in others, it's a means for the spirit to answer questions or pass messages to the living.

Automatic writing was extremely popular for several decades during the 1800s but, with the turn of the century and the popular dissemination of psychological literature, a second, more grounded theory became feasible. So much automatic writing appeared as fragmentary thoughts with fantastic elements that psychologists postulated that the medium, instead of being adept at contacting the dead, was actually incredibly adept at making contact with the writer's own subconscious, an unusual talent in itself.

In recent times, the channelers' ability to assume a personality other than their own has begun to intrigue psychologists. Some suspect that it may be channelers who open doors into our own unconsciousness—a world as mysterious as the afterlife.

In the realm of the séance, automatic writing seldom occurred, but another expression of a spirit's presence, automatism, allowed the group to act as one with the medium. The Ouija board, one of the most common tools of automatism, even allowed the séance's traditional circle of hands to remain unbroken. In response to accusations that devices like the Ouija board could be manipulated, spiritualists have responded that the séance itself allowed certain subliminal thoughts and messages to be received. That they were *expressed* through the Ouija made them no less relevant; the medium's role is to provide an environment where the *average person* could contact the spirit world, even if unknowingly.

Many channelers believe that channeling, the act of a single individual, is actually an evolution of the séance. They claim that with our inhibitions broken down, *anyone* can contact other realms.

Where in the World? British Columbia!

Though *The X-Files* cases have supposedly taken Mulder and Scully over most of the country, even to Puerto Rico and Norway, in reality the show's producers have found all those exotic locales in and around British Columbia, Canada. Like a long list of programs, *The X-Files* does its primary shooting out of North Vancouver. It was the pilot episode that originally brought the crew to British Columbia. Unable to find a forest in or around Los Angeles, the X-crew found plenty of forest in Canada.

Here are some other location surprises:

- "Tooms" wasn't filmed at 66 Exeter Street or anywhere else in Baltimore. Instead, the liver-eating mutant tried to make a happy nest for itself under the escalator at Vancouver's City Square Mall.
- Standing in for Lake Okobogee, where a woman's trailer was nearly fried and her daughter abducted, was Buntzen Lake in Port Coquitlan.
- While the audience may have thought the Flukeman was swimming happily through the pipes and tanks of the Newark Sewage System, he actually had a slightly tighter fit at the Iona Island Sewage Treatment Plant.

Easy Stuff: Give yourself 1 point for each correct answer.

1. What pet name did Scully call her father?
2. What is Scully's mother's name?
3. What did Scully's father call her?
4. What song played at the wedding of Scully's parents?
5. How did Scully's father die?

Getting Tougher: Give yourself 2 points for each correct answer.

6. For what crime was Boggs incarcerated and sentenced to death?
7. What item of clothing did Mulder give Boggs to use during Boggs's channeling session?
8. What other prop did Mulder try to trick Boggs with?
9. What object did Boggs warn Mulder to avoid?
10. What famous musician did Mulder ask Boggs to channel?

ANSWERS

1. Ahab.
2. Margaret.
3. Starbuck.
4. *Beyond the Sea.*
5. He had a heart attack.
6. Multiple murder. He strangled five members of his family over Thanksgiving dinner.
7. A piece of Mulder's New York Knicks T-shirt.
8. A fake newspaper with a headline reading: "KIDNAPPED COLLEGE STUDENTS FOUND SAFE. POLICE SEEK SUSPECT."
9. A white cross.
10. Jimi Hendrix.

YOUR SCORE: 9

- By mixing some previously shot stock footage of the famous J. Edgar Hoover Building with location shots of Simon Fraser University in Burnaby, the crew created the illusion that Mulder and Scully could just dart down to the office any time to research their latest case. Propping the J. Edgar Hoover Building sign on SFU's ugliest building was probably an improvement.
- West Vancouver's Lighthouse Park played host for the EMA-winning episode "Darkness Falls." Just across the border from Washington State, where the episode was supposedly set, the scenery needed to mimic Olympic National Forest wasn't difficult to find.
- When the crew needed a restricted facility to house an alien, Powertech Labs, Inc., in Surrey became Mattawa, Inc., Washington—complete right down to level six where Mulder just missed his best chance to view an alien.
- Some places are just so good you could visit them twice, which is exactly what *The X-Files'* crew did in Stevenson Village, Richmond. First it became Steveston, Maine, home to the Kindred. Then, when a home was needed for the Miracle Ministry's traveling tent show, it became Kenwood, Tennessee.
- Instead of jumping off a pier into an anonymous Maryland harbor in "The Erlenmeyer Flask," Dr. Secare flew off the end of the Versatile Shipyards into North Vancouver's chilly water.
- Boundary Bay Airport, in Ladner, is usually home to a few light aircraft and gliders, but for "Deep Throat," the quiet little airfield became Ellens Air Force Base in Idaho.
- For David Duchovny's dangling-off-the-side-of-a-Skytram scene in "Duane Barry," filming moved to two local ski hills, Grouse Mountain and Seymour Mountain.
- In "Blood," the crew made use of a perfectly good tower at University of British Columbia, allowing the phobic sniper to use it as a vantage point.
- The home of Vancouver Canuck Pavel Bure was briefly the residence of a vampire-fetishist when the episode "3" was filmed there just prior to the hockey player's taking occupation of his new house.
- For the odd scene that absolutely demands the perfect location shoot, there are ways to work around the necessity of having your actors and the location in proximity to one another. When a scene of Mr. X leaving his opera at the Kennedy Center was

required, a second production team went on-site to shoot the location. The gentleman seen leaving the center isn't actually Steven Williams, who plays Mr. X, but a member of the District of Columbia Film Commissioner's office who happened to be there and fit the physical profile well enough to carry it off.

For X-Philes living in the Vancouver area who can't get enough of their favorite duo, the black and orange signs with "X-FILES" sprayed across them are close enough to the real thing—even if it's just a crew catching those all-important establishing shots and none of the actors is anywhere to be seen.

The song played as Captain Scully's ashes are scattered, and which inspired the title of the episode, is Bobby Darin's "Beyond the Sea."

Case #: X-1.14-012194

Code Name: "GenderBender"

CASE SUMMARY

When the victims of a serial sex killer include both men and women, Scully wonders if they're dealing with a bisexual or a transvestite. Mulder's response, that the killer's variable sexual practices might extend beyond a simple change of clothes or partner, seems incredible. Then he and Scully discover a small cult whose members exert a strange pull on outsiders.

DEEP BACKGROUND

Pheromones

If Mulder thought it odd to find his smooth, sophisticated partner rumpling the sheets with Brother Andrew on the basis of nothing more than a scent, he didn't know as much about pheromones as he seemed to when he first suggested them as a plausible explanation for the string of deaths that began "GenderBender."

The pheromone is perhaps the most widespread chemical in nature, seeming to affect all animals except birds. Specifically, a pheromone is any chemical secreted by one organism to affect another, expressed through special organs or through sweat, urine, breath, even the oils of the hair or skin. They can be released in a general sense, to float on the air and whatever else comes in contact with the body, or they can be directed to carefully chosen locations. They aren't even restricted to the animal kingdom. Some mushrooms, slime molds, and algae release pheromones that encourage parts of the organism to clump and grow together.

As in the algae, the purpose of phero-

EYEWITNESS STATEMENT

I know what I saw, Scully—I saw you about to do the wild thing with some stranger!

—Mulder, "GenderBender"

mones has been found to be the promotion of togetherness, to encourage individuals to gather together so that the group can act as a single unit for particular tasks. Ants who find food will leave a scent trail behind them as they return to the nest. Not surprisingly, something that can cause grouping can also inspire swift dispersal. In schooling fish, it's not uncommon for a wounded member to release a particular scent that acts as an alarm to the rest.

Undoubtedly though, it's the pheromones related to sexual togetherness that attract the most attention from both scientists and lay readers. The ability of a sexual pheromone to linger for many times the duration of an alarm pheromone strongly suggests that they're more important to the pheromone producers as well. Alarm scents among moths may carry up to three miles, but moth mating pheromones have been known to affect moths *ten miles* away. In some mammals, the presence of pheromones in the area is a necessity if the animal is to mature sexually; individuals raised away from the group may remain in a stunted state of growth until death. A different scent invokes the parent/young response, creating a desire to nurture and protect the vulnerable. There are strong indications that the young of almost every species first recognize their providers by scent alone.

Interest in the possibility of human pheromones is now growing, having probably been delayed by a number of prevalent misconceptions about the human ability to smell. Compared to other animals, humans were once believed to have limited olfactory senses. While a newborn rabbit has as many olfactory cells as skin cells, the human ratio is closer to one olfactory cell to ten thousand skin cells. We aren't even playing the same game as a shark, whose 50:1 ratio in favor of olfactory cells allows it to smell at a mile's distance something we wouldn't smell if we were standing in it.

However, what we lack in quantity, we make up in other ways that are only recently being understood. What we *do* have that's lacking in many other animals are *pain* receptors where our olfactory cells should be. Humans don't perceive all smells equally; there are some we'll avoid at all cost, others we'd just as soon avoid, and still others we actively seek out. Though research is still sketchy, it might be because somewhere in our development, evolution decided that some smells are dangerous and should be perceived by our pain receptors as unpleasant, even if nothing is about to bite us. One example of an odor triggering pain, as opposed to olfactory nerves, is spoiled meat. Though we can't find a McDonald's without the golden

Easy Stuff: Give yourself 1 point for each correct answer.

1. What did the members of the religious community call themselves?
2. What is the major commercial product of the religious community?
3. What did the victims die of?
4. Mulder found something unusual in the barn cellar. What?
5. What did Mulder and Scully find in the field after the disappearance of all the people?

Getting Tougher: Give yourself 2 points for each correct answer.

6. What unusual chemical was associated with the victims' deaths?
7. What magazine topped the stack Brother Andrew had hidden in his room?
8. On a scale of one to ten, where did Marty's surviving victim put him/her?
9. When Scully and Mulder arrived in the religious community, the residents were engaged in some rather odd activities for a rainy afternoon. Name one.
10. What was the horse's name?

ANSWERS

1. The Kindred.
2. Pottery.
3. Coronary failure.
4. A series of tunnels where the Kindred "buried" their members.
5. A single crop circle.
6. Pheromones, human pheromones.
7. *Bazaar.*
8. "A kind three."
9. Pick one of:
   A. hanging laundry in the rain.
   B. cutting grass to lie on wet ground.
   C. chopping wood in the rain.
10. Alice.

YOUR SCORE: _15_

arches, a dog, whose acute sense of smell we've co-opted for our own use, is ten times as likely as we are to eat tainted meat.

Pain endings are more widely distributed among the nasal cavities of humans than olfactory receptors — ask anyone who's been punched in the nose — and those nerves are exquisitely capable of reacting to even mild irritants like orange oils. Strong irritants, like ammonia, produce responses active enough to rouse the semiconscious.

If humans are so sensitive, even if the rest of the animal kingdom might term us differently abled, how do we manage to avoid being in a constant state of pain?

By adaptation. Humans adapt to odors, basically ignoring them on all practical levels. How we do it is still a question, but human beings who enter a slaughterhouse and immediately begin gagging, can, within an hour, "tune out" the scent. Oddly, the adaptation rate rises with the strength of the odor. The scent of something burning on the stove will remain with us twenty times longer than the smell of the slaughterhouse.

The fact that humans classify tastes like tart and sweet isn't news: Most people agree that lemons are sour, sugar is sweet, and cloves are bitter. One item will elicit the same taste response from the vast majority of people. What *is* new is that we do the same things with odors. Because wintergreen and eucalyptus, for example, fall within the same *odor* category for the majority of people, we can sniff wintergreen until it fails to invoke a scent response — until we tune it out — and then be completely unable to smell the new scent of eucalyptus.

This new understanding of the human sense of smell has prompted the recent study of our response to pheromones. Could we smell pheromones, and produce them as well?

Yes. And yes.

With hindsight, the signs were always there. Perfumeries have long included musk, a pheromone, in their products. In households where several women of menstruating age live together, there's a tendency for their menstrual cycles to synchronize. That females become incredibly sensitive to musklike odors around the time of ovulation is a strong indication that human males must, either currently, or at some point in our past development, produce a musky pheromone. Once the evidence was gathered supporting human reactions to pheromones, some studies were begun to *find* the human pheromones.

In testing human vaginal secretions, certain fatty acids came to light, chemicals that are nearly identical to combinations known to act as pheromones among other primates. Scent testing swiftly revealed that human males react strongly to these fatty acids. What remains to be seen now is whether a source for male pheromones can be found. As males tended to be the aggressors throughout early history, it's possible that no such chemical exists in modern man, but, as most modern species do have mirrored pheromones in males and females, the search will continue. The existence of human pheromones may even explain love at first sight.

Nicholas Lea, who later appears as Mulder's new partner, Alex Krycek, makes a brief appearance in "Gender-Bender." You can also see him as Jake in *Bad Company*, and as Baines in *Xtro II: The Second Encounter*.

IT'S A BOY! IT'S A GIRL! IT'S . . . !?

While "GenderBender" took alternative sexuality over the top, it's old news to most biologists. A number of species have the potential to adjust at will either their own sex or that of their offspring. Even among human beings, the genetic potential for either sex is present for a considerable time after conception and most embryos go through a phase where both sexes are at least partially expressed. The ability to change sex completely as adults, however, isn't among our usual talents.

Some of the species that can change sex at will—or at least in response to environmental factors—are: guppies who respond to population pressures; certain frogs who begin tadpole life as one sex, but finish it as the opposite; and several of the larger amphibians of South America who appear to express both sexes into adulthood and then adopt the sex of the most needed gender.

The social insects like ants or bees usually produce offspring of a particular sex (or no sex at all) by flooding their environments with a sex-specific pheromone (ants) or by feeding them specific foods like royal jelly (bees).

What was truly extraordinary about the Kindred was their ability to not only switch genders but to shift back and forth! Only a few of the Earth's species have ever been suspected of shifting more than once per lifetime and even their capabilities have yet to be confirmed.

Code Name: "Lazarus"

CASE SUMMARY   During a bank stakeout to capture a modern-day Bonnie and Clyde, Scully's former lover and fellow agent, Jack Willis, is gunned down along with criminal Warren Dupree. Though her desperate efforts to bring Willis back from the edge of death seem successful, Mulder's not so sure Willis is really Willis.

DEEP BACKGROUND

Agents We Have Known

Whether skeptical, open-minded, or credulous, the FBI agents we've met through the episodes have taken different positions on the X-Files. With questionable characters like Krycek and Mr. X surrounding them, who might Mulder and Scully trust?

SPECIAL AGENT TOM COLTON
X-1.03-092493
While Agent Colton is competent and well-placed within the Bureau, even Scully, a former classmate, has displayed her displeasure with his inability to evaluate the evidence as given. His attempt to pump Mulder for information without sharing credit for it has not gone unnoticed.

SPECIAL AGENT NANCY SPILLER
X-1.07-102993
Contact with this agent has been limited. Agent Scully studied under her as a forensics student at the academy and, while finding humor in the woman's nickname—the Iron Maiden—appears to have considerable respect for her as an agent. Her openness to exotic theories has yet to be tested.

EYEWITNESS STATEMENT

You *are* Jack Willis!

—Scully, "Lazarus"

Special Agent Jerry Lamana
X-1.07-102993

As one of Mulder's previous partners, Agent Jerry Lamana might have been expected to support the work of the X-Files division. Instead, his current probationary status within the Bureau has had the opposite effect. While refusing to consider Mulder's theories about sentient computer systems, Lamana was willing to steal and present Mulder's criminal profile as his own. Agent Lamana's future support became a moot point when he died during the investigation of this case.

Special Agent Jack Willis
X-1.15-020494

While Agent Willis had few professional dealings with the X-Files (the lone instance being a stakeout), he and Agent Scully had a relationship while he was an instructor and she was a student at the Quantico training facility. If, as is often the case when agents form personal relationships, that trust carried over into their field work, he might have been a supporter. However, Jack Willis died during the investigation of this case.

Special Agent Reggie Purdue
X-1.16-021194

While Reggie Purdue was no wide-eyed rookie, he hadn't developed a mindset so fixed as to ignore the theories of an agent already acknowledged to be one of the Bureau's best and brightest. Without becoming a slave to Mulder's interpretations, Agent Purdue was perfectly capable of thinking beyond traditional possibilities if the situation required it. He was killed by John Barnett.

Special Agent Henderson
X-1.16-021194

A technician in the area of document examination, Agent Henderson has been willing to consider Mulder's theories. It seems entirely possible that future dealings with this agent would proceed on a footing of mutual respect.

Special Agent Lucy Kazdin
X-2.05-101494

Initially distrustful of Mulder's theories, Agent Kazdin wasn't so close-minded as to ignore evidence put in front of her. She also admitted she might have misjudged the Duane Barry situation. In the event that Agent Kazdin should happen to encounter either Agent Scully or Mulder, cooperation wouldn't be an unreasonable expectation.

Easy Stuff: Give yourself 1 point for each correct answer.

1. What did Scully give Jack Willis for his birthday?
2. What did "Willis" retrieve from the body of Warren James Dupree?
3. What physical feature of Warren Dupree was transferred to Jack Willis?
4. Jack Willis had a life-threatening medical condition. What was it?
5. Where did Scully and Willis spend a weekend?

Getting Tougher: Give yourself 2 points for each correct answer.

6. What birth date did Scully and Willis share?
7. What crime is in progress when Willis and Dupree are shot?
8. Something about Scully's birthday card warned Mulder that Willis might not be what he seemed. What was it?
9. Where did Dupree and Lula Phillips normally hide things they didn't want found?
10. Where did Scully and Willis meet?

SPECIAL AGENT BOCKS
X-2.13-011395
Agent Bocks, unlike the majority of Bureau personnel, has no difficulty formulating implausible theories, impressing even Mulder with his skill in applying paranormal circumstances to earthly events. While Agent Scully questions Bocks's ability to objectively assess a crime scene, there's little doubt that he would continue to provide support to the X-Files' agents.

SPECIAL AGENT BARRY WEISS
X-2.16-021095
Though Mulder and Scully's association with this agent was cut short by his murder, he was willing to throw the support of his section behind the Washington agents.

In this episode, Scully can't be located by the signal from her cellular phone. At the end of season two, however, the Smoking Man has no difficulty locating Mulder in the middle of the desert by *his* cellular signal.

Code Name: "Young at Heart"

CASE SUMMARY

A painful case is resurrected when the subject of the investigation, supposedly dead for five years, begins writing threatening notes to Mulder and killing his friends. When Scully's medical contacts turn up an alarming connection between Mulder's suspect, John Barnett, and a modern-day Dr. Frankenstein, the pieces begin to fall into place. The question now is will Mulder find Barnett before Barnett finds Scully?

Between the Lines

DEEP BACKGROUND

The handwriting analyst in "Young at Heart" said she was showing off when she claimed to know some extraordinary things about John Barnett. Maybe she was, but maybe not. Back in 1933 an expert analyst convicted a rumrunner by determining from his writing alone that he had a stiffened middle joint in the thumb of his right hand.

The work of the "questioned document examiner" isn't limited to handwriting; it also encompasses the examination of typewriting, inks, papers, and typography, and covers such problems as the identification of handwriting and typewriting, the sequence of events involved in the preparation and handling of a document, the alteration of a document, and the age of documents.

Handwriting, like all other evidence, is identified on the basis of individuality. Children are taught specific ways of forming letters, but they rapidly begin to project their own individuality into letter formation and writing execution. By the time people reach maturity, their writing has acquired peculiarities that serve to identify them.

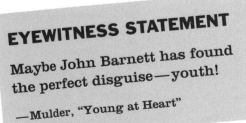

EYEWITNESS STATEMENT

Maybe John Barnett has found the perfect disguise—youth!

—Mulder, "Young at Heart"

Handwriting experts believe it's impossible for anyone to mimic another's writing perfectly. Body position, dexterity, the angle of the pen, and other factors, a lifetime's worth of idiosyncrasies can't be learned in a moment, or even in several days, regardless of the forger's skill. To the distinguishing eye of a professional, the slant of a stroke, the pressure on a curve, the type of dot over an *i*—all combine to create a style as individual as a face.

If the writing itself isn't enough, document examiners can add a lot to their profiles by taking into account tangential evidence. For example, far from ensuring anonymity, the use of a typewriter can make the examiner's job easier. The make and model of any typewriter used to prepare a document can be determined by examining typeface designs and comparing them to information contained in

Just for fun, have a look at your own handwriting and see if you can spot any of these characteristics:

- **Big loops, indicative of an outgoing and confident nature.**
- **Sharp angles, the mark of the decision-maker.**
- **Circles instead of dots over the *i*, representative of a fun-loving personality.**
- **Longer descenders (the parts of letters below the body, like the downstroke in *y*) than ascenders (the parts of letters above the body of the letter, like the upstroke in *d*), often found in those with latent psychic ability. The opposite situation is thought to represent the logical side of human nature.**
- **Overall tiny construction, frequently seen in those with the best organizational skills.**
- **Overall large construction suggests an artistic nature.**
- **Illegible writing, a sure sign of a future or current medical professional.**

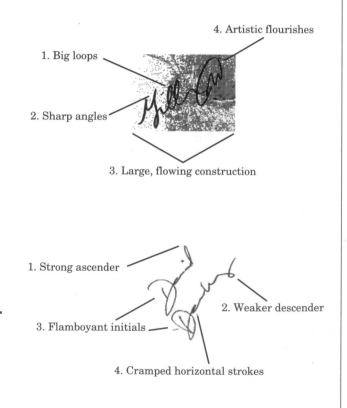

4. Artistic flourishes
1. Big loops
2. Sharp angles
3. Large, flowing construction

1. Strong ascender
2. Weaker descender
3. Flamboyant initials
4. Cramped horizontal strokes

reference files and differentiation charts. The work of a specific typewriter can be identified if it contains sufficient "identifying individuality," based on broken or tilting characters, badly aligned characters, characters that print more heavily on one side than on another, and rebounding characters.

Mechanical conditions affecting the type basket or the escapement may also have identifying value. Since it is impossible to reinsert a document into a typewriter in its exact former position, it can be determined, using a ruled screen, if a document has been prepared at one sitting or has been reinserted.

Ink comparisons provide compelling evidence that is frequently of value, but it is not possible to individualize ink; that is, to identify it as coming from a unique source. Chemical tests of various kinds are used for ink comparisons, however, and it is possible to eliminate possibilities on the basis of an ink's composition.

Papers can be differentiated on the basis of fiber, filler, and sizing constituents. Fibers can be identified by differential staining and microscopic examination. Fillers can be identified by X-ray diffraction because they are crystalline substances. Chemical tests are used for the identification of paper constituents, making it possible to identify the source of specific batches of paper.

Questions concerning the sequence of writing—for example, whether the ink signature is over or under the typewritten portion of a document—can be important in proving the authenticity of a document. In this and related problems, such as deciphering and restoration of eradicated or erased writing, examinations are carried out using stereomicroscopes, ultraviolet and infrared techniques, or chemical tests, depending on the specific problem.

While the general approach of the experts is usually the same, some place more emphasis on certain characteristics than others. Most pay special attention to word terminals—upward, horizontal, or downward—and to connections between letters, as these are the easiest points of comparison. Today's experts undertaking a complicated study use their microscopes to examine every stroke of the pen or pencil.

On rare occasions, experts are confronted by puzzling problems arising from the practice of using invisible writing materials like milk, lemon juice, or saliva. It has been found, however, that with proper scientific treatment and illumination such writing can be made legible once again. In some instances, forgers will trace a signature onto another piece of paper; less frequently, they will attempt to erase using ink eradicators, rubber, or knives. But if the paper has

Easy Stuff: Give yourself 1 point for each correct answer.

1. Who was the subject of Mulder's first case?
2. How old was Mulder when he joined the FBI?
3. What did the first note say?
4. How long was Barnett's sentence supposed to be?
5. What cause of death was listed on the official certificate?

Getting Tougher: Give yourself 2 points for each correct answer.

6. Where were the crematory ashes scattered?
7. Which state was Barnett from?
8. What disease was Dr. Ridley treating at the National Institutes of Health?
9. Under what ruse did Barnett gain access to the music hall?
10. In what locker did Barnett hide the research material?

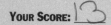
been altered, erasure can be detected with little difficulty, usually with the help of ultraviolet light.

For future document examiners, the real challenges are created not by human hands but with high technologies. Photocopiers have become so good that currency copied on high-end machines is known to get by bank clerks. Desktop publishing has become so easy to access that almost anyone can create checks indistinguishable from the real thing. Laser jet printers never come in contact with the paper they print on, so physical evidence like typewriter key marks doesn't apply. While previous efforts have been aimed at detecting forgeries after the fact, modern attempts to eliminate forgery will likely center on methods of creating irreproducible images. Far from being a waning field, document examination is entering its most innovative era.

PROGERIA, Dr. Ridley's specialty, a disease that causes such rapid aging that a ten-year-old child can not only appear to be ninety, but experience all the medical complications of that age. Its victims seldom live beyond their teenage years. Though rare, the disease receives an unusually large share of research funding as many scientists believe that a cure for progeria may hold the ultimate key to aging in general.

Duchovny
(doo-KUV-nee), from the Russian, "spiritual."

David William Duchovny

DOB: August 7, 1960
Hometown: New York City
Height: 6'   Hair: Brown   Eyes: Hazel
Identifying marks: Mole on right cheek
Marital status: Single, never married, but is cur-
                            rently in a committed relationship.
Dependents: Blue, a dog of mixed breed, female.
Parents: Amram and Margaret Ducovny
Siblings: Daniel (older), living in Los Angeles
              Laurie (younger), living in New York City
Interests: Sports, both individual (jogging, swimming, and
              yoga) and team (basketball and baseball). Writing,
              including poetry. Music. Theater.

Educational Information

Collegiate Prep, Manhattan
Princeton University, B.A.
Yale University, M.A. (English), Ph.D.
  (unfinished)
Dissertation: "Magic and Technology
  in Contemporary Poetry and Prose"
The Actor's Studio

Filmography

Working Girl (1988)
New Year's Day (1989)
Twin Peaks (1990)
Bad Influence (1990)
Julia Has Two Lovers (1991)
Denial (1991)
Don't Tell Mom the Babysitter's Dead (1991)
The Rapture (1991)
Beethoven (1992)
Baby Snatcher (TV, 1992)
Ruby (1992)
Chaplin (1992)
Red Shoe Diaries (TV, 1992-)
Venice/Venice (1992)
Kalifornia (1993)

He's also done three television commercials:
Lowenbrau Beer (1987), AT&T (1993),
NYNEX (1995).

Code Name: "E.B.E."

CASE SUMMARY

Vague hints from obscure sources and a dramatic increase in UFO sightings lead Mulder to think he might be on the trail of an Extraterrestrial Biological Entity—a live one! Scully, wary of the machinations of Deep Throat, isn't so sure. The involvement of The Lone Gunmen, an organization as paranoid as Mulder himself, does little to ease her concerns.

DEEP BACKGROUND

The Lone Gunmen

The Lone Gunmen embody paranoia come to life. Though they only appeared in five episodes during the first two seasons, each has provided fascinating tidbits about this group that takes its name and the name of its newsletter from the "Lone Gunman Theory" of President Kennedy's assassination.

Whether they were hiding behind the grassy knoll, or just had enough sense to keep their heads down, sixteen episodes were already in the can before The Lone Gunmen first appeared in "E.B.E.," when Mulder approached the trio for information on recent UFO sightings. At the time, their ability to pick up one another's sentences, their common pool of knowledge, and their joint cynicism, made them difficult to differentiate as individuals.

The Lone Gunmen also appeared together briefly in "Blood," and "One Breath," allowing viewers to begin to pick them apart. Most easy to separate from the other two was Frohike, whose interest in Scully was shown through a genial, half-joking "She's tasty," and a more conservative concern that extended to flowers, combed hair, and

EYEWITNESS STATEMENT

That's why I like you, Mulder. Your ideas are even weirder than ours.

—The Lone Gunmen, "E.B.E."

a suit. From a man who trades night goggles for phone numbers, a comb and Brillo may equal true love.

In "One Breath," we were also introduced to the most mysterious member of this strange cabal, a hacker known only as The Thinker. While we couldn't pin a face to the images streaming across a computer screen, this latest member may have been all the more intriguing for the mystery. And "Fearful Symmetry" provided the opportunity to *finally* put names to faces. Because Langly was absent from the tight trio, Byers was the dark-haired man with the fetish for IBM-styled clothes. The blond was, by default, Langly.

"Anasazi" left us dangling in many ways, but, for those interested in The Lone Gunmen, it seemed to hold the final piece of the puzzle: The Thinker. For the first time, we saw the Gunmen come to Mulder instead of the other way around. One of their number was in trouble and would speak only to Mulder. At last, we had a name. Kenneth Soona. Even the name, however, is discovered to be probably a pseudonym. Mulder meets Soona, and we have a face, but that's about all.

The mysteries continue.

U.S. ARMY TO EXAMINE A "FLYING DISK"

FROM OUR CORRESPONDENT

WASHINGTON, July 8

After an Army announcement from Roswell, New Mexico, that an object resembling a " flying disk " had been found there, the commander of the Eighth Air Force said here to-night that the object was being sent to the research centre at Wright Field, Ohio, for examination.

The first well-publicized E.B.E. crash.

sfX

Special effects is *the* fastest growing and most quickly changing area of film and television production. Increasingly sophisticated audiences are demanding more and more from their television entertainment as well as from the big screen.

The advent of computer technology has undoubtedly pushed the field ahead. On programs like *Babylon 5,* for example, entire scenes that never existed outside a computer system are displayed on a regular basis. But while computer technology has made it possible to create spectacular visual effects like people-eating shadows in "Soft Light" and the smooth morphs in "Colony," it is by no means the only trick in the special effects department's little bag.

Special effects embraces a wide array of photographic, mechanical, pyrotechnic, and model-making skills, and makes use of makeup artists and wardrobes as well as technicians. Over 200 people have

Easy Stuff: Give yourself 1 point for each correct answer.

1. Where was the bug hidden in Mulder's apartment?
2. What did Scully blame the trucker's illness on?
3. What's an E.B.E.?
4. What was in the $20 bill?
5. Name The Lone Gunmen.

Getting Tougher: Give yourself 2 points for each correct answer.

6. How do Mulder and Deep Throat contact each other?
7. What did Scully find in her pen?
8. What was wrong with the moon in the photo?
9. What organization does Deep Throat claim to have been a member of during the Vietnam War?
10. What level of the facility were the agents trying to reach?

contributed to *The X-Files'* effects. Optical and physical effects can be used together or singly depending on the desired image, which means that, on occasion, an entire outside company may be required, as was the case with the whirlwind in the pilot episode.

Perhaps the most important piece of equipment for optical effects like mattes, blue screen, off-speed shots, and fades, is the optical printer, a camera-projector combination that allows the operator to take a picture of a picture. Frames can be printed more than once to slow a scene or freeze an image, which can extend costly effects like Samantha's floating body. By skipping frames, the audience perceives an increase in speed.

By mixing the trailing frames of one scene with the opening frames of the next, a simple dissolve is easily accomplished. More complex manipulations allow sophisticated superimposition, the combination of several live-action shots, and the addition of animated sequences to live action (or vice versa)—combining "Fire's" flames and the live-action actors. The use of an aerial image optical printer (which is aimed at a platform of ground glass that can hold an image projected from below) allows artists to position artwork and live action so precisely that both images can be filmed in a single pass—an enormous time-saver for the production crew.

Optical printing's ability to combine two tracks of film to form a third that incorporates both can be used in conjunction with other techniques to further increase the variety of images produced. An optical printer with blue-screen photography, for example, can create seamless images of flying (or floating) characters (like Duane Barry in the episode of the same name) to which eerie glows and audio elements can be added later without any of the background bleeding through the moving character.

Blue-screen technology exploits film's sensitivity to blue light. By having an actor work in front of a blue screen lit from the back to avoid shadows, and recording the action on Eastman No. 5247 film to create a dense black-silver image everywhere the blue would have been visible, other images can be imposed on the positive print. The images of the actor and the background can then be combined on a single film, allowing actors to vicariously visit any number of locations they'd never approach in the flesh. For big effects like raging fires, blue-screen is a favorite among actors and sfX personnel alike.

Smaller effects are often called for as well, and, while optical effects have certainly progressed, some things are best handled by talented physical effects personnel. Exploding pustules, character aging, erupting fungi, and subcutaneous parasites, for example, are products of both the special effects and makeup departments. Prosthetics (literally replacement body parts but with a slightly broader meaning for effects artists) receive incredibly detailed examinations before an actor is allowed to use them. Even the tiniest prosthetic can be painful if an actor hasn't been properly fitted, if it's applied incorrectly, or if the actor has a reaction to the composite material. So complex is the process for a full-body prosthetic application, like that of the Flukeman in the episode "The Host," that actors are often filmed reacting to creatures that are still being made by technicians.

Prosthetics can be relatively simple, like the black dots that showed up in "Ice," or complex, incorporating hidden water bulbs or mechanical elements to produce movement, as well as bladders of other fluids that should seep, squirt, or bubble from the prosthetic. Prosthetics that have to be mutilated in some way present other complications and it's sometimes necessary to cast and reproduce an actor's entire limb, or create another model, so that live action and optical action can be joined without obvious breaks in filming. Certainly actor Darin Morgan had no desire to really hang around under the falling grate that chopped Flukeman in half.

The most common models, of course, are scale models where huge items are made small enough to be filmed easily or tiny objects are re-created at many times their normal size. Creating scaled models that will look realistic on screen is actually a two-part problem. The obvious problem, that of creating a reasonable facsimile of the original item, is actually the easier of the two to resolve. Talented modelers will often spend huge amounts of time observing their subject and making rough sketches and sculptures before tackling the model itself.

The real problem is one of filming technique. For moving models, maintaining a smooth movement that's proportional to other objects or backgrounds is difficult. Without attention to detail, miniatures have a tendency to appear jerky and flimsy. The usual response to the tracking problem has been twofold. First, off-speed filming at a higher rate produces a slow-motion effect and smooths movements. So does rigging the model and camera so they remain steady relative to one another. A mobile camera and fixed model make swooping actions, even close up, realistic and smooth.

While *The X-Files* allows the audience to supply many effects by having action take place off screen and letting the viewer's imagination fill in the blanks, it has tackled both big and small effects. From floating letter openers to pulsating pustules to alien silhouettes to hovering children, there's little the show won't attempt.

Code Name: "Miracle Man"

CASE SUMMARY

The Miracle Ministry's claims to heal the sick and even raise the dead were old news. So were complaints about them. If not for a rash of deaths in the Miracle Ministry's tent, the FBI wouldn't have sent in Mulder and Scully. What should have been a straightforward murder investigation becomes much more when Mulder's long-lost sister begins appearing and the dead really do rise.

DEEP BACKGROUND

The Healing Touch

Psychic healing, faith healing, or miracle—by whatever name you call them, claims of instant cures beyond the ability of contemporary science have been with us as long as diseases and accidents. Equally timeless and usually ignored by the miracle worker is the question, "Did it work?"

In an age of televised miracles, answering that question should be easier than ever: Set your VCR to record any television evangelist's show, track down its miraculously healed congregants, and ask them. Nothing could sound easier. In fact, it's the model that dozens of investigators have tried to put into action, the same model Mulder and Scully tried to use in "Miracle Man" to substantiate the minister's talent.

Like all investigators before them, they quickly discovered that while medicine, a science, welcomes peer critique, faith healers often claim their methods depend on mutual belief between a healer—as a stand-in for a greater force—and the healed. Doubt, expressed or implied by a need to confirm the obvious, might negate the benefits gained. Before expecting cooperation from healers or the healed, the investigator is urged to explore faith-healing by first dropping all efforts to apply scientific methods to spiritual experiences, and encouraged to approach it from a historical and holistic perspective.

THE MODERN TRAVELING MISSION

Tent missions were once popular events in America. Their tendency to follow a fair or circus route, the charismatic style of most evangelists, and the cheer with which assistants passed the hat gave the whole thing something of a carnival air. If the evangelist threatened fire and brimstone, so much the better; after evoking a fear level about on par with a Saturday afternoon horror matinee, the attendee left feeling a cathartic release from sin. The addition of faith healers to the evangelist's entourage was a natural, the equivalent of the circus sideshow.

It was when the faith healers *became* the show, around 1950, that some people began to worry that something dangerous was happening under the white tents, that faith healers were lying, and that those lies might begin to cost lives.

One researcher to seriously address the issue was Peter May. He didn't just watch the tent shows on television, he attended—and left with deep reservations. He'd seen people throwing away medicine and walkers, glasses and hearing aids being taken from children, supplicants declaring themselves healed of cancers and free of doctors. If it was all true, wonderful; if not, these people were in a desperate situation.

In the cases May studied from one particular ministry in London, he had several years worth of flyers and advertising spots to consult, all full of claims, and, at least initially, the cooperation of the faith healer's people. It was a promising beginning, but the difficulties he encountered could have formed a textbook for the fictional confrontation between the Miracle Ministry and Scully and Mulder. Within weeks, May found himself hip-deep in confused diagnoses and prognoses, unproven therapies, contradictions between doctor and patient reports, and, most importantly, fear. Whether it was fear about their illnesses or what would happen if they allowed themselves to be reexamined, fear cast its shadow across every case. Even with all the testimonials in hand, dredging up the truth was difficult.

May put aside his own research material and asked the faith

healer to produce what he felt were his three best cases from the recent ministry. While awaiting a response, May discovered that the ministry's claim that everyone was coming to be healed was false. At one meeting, fully 450 of the people present claimed to have *already* been healed. May then took a list of five names provided to him by the faith healers and began a case-by-case investigation.

Sheila L., a forty-five-year-old with a fifteen-year history of constant back pain attributed to a slipped disk, had left her job and been confined to a wheelchair when outdoors and a walker when in her home. She'd been through the gamut of analgesics, physiotherapy, acupuncture, and corsets. At one meeting, a hand was laid over her and the faith healer prayed for her recovery. The pain disappeared immediately and, according to the ministry's advertising, she'd remained healthy ever since. All the trademarks of a psychic healing were present.

A check of her medical records turned up X-rays showing a narrowing of the L5/S1 disk space. Osteophytes, bone growth, had also intruded into the space. Her orthopedic surgeon agreed that the degree of degeneration was severe, certainly capable of causing considerable pain. In his large practice, the surgeon had seen many cases like Sheila's but she was the only one in a wheelchair. She was also the most depressed of his patients. She was sometimes suicidal and her pain, which extended to her arms and neck, was inconsistent with an L5/S1 problem.

May found that an X-ray taken after the healing showed absolutely no change. Sheila's record included a notation of a further period of back pain following the meeting, for which she was treated with medication. Whether or not Sheila believed herself healed is unknowable, but the facts of her record directly contradict the way her case was used in the ministry's advertising.

Of the children who were healed of visual impairments, all had their glasses taken from them and only one set of parents were willing to have their son, in this case three-year-old Azam, retested. Once again, a documented medical record existed. Just before attending the mission, Azam's home-care worker had begun to think the boy had a squint and arranged to have it checked. As suspected, Azam was found to have a lazy left eye caused by farsightedness and astigmatism.

After attending the mission, more comprehensive testing showed results for the left eye that were slightly better than the rough original estimate. Though Azam's mother believed a miracle had happened, the ophthalmologist pointed out that not only had the testing conditions changed, but it was earlier in the day, Azam wasn't as tired as he'd been on the first visit, and the underlying problems, astigmatism and farsightedness in one eye, hadn't changed.

Under warning from the physician that Azam could lose all vision in the eye if it wasn't used, his parents returned his glasses. Though they requested that the faith healer refrain from using their son in the testimonial flyer, the following continued to show up: "My son had very poor eyesight and could not see out of his left eye. . . . Since MTL, he has been healed and is now able to see clearly out of both of his eyes."

Georgina M., a forty-six-year-old woman claiming to have been healed of a fibroid tumor, was high on the faith healer's list of substantiating cases. Her doctor disagreed. Prior to the "healing," Georgina had sought medical attention in April 1992 for excessively heavy menstruation. Hormone studies indicated she was experiencing a fairly common symptom of imminent menopause. To *eliminate* the possibility of fibroids or other masses, her doctor arranged an ultrasound examination. No fibroids were found. Subsequent testing by a different physician didn't find any fibroids either. Hardly surprising. In May's opinion, what he was seeing were patterns of behavior and belief that, in the wrong circumstances, could be deadly.

Small wonder the X-crew found grist for a horror story within the lights and flash of a tent ministry. However, never willing to accept stereotypes, they refused to let their faith healer, or even the diamond-flashing lead minister, be the bad guy. Instead, perhaps more surprisingly at a time when contemporary teleministries are rocked by scandal after scandal, Mulder's faith in Samuel turns out to have been well placed.

Samantha's Shadowy Influence

In the days of show-it-all-preferably-graphically television, it's rare to encounter the "invisible character" whose very absence provides motivation to other characters and moves both plot and action forward. Samantha Mulder is just such a character (regardless of what the audience thinks it has seen when a Samantha or two has appeared).

From episode one, we've seen Mulder's passion, his search for the truth about his sister, his desperate need to know. We've supported his questionable antics, recognizing the greater good of his cause on those occasions when we're just as happy we aren't the subject of his searching scrutiny. His survivor syndrome, the guilt he seems to

TRIVIA BUSTER 18

Easy Stuff: Give yourself 1 point for each correct answer.

1. What came through the air vents of the courtroom the day Samuel was arraigned?
2. What was Leonard Vance's claim to fame?
3. What was the name of the traveling tent ministry?
4. Who did Samuel raise from the dead?
5. How did Samuel die?

Getting Tougher: Give yourself 2 points for each correct answer.

6. What did Samuel supposedly have in common with the biblical Moses?
7. What did the vanity plate on Rev. Hartley's Caddie say?
8. To what religious denomination does Scully belong?
9. How were the victims actually killed?
10. What did Nurse Salinger claim happened to Samuel's body?

wear somewhere between his skin and his clothes, yanks at our heartstrings. Knowing the history of this intense man, we build up expectations that never need to be spelled out in dialogue or action.

When Chris Carter presented his audience with a man who consistently saw a little further than his colleagues, whose vision seemed clear enough to take him through the jibes and snickers, and who would be tackling huge, impersonal organizations, he must have recognized that this character's weaknesses must equal his strengths. In many ways, Carter had created a mythic hero and set Samantha up as the Holy Grail. Without her, this odd hero might have settled into a life too like the average American's to be of interest. Who would watch a civil servant plod through his day?

On rare occasions Samantha Mulder has appeared to play a more direct role in Fox Mulder's life. In "Miracle Man," for example, Samuel's apparent ability to project her image or dredge it up from Mulder's mind sent Mulder searching for answers in what might otherwise have been an interesting case, but one tangential to his real life's work. The appearance of an adult Samantha, a living, breathing woman who appeared ready to pick up the old Stratego pieces, would not only renew Mulder's efforts to find the real woman, but tie in yet another floating mystery, why these green-blooded clones should deserve so much of Mulder's attention.

At every turn, this absentee character's influence affects her brother's work and, with those subtle touches, the direction of *The X-Files*.

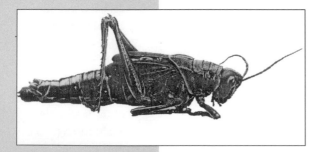

Code Name: "Shapes"

CASE SUMMARY

When a Native American youth is gunned down by a rancher claiming to have shot at an animal, Mulder's suggestion of lycanthropy brings swift rebuttal from Scully. Not even the very first X-File, another lycanthropy case opened *before* Mulder's revival of the dusty division, convinces her that men can defy the restraints of their physiology—at least not without some hard physical evidence. A bizarre footprint trail, a scrap of skin, and tales told in smoky reservation taverns aren't exactly what she had in mind.

Under the Moon: Lycanthropies Among Us

DEEP BACKGROUND

As the werewolf prowls the underbrush, waiting to leap from the shadows and settle its teeth deep into the pulsating throat of its victim, the uninformed would be hard-pressed to separate it from its kissing-cousin, the vampire. They might consider the werewolf (or lycanthrope) a hairy vampire, but a vampire nonetheless. In *Dracula and the Werewolf* and a host of *Son of . . .* films that delight and terrify children at Saturday matinees, the werewolf often appears as little more than an adjunct to the great vampires, a pet sharing its master's feasts.

But long ago, in Romania, China, even Paris, the differences, blatantly displayed in headlines and news stories that read like macabre autopsy reports, were evident. The vampire thirsts for blood, needs it to survive, and without it suffers the cramping hunger that a human would if confined for days without food. A failure to hunt is tantamount to suicide. The vampire is a vampire for eternity, incapable of crossing back to

EYEWITNESS STATEMENT

I coulda sworn I saw . . . red eyes . . . and fangs.

—Jim Parker, "Shapes"

87

the mortal world: inhuman. The dead are of no interest to the vampire and it disturbs no grave but its own. In a number of myths, far from being a killer by design, the vampire is a hungry shepherd fervently concerned with the survival of his flock.

Compare that to the classic lycanthropy case of a Parisian by the name of Bertrand who, as but one of the highlights of a checkered career, dug a fifty-year-old woman out of a week-old grave. Using the shovel only for those bony bits he couldn't manage with his bare hands, he tore her to shreds, threw the pieces back into the grave, and proceeded to grovel among them before gnawing on a stray finger as exhaustion overwhelmed him. When captured, shortly after raiding a booby-trapped cemetery, Bertrand swiftly spilled his entire history to the police. His confirmed acts included desecrating the grave of a seven-year-old child, who he literally tore in half. His first insatiable longing had come over him as he and a friend walked past a funeral.

Woodcut, circa 1792.

While both lycanthrope and vampire have been called creatures of the night, there exist between the two more folkloric differences than similarities. Perhaps the most significant disparity is in their very creation, or origination. This might explain why the vampire has come to symbolize, for many, an evolution of humanity, while the werewolf languishes in Western literature and film. The vampire doesn't choose its fate. Once a normal mortal, helpless before the vampire's formidable ability to lure, to coerce, to seduce, a new vampire begins existence as a victim. The vampire's strength and dexterity, its charisma, its magical abilities, simply overwhelm the chosen subject. Not so the werewolf. In nearly every legend, the werewolf *chooses* its fate. While folktales can romanticize the victimized vampire, create heroism in its struggle to find dignity in its new life, it's difficult to find anything noble about a creature whose greatest joy is to gnaw on the rotting carcasses of its own kind. Though both vampire and werewolf prey on humankind in bizarre forms of cannibalism, the vampire's need can be rationalized. The werewolf's motivation escapes us, so we have no empathy for it. Dr. Park Deitz, a forensic psychiatrist who has worked on cases as notorious as Jeffrey Dahmer's and who taught at FBI's Quantico training center, has speculated that our inability to understand and accept our bestial impulses has brought about the werewolf myth. Through his work, Deitz has concluded that there's very little human beings *aren't* capable of. But some acts are so bestial, so savage, it's nearly impossible for us to include them in any range of human behavior. A beast-man, a were-creature, even if mythical, can assume the mantle of such crimes without forcing humanity to accept responsibility.

The sheer number and variety of werewolves in human history give that theory credence. In modern times, Post-Traumatic Stress Disorder has been recognized as a psychological illness with distinct symptoms, symptoms so precisely articulated that it's a relatively easy matter to recognize. PTSD was centuries in the future when the Norsemen's societal demands forced them into battle, but these people, also known as the Wolfheads because of the wolf skins they wore in combat, may have found a different way to cope with the mental and emotional scars of war.

In dozens of Norse lays and poems, a mindset known as a berserker state or berserker rage has been described in detail. Like Bertrand the Parisian, the Wolfheads would fall upon the bodies of their victims, often destroying corpses and living enemies alike with their teeth and hands. Time appeared to warp and their attention narrowed to the immediate task. In some, the altered state resulted in amnesia so complete that the berserker retained no memory of his action from the time the battle began until he came to his senses hours or days later. The berserkers succumbed to a weariness deeper than would have been normal after days of strenuous labor.

In a very real sense, by wrapping themselves in the skins of animals, the Norse warriors had left their humanity behind when they'd stepped on the battlefield. The theme of *choice,* symbolized by the deliberate donning of the skins, is reflected in tales like those of the were-hyena of Abyssinia, warriors who coursed across the savannah in hyena skins to break open the graves of neighboring tribes.

Even those who didn't wrap themselves in skins enacted elaborate rituals to accomplish transformations from the human state. It's the skinless ceremonies that seem to have propagated the notion that a werewolf's fur could be found on the underside of his skin, just waiting to be called forth. The Russian werewolf, the

Easy Stuff: Give yourself 1 point for each correct answer.

1. What object, once owned by her brother, did Gwen Goodensnake pass on to Scully?
2. How do the Trego dispose of their dead?
3. How did Ish refer to the creature?
4. The Parkers were keeping an unusual animal on their property. What was it?
5. What did Mulder shoot in the Parkers' house?

Getting Tougher: Give yourself 2 points for each correct answer.

6. What peculiar trace evidence did Mulder use to convince Scully to consider the lycanthropy theory?
7. What unusual feature was discovered in Joe Goodensnake's mouth?
8. What disturbed the doctor about Lyle Parker's medical workup?
9. Who opened the first X-File?
10. When was it opened?

ANSWERS

1. A claw nearly as long
   as Scully's hand.
2. By cremation.
3. By its Algonquin
   name, the Manitou.
4. A mountain lion.
5. A stuffed bear.
6. Take 2 points for
   naming any of these
   items: shreds of shed
   skin, tufts of fur,
   tracks that appeared
   to morph from human
   to animal.
7. Fangs.
8. They found traces of
   his father's blood
   type in Lyle's system
   —presumably the
   result of ingestion!
9. J. Edgar Hoover.
10. 1946.

YOUR SCORE: 13

orborot, entered the lupine state every bit as deliberately as the Norsemen. A person wishing to become a werewolf went off alone to the woods where he'd search for a fallen tree to stab with a copper knife while chanting an incantation. As he circled the tree trunk, his perception would shift and, before long, the *spirit* of the wolf would possess him. Though he might not remember the details afterward, it was common knowledge that once possessed by the wolf spirit, the skin would become apparent.

While there are few tales of anyone being forcibly made into a were-being, cases abound where mysterious were-figures appeared from nowhere to tempt others to join them on their nightly romps. Perhaps the most famous—certainly the most detailed—account comes from the lips of Jean Grenier, a French teenager who'd confessed to numerous gory murders. In his tale, a man named Pierre Labourant, who constantly gnawed at his iron collar with the werewolf's dislocatable jaw and ruled over a place where his many companions sat on iron chairs set amid glowing coals, offered him the ability to roam as a wolf in exchange for his soul. Grenier, poor and without prospects, agreed. This Labourant, who Grenier called M. de la Forest, gave him a wolf skin and a magical salve along with instructions on how to use them. Grenier claimed that, within days, he'd mastered the transformation, and embarked on hunts and eaten five children.

That an adolescent should create such a tale was unsettling. Even more disturbing were the number of incidents the boy described and how uncannily his descriptions matched known facts. Though some of his claims were outright lies, his ability to recount the color of a murdered child's dress and give exact testimonials about its wounds, and to corroborate eyewitness testimony of one victim who'd escaped him were convincing enough for a court to convict him on several counts of murder. However, the oddest part of the trial was yet to come.

In her testimony, a witness named Marguerite Poirier, who'd driven Jean off with a shepherd's crook, described a startling change in his appearance. Never particularly attractive, the boy had dropped to all fours, becoming lean and sharp-boned as his teeth protruded beyond his lips and his face lengthened. Before leaving the stand, Marguerite described Jean as a larger-than-average wolf —a claim that was upheld by the parents of one of his victims who'd said all along that their child was snatched by a wolf. However, the judge, apparently quite progressive during an era when looking oddly at a neighbor's cow could get you burned, considered all this testimony and returned a verdict that Jean Grenier, though certainly guilty of murder, was more likely insane than a werewolf.

Instead of the hanging most people expected, Jean Grenier was confined to a monastery for the remainder of his life on the condition that he not try to escape. The monks could, of course, attempt to disabuse Grenier of his strange notions, but there was little hope of recovery. On being forced into the monastery's precincts, Grenier appeared to go mad for a time, racing about on all fours, howling, and gobbling down the offal he found near the monastery's slaughterhouse.

Seven years later, the judge found Grenier still at the monastery, but nearly unrecognizable. The boy had barely grown two inches, he lurked in dark corners and shyly turned his face away from strangers. Behind restless eyes, it seemed his mind was a blank. His lips drooped, but not enough to cover his elongated canines. The hands he constantly clenched and unclenched had black nails that naturally grew to a point. He died shortly after the judge's visit.

Silver Bullets and Iron Rods: How to Kill a Werewolf

There are a dozen explanations for how werewolves arise, and many more than one way to kill them. Should you find yourself faced with a rumbling growl echoing from the surrounding woods, try one of these:

1. Whether in bullets, crosses, or simple jewelry, silver is anathema to werewolves. Even if it doesn't kill them, the burns it causes will normally drive them off.
2. Like wizards, werewolves are also vulnerable to cold iron. A single blow from an iron rod to a werewolf's forehead is reputed to split the werewolf apart, allowing the man within to be freed.
3. Salt, saltwater, or any salted food you can trick a werewolf into eating or drinking are said to be deadly.
4. If your werewolf happens to have been a Christian, you could try splashing it with holy water or somehow forcing a eucharistic wafer into its mouth. Both are instantly fatal.
5. Asiatic werewolves are best disposed of by luring them into a pit of saltwater or onto ice over saltwater that can then be broken.

DARK DAYS

Code Name: "Darkness Falls"

CASE SUMMARY People are disappearing in the woods of Washington State. Not hikers or casual campers, but experienced woodsmen and the rangers sent in to find them. While a local logging company points fingers at an active ecoterrorist group in the area, both Mulder and Scully think it's a big jump from spiking a tree to murder. She doesn't put much more weight in a local's theory of what sounds like swarming, intelligent, killer fireflies.

DEEP BACKGROUND

All That Glows

Strange things *are* at work in the woods.

Fireflies, the very ordinary bugs we caught in jars as kids, are doing something absolutely extraordinary. Anyone who's ever stared up through the branches of their backyard trees knows that each firefly has its own rhythm, its own beat. Flash. Flash. Flash. Or maybe, flash-flash. Flash. Flash-flash. If any two flashed in unison, it was briefly interesting if only because you knew it wouldn't happen again. Like watching stars twinkle, half the intrigue of fireflies is their unpredictability.

So, when reports started coming out of Tennessee about not just two or three synchronous fireflies, but acres of them, entomologists' ears perked up quickly. Deep in the Great Smoky Mountains, a light show was warming up. The eerie sight had become almost old hat to generations of the Faust family whose cabin sits seemingly in the center of the rhythmic insects. In addition to the regular flashes, they'd even seen

EYEWITNESS STATEMENT

It'll be a nice trip to the forest.

—Mulder, "Darkness Falls"

a ripple of flashes run down the mountainside. And these bugs do more than just flash together. They also *stop* flashing together. It's not a simple continuous pattern but a complex combination of responses that would be closer to language-styled communication than signaling if not for the automatic aspect of the reply.

The Faust fireflies aren't alone. On the other side of the world, in Southeast Asia, throughout the firefly breeding season trees are observed flashing as though they were decked out for Christmas. After reading an article about the well-known Asian insects, Lynn Faust wrote a letter that caught the attention of ethnologist Grant Copeland, who recorded the activity with video cameras.

While he hasn't yet figured out why bugs on two different sides of the world just happen to have decided to form light orchestras, he does have some basic starting points. Fireflies, it's generally thought, achieve synchrony in much the same way that a crowd of people clap in unison at a baseball game. If you begin to clap by yourself, you pick a tempo of your own, but as you hear others clapping you adjust the interval of your claps so that your next one will be closer to theirs.

A synchronous firefly flashes rhythmically if it is alone. The rhythm, researchers believe, is an involuntary response, a biological means of completing a sensory circuit. If you imitate another firefly, by flashing a light in the first insect's eye, its rhythm will slowly adjust until it matches your light. So what could explain the fact that these two groups of fireflies appear to be gifted with a preprogrammed beat?

Researchers have determined that in both Asia and Tennessee it's the male fireflies that flash in unison. Regardless of the species or method of signaling, if all the signaling members are of the same sex, it's likely the signals are meant to attract the opposite gender. As normal signaling among fireflies is known to be a premating ritual, the question appears to be why the males of this species would sacrifice their individual flash patterns and join the crowd.

Copeland and others in the field believe the joint flashing is a means of attracting females who might be confused by the presence of other firefly species. Rather than risk a female passing all of them by, they cooperate to create a larger light signature. Once they've caught the female's attention, it's every insect for himself.

While a fascinating puzzle in its own right, the synchronous flashing of fireflies raises new questions about what insects, as a group, are capable of. Bees, termites, and ants have been frequent subjects

Easy Stuff: Give yourself 1 point for each correct answer.

1. What explanation did Spinney give for being up in the logging area?
2. What's a monkey-wrencher?
3. How did Spinney suggest they keep the bugs away?
4. In what unusual wrapping did they find one of the missing loggers?
5. What's a caltrop?

Getting Tougher: Give yourself 2 points for each correct answer.

6. Where did Larry Moore of the Federal Forest Service find a nest of the glowing insects?
7. What's a Freddie?
8. What prevented the environmentalists from leaving?
9. How had the lumber company's vehicles been sabotaged?
10. Who decided to let Doug Spinney go back to his camp?

of study but scientists are beginning to think they should broaden that test pool to include fireflies and all bioluminescent insects.

Awards!

Though success seemed to creep up on *The X-Files,* there were hints along the way that someone was noticing the show's many innovations.

John Bartley, who Chris Carter once called his "secret weapon," has consistently provided a steady influence on the images making their way into our homes each week. The film noir quality, the intriguing use of spaces and cameras, the hundreds of tiny details that make each episode unique, all come under his watchful eye. In 1994, his work was recognized by his nomination for an American Society of Cinematographers Outstanding Achievement Award for his work on "Duane Barry."

The technical staff received an Emmy nomination in the show's first year out for Best Music for a Title Sequence, and won the award for Best Title Sequence. That same year, the Viewers for Quality Television named *The X-Files* one of the best shows on the air—an unusual accolade for a sci-fi–horror–drama.

This episode, a fan favorite, won *The X-Files* the Best Drama Series at the Environmental Media Awards. Though Carter, in accepting the award, admitted the intent of the episode had been to frighten, not necessarily educate, the television audience, the episode was more effective for its lack of preachiness. Like most aspects of *The X-Files,* the subtle touch worked best. "The Erlenmeyer Flask," a favorite of both cast and crew, was nominated for an Edgar Award by the Mystery Writers of America for Best Episode in a Television Series.

In its second year, *The X-Files* seems to have shed whatever stigma might have been attached to its unusual subject matter. *Entertainment Weekly,* which had declared the show a "goner" in its first month on the air, now chose it the Best Drama of 1994.

Finally, the Golden Globes broke with its trend toward doctor and lawyer shows when it awarded *The X-Files* the coveted award for Best Television Drama. Beating out shows like *ER* and *Chicago Hope,* this was, for many non-Philes, the first indication that here was a series to be reckoned with.

THOSE AMAZING BUGS

How could some itsy-bitsy mites manage to get at least one of the husky woodsmen in this episode ("manly men at the height of their manliness," according to Mulder) all the way up a tree?

Always in search of the possible, if not the plausible, dozens of theories have circulated, including the idea that the loggers were somehow "treed" by swarming bugs. Although no less incredible, the true answer may be more realistic than that.

As Scully pointed out when she "unwrapped" an unfortunate woodsman, his (or her) body was thoroughly desiccated: completely dried out. What viewers may not be aware of is just how light a human body is once its fluids are removed. If these mites were as effective as their modern cousins, the spiders, they could have sucked out as much as *80 percent* of the logger's weight. Even a man of, say, 200 pounds becomes a lot more manageable once he's turned into a dried husk of less than 50 pounds.

Still, for an insect that weighs less than a grain of rice, 50 pounds might seem like a mountain. But the fact that these deadly little goobers were *glowing* goobers opens the door to a whole different scenario, because bioluminescence allows a bunch of individuals to work together. With that in mind, we no longer have just one glowing goober trying to heft a husky logger into a tree; we have thousands.

The final key to the mystery is the most obviously frightening aspect of the mites' activities: the way they cocoon their victims. If you assume the logger's body wasn't lifted into the tree until it was relieved of most of its fluids, that numerous bugs were working together to do the lifting, and that mites, like spiders, *have silk that shrinks,* the whole thing begins to come together and we can put aside the image of a full-grown man being lifted off his feet by tiny insects.

With their victim on the ground, the mites could have rather easily drained him of fluids, wrapped him in strands of silk that would naturally start the lifting process as it dried, and then pulled the body the remaining distance. Not as outlandish as being treed, but perhaps more incredible for being possible.

Jason Beghe, who plays Ranger Larry Moore in this episode, was instrumental in David Duchovny's decision to take up acting. The two wound up tending bar in New York and taking acting classes.

Could you imagine even a *bunch* of these lifting a logger into a tree?

Code Name: "Tooms"

CASE SUMMARY

When a psychiatric board frees mutant killer Eugene Victor Tooms, Mulder and Scully race against time in search of the down-to-earth evidence to put him back behind bars. While Scully exhumes one of Tooms's previous victims, Mulder attempts to avoid becoming the next.

DEEP BACKGROUND

Don't Forget to Pack Your Gloves

In "Soft Light," Mulder casually asks Scully for a "prophylactic" and is promptly handed a rubber glove from her seemingly endless supply. During his investigation of "The Host," he suggests that his latest corpse be wrapped in plastic as a "to go" order and sent to her. On one of the rare occasions when Mulder didn't have a body for Scully to work on, the CIA got in on the act and brought both her and

Oh, the places that scalpel has been. . . .

Mulder in to give their expert opinions on remains found two states away!

Even a lack of fresh material seems to be no impediment to having Scully muck about with dead bodies—especially with characters like Tooms, who provides the sixty-year-old cadaver she examines in this episode. Amid the charming aroma of Eau du Formaldehyde, Scully had, by the end of the second season, examined:

- something she believed to be an orangutan;
- a "wild woman" with human bone fragments in her stomach;
- bodies whose throats were crushed *from the inside*;
- scientists whose bodies contained prehistoric worms;
- sanitation workers infested by irradiated flukes;
- victims who died of extreme sexual excitement;
- soldiers with parts of their brains chopped out;
- scientists whose lungs had mysteriously filled with sand—just before something forced its way out through their necks;
- sailors whose bodies appeared to have turned to salt;
- at least a dozen bodies boiled in a pot; and
- the cavernous interior of an elephant.

If not for some religious taboos, she'd even have been elbow deep in the reputed remains of a werewolf!

Forensic Science: The Crime Scene Speaks

Though hardly as concerned with scientific accuracy as, say, *Quincy, The X-Files* has attempted to use the correct terminology, appropriate technique, and existing science wherever called for. If, from time to time, they've over- or underestimated the scope of those sciences, they've made forgivable errors in a field that's advancing so rapidly even its own experts would be hard-pressed to define the cutting edge. Not only is the frontier for forensic science advancing faster than ever before, but that frontier is breaking into narrower and narrower specialties.

PHOTOGRAPHY

Of all the fields, photography has likely progressed the most quickly and consistently. Certainly, photographers won't be found hunched under a tarpaulin anymore with a tray of gunpowder held high overhead. Though complex renderings such as the three-dimensional re-creation of Tooms's teeth are mostly theoretical at this point, as was the modeling of the victims' slashed chests in "Aubrey," incredibly detailed images, from odd sources, are being captured every day.

Just as color photography was a vast technological improvement

---

Easy Stuff: Give yourself 1 point for each correct answer.

1. How long is Eugene's hibernation period?
2. Where was Eugene's missing victim found?
3. What injury did Eugene have when he was admitted to the hospital emergency room?
4. Who was Eugene's doctor?
5. What hobby did Eugene's doctor mistakenly believe Eugene had taken up for entertainment?

Getting Tougher: Give yourself 2 points for each correct answer.

6. What was the name of the asylum where Eugene was held?
7. What breed is Mulder's fictional dog? (Extra point if you can name it as well.)
8. Where does Det. Frank Briggs live?
9. What's Mulder's preferred drink for stakeouts?
10. With his old apartment house torn down, where did Eugene build his new nest?

1. Thirty years.
2. Under the concrete floor of the Ruxton Chemical plant.
3. A dislocated shoulder.
4. Dr. Aaron Monte.
5. Papier-mâché.
6. The Druid Hill Sanitarium.
7. Norwegian elkhound, named Heinrich.
8. Lynne Acres Retirement Home.
9. Iced tea.
10. Under an escalator in a shopping center/office building on the same site.

YOUR SCORE: 14

over black-and-white images, color images are now losing prominence to the even more exotic spectrums of the infrared and ultraviolet. With these lightwaves, invisible to the human eye, the trained criminalist can detect—and record—hidden stains, alteration by chemicals, or physical manipulation of documents, and even invisible inks.

To capture details, details fine enough to separate the ink trail of one ballpoint pen from another, criminalists use instruments that began life in science labs before moving into the forensics department. Photomicroscopy (photography through microscopes) has proven invaluable in the examination of bullets, and radiography has recovered elusive fingerprints from difficult surfaces.

HAIR AND FIBERS

One of the most technically difficult areas of forensic science is the examination of hairs and fibers found at the scene of a crime. Identifying perfect matches that will stand up in the courts is often a challenge. For example, when Mulder spotted the red strands of hair on Duane Barry's medical band, there were many things he could have determined from them—but not that they were, without doubt, Scully's. It's impossible, on the basis of hair examination alone, to match a particular hair to a particular person. If, however, the strand of hair has a root that provides further DNA evidence, or if there is strong circumstantial evidence, hair can form vital links between victims, perpetrators, and crime scenes.

The fact that perfect matches aren't really possible doesn't render the field useless. What *can* be discovered from these slender strands of organic matter is quite remarkable. In the past fifty years, researchers have found methods to distinguish human hair from animal hair, the part of the body a hair originated from, and, within reason, the ethnic background of the hair's owner. Hair from natives of several African cultures, for example, is elliptical when seen in cross-section whereas that of Native Americans is rounder and more coarse.

Microscopic and chemical examination can tell us even more. Chemical tests quickly determine whether hair has been dyed, bleached, tinted, permed, or straightened. Close scrutiny by an experienced examiner can even tell how long ago the hair was cut. Trace elements that have built up in the shaft of the hair can be differentiated by neutron activation. A chemical history, laid down over the length of a hair, has even been admitted in courts to prove long-term poisoning.

If hair, a single substance, can spawn a dozen subspecialties, imagine for a moment how many points of comparison there must be for the multitude of fibers the average person contacts over the course of a single day. As with hair, fiber examination begins under the microscope. By gross observation, even minute fibers can be classified as either synthetic or organic. From there, the organics are broken into animal, vegetable, or mineral in origin while chemical tests can often sort the synthetics. Like hair, fiber can't be matched perfectly, so solubility, color, trace elements, and even the chemicals used at laundries are painstakingly determined from tiny snippets. Tear patterns and, if appropriate, even DNA sequencing from cells found on clothing are also recorded. With these key points, a "profile" of sorts can be assembled.

TOXICOLOGY

Toxicology, the study of substances and their interaction, is one of the most delicate and precise fields open to the forensic scientist—and one of the widest. While some toxicologists unlock the mysteries of poisons, their colleagues create desperately needed new drugs. Of course, the difference between poison and medicine is often nothing more than dosage.

In the field of forensics, toxicologists frequently find themselves attempting to identify unknown substances (the X factor), from a variety of sources. Confiscated drug evidence, stomach contents, even body organs come under their intense scrutiny.

At their disposal in the lab is some of the most high-tech equipment in existence. Laboratory test methods for specific chemical substances include color reaction tests, crystal tests, chromatography, even infrared spectrophotometry. In the case of body organ exams to screen for poisonous materials, an involved and tedious extraction procedure, accompanied by a series of tests to confirm or eliminate the presence of toxic materials, is required. Despite the costs involved—which are growing as fast as the technology—a battery of tests is routinely thrown at every sample because, of all the forensic fields, toxicology can be the most damning to a suspect.

DNA from a single hair: the new forensics "fingerprint."

In the interest of artistic integrity, Doug Hutchison went nude for the scene that required him to explode, bile-covered, from Tooms's latest nest. As the goo covering his entire body was supersticky, it made for some uncomfortable problems while crawling along a tin chute on his belly.

Code Name: "Born Again"

CASE SUMMARY

A young girl claims to have seen a dead policeman in the room when a second officer jumps to his death from the window of an interrogation room. Within twenty-four hours, another man dies in her presence. At Mulder's suggestion, the child is hypnotically regressed and Mulder comes to believe the girl is the reincarnation of the dead cop she "saw." Now he has to convince both her mother and Scully if they're to have any chance of preventing more deaths.

DEEP BACKGROUND

Hypnotic Regression: Take Me Back

New Age miracle medicine or stage-show attraction? Hypnosis has been psychology's darling—and its devil. Daily reports of three-pack-a-day smokers quitting without discomfort make it impossible for psychologists to refute its medicinal value, yet the inability of hypnosis to satisfy that most basic requirement of all medical treatments—repeatability—leads to genuine doubt about the technique's efficacy. Can hypnotherapy really take credit for the one-in-five smokers who quit if it can't explain the four out of five who don't?

Following the I-needn't-be-a-mechanic-to-drive theory, some practitioners elect to leave comprehension of the process to others and simply employ the method in the belief that it is better to help one in five than none. For others, that action implies a cavalier and potentially dangerous attitude similar to dosing a patient with drugs, the side effects of which are unknown. Without any middle ground, the field of hyp-

EYEWITNESS STATEMENT

Jumpers tend to open the window before they jump.

—Mulder, "Born Again"

notherapy has been relegated to the category of "marginal" or "alternative" medicine.

Hypnosis's subdisciplines, including hypnotic regression, fare even worse, often regarded as outright quackery by most Western medical practitioners. However, in the middle of this century, even the moderate successes with the technique encouraged some people to explore it objectively. In studying regression therapy, these researchers concentrated on two distinct categories: single-life regression, which attempts to recall memories of earlier events in a patient's life, and past-life regression, which claims to connect your present consciousness with earlier *incarnations* of itself.

Single-life regression, the technique that supposedly allowed Mulder to recall memories of Samantha's disappearance that he'd been unable to access in the usual way, is today by far the more commonly employed technique. It was the first of the two regressions to come under scrutiny by researchers, as there was evidence of its value in the statements of witnesses who could recall license numbers and similar details accurately under its influence, and its results were easier to verify. If a hypnotherapist knew the relevant information, it should be possible to determine if forgotten knowledge could be retrieved through regression.

One doctor, Robert True, decided to begin his research into hypnotherapy at precisely that point and, in 1949, devised a simple test. He gathered groups of people, hypnotized them, and regressed them to various events in their lives. If they could answer questions while hypnotized that they were unable to answer while awake, it would support the single-life regressionist's claims. After hypnotizing his subjects, True regressed them to their tenth, seventh, and fourth birthdays and asked them what day of the week it was, something that could be easily checked. Random chance should have yielded results no better than one in seven, or 14 percent correct, but True's subjects had the right answer in 82 percent of the cases! Once in their normal states of mind, the subjects were unable to recall what day their birthdays had fallen on. The results of True's investigation, with the raw data, were published in the prestigious journal *Science*.

His procedure of verified testing, known as the scientific method, would have satisfied even a dedicated skeptic like Scully. Unfortunately, though others tried to replicate his results, no one could. Some claimed True had fudged his results, a charge he vehemently denied, but, until 1982, no one actually asked *him* what sources of error might have snuck in.

A scientist named Martin Orne, with a copy of the original article in hand, undertook to speak to True himself. It took Orne mere minutes to find the problem. *Science* had edited the question down to "What day is it?" In actuality, True, who knew the answers, had asked, "Is it Monday? Is it Tuesday? Is it Wednesday? . . ." until the subject stopped him! True was clearly unaware of the implications of "subliminal hints," but Orne, thirty years later, understood them all too well. Using True's flawed method, he easily reproduced True's results. To further illustrate the experiment's weakness, Orne asked ten four-year-olds what day it currently was. None of them knew. If regression really was a state of heightened memory, the adults should recall only information they'd actually known *at the time*. Few, if any, of them would ever have known the day of their fourth birthday at the time.

Knowing the pitfalls to avoid, other researchers designed new experiments. Within a few years, new, repeatable data proved beyond a doubt that adults could reliably recall the minutiae of their early lives—even if the hypnotherapist scrupulously avoided leading questions. (It was just such leading questions that were blamed for the occasional instances of *past-life* regression that arose spontaneously during experimentation.)

Same-life regression had caused dissent; discussion of past-life regression precipitated a storm of controversy and even more rigorous experimentation.

Despite stringent controls, one twenty-four-year-old woman with the case name Beth was able to perform feats that defied explanation. Beth displayed none of the fantastical regressive elements that caused serious scientists to dismiss past lives. She didn't claim to be a famous person. (Henry VIII and Joan of Arc are quite popular in past-life regressions.) She didn't claim to have had an unusual occupation or to have witnessed any well-known historical event. What she did do, consistently, was describe the everyday details of the life of a French housewife born in 1724. In the presence of a museum curator who could verify her statements, she was given a wide variety of period implements, all of which she identified by name and function without the least hesitation. In her hypnotized state, Beth spoke the French of the era fluently—though she'd never taken a French lesson in her life.

Cases like Beth's are rare, and, though no one could come up with any motivation for her to do so, Beth was frequently accused of secretly researching her part before presenting herself to the experimenters. No one was ever able to prove it.

If Beth's case is difficult to explain, Scott's is a real stumper. Scott, unlike Beth, wasn't randomly chosen as a subject. His parents, frightened by their son's nightmares, brought him to their family doctor who suggested they speak to regression researchers. Scott, a sunny eight-year-old Caucasian boy, dreamed of uniformed men, muskets, and death. In his dreams, and later in regressions, Scott described himself as a black soldier who'd been killed at an insignificant battle during the American Civil War. Like Beth, he described events in eerie detail, right down to the technique of cleaning and loading a type of gun that in reality he'd never even seen.

For those determined to disbelieve, these incidents are either the result of retentive and inventive memories, the supersaturation of our culture with television programming, or careful coaching. They point to other regressed subjects who claimed to have been Japanese fighter pilots but couldn't name the emperor of Japan at the time, couldn't explain the simplest flying maneuvers, or even give their own name. Without doubt there have been hoaxes, but, if even one Beth or one Scott turns out to be legitimate, psychology will spend the next several decades rewriting its textbooks.

Old Souls, Young Bodies

Reincarnation, transmigration, and metempsychosis all describe the religious or philosophical rebirth of the soul, the essence of a human being, in one or more successive lives. Depending on tradition, those lives may be limited to another human being, or include animals and even plants.

In some religions, including vodun and several Caribe faiths, belief in multiple souls is common. The philosophy is as follows: There is one aspect of the soul unique to each individual that returns to a greater being, and a second part that belongs to a greater cosmic soul and is reborn into the next generation. The soul is frequently viewed as capable of leaving the body through the mouth or nostril and of being reborn as a bird, for example, or a butterfly. The Venda of southern Africa believe that when a person dies, the soul stays near the grave for a short time and then seeks a new resting place or another body—human, other mammalian, or reptilian. Some priests have the job of watching over the body to ensure that no creature or person is available to be the receptacle for its newly freed soul.

Among the ancient Greeks, a belief called Orphism held that a preexistent soul survived bodily death and was later reincarnated in a human or other mammalian body, eventually receiving release

1. Origami, the art of Japanese paper folding.
2. A tank aerator shaped like a diver.
3. She ripped off the left arm and disfigured the right eye.
4. The 14th.
5. The 27th.
6. Flour.
7. Ten years.
8. The giraffe.
9. Twenty-four.
10. Thorazine, an antidepressant.

YOUR SCORE: 7

from the cycle of birth and death and regaining its former pure state. Plato (ca. 428–348 B.C.) believed in an immortal soul that participates in frequent incarnations.

The major religions that hold a belief in reincarnation, however, are the Asian religions, especially Hinduism, Jainism, Buddhism, and Sikhism, all of which arose in India. They hold in common a doctrine of karma (results of an act), the law of cause and effect, which states that what one does in this present life will have its effect in the next life. In Hinduism, the process of birth and rebirth—transmigration of souls—is endless until one achieves moksha, or salvation, by realizing the truth that liberates: that the individual soul (atman) and the absolute soul (Brahman) are one. Thus, one can escape from the wheel of birth and rebirth (samsara).

Jainism, reflecting a belief in an absolute soul, holds that karma is affected in its density by the deeds that a person does. Thus, the burden of the old karma is added to the new karma that is acquired during the next existence until the soul frees itself by religious disciplines—especially by the practice of ahimsa (nonviolence) and rises to the place of liberated souls at the top of the universe.

Although Buddhism denies the existence of an unchanging substantial soul, it holds to a belief in the transmigration of the karma of souls. A complex of psychophysical elements and states changing from moment to moment, after death the soul, with its five skandhas (groups of elements) ceases to exist; but the karma of the deceased survives and becomes a vijana (germ of consciousness) in the womb of the mother. This vijana is that aspect of the soul reincarnated in a new individual. By gaining a state of complete passiveness through discipline and meditation, one can leave the wheel of birth and rebirth and achieve nirvana, the state of the extinction of desires.

Sikhism teaches a doctrine of reincarnation based on the Hindu view, but in addition holds that, after the Last Judgment, souls that have been reincarnated in several existences will be absorbed by God.

Code Name: "Roland"

CASE SUMMARY

Members of a high-security jet propulsion team are being killed, one by one, and the only person with access is a mentally challenged maintenance man named Roland. Though Scully is ready to dismiss him as a suspect after discovering highly theoretical notations at the crime scene, Mulder's not so sure. Somewhere there has to be a connection.

Suda's Cat and Cryonics 101

DEEP BACKGROUND

The end of this episode—when the frozen head of Roland's brother is revealed as an unexpected player in the action—would have dismayed cryogenic supporters who are still trying to correct the many misconceptions that science fiction and horror genres have spread about this emerging science. Even before early theories had amounted to more than a few scientific abstracts, *The Twilight Zone* was regularly freezing characters to thaw out later and embroil in the situation of the week. Later, in *Forever Young,* a cryonics experiment gone wrong leads to a touchingly unorthodox love story. *Demolition Man* gave us two hours of rip-roaring cryonic action; *The Ice Man* brought audiences to tears while *Encino Man* left them rolling in the aisles. Between 1954 and 1994, literally hundreds of films and television episodes were inspired by cryonics.

So when a young *X-Files* writer named Chris Ruppenthal took on the subject almost half a century after the *TZ* writers first flash-froze a USAF pilot, he faced a daunting task. After all, he was writing for *X-Philes*. Imitation, even of the earliest cry-

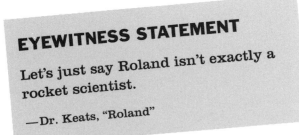

EYEWITNESS STATEMENT

Let's just say Roland isn't exactly a rocket scientist.

—Dr. Keats, "Roland"

onics plots, wasn't an option with fans who could pluck the reference almost out of thin air. Cryonics wasn't new or exciting anymore. So Ruppenthal needed an exceptional *story* where cryonics was but one thread of a complex plot, and he needed a good base of knowledge to build that story on.

Going back almost to the beginning takes us to 1966 and Japan's Kobe University, where a scientist named Isamu Suda was contemplating the very new work of England's Audrey Smith. Smith, one of the first cryogenics researchers, had been attempting, with some success, to freeze and revive hamsters.

The second home of Suda's cat.

Suda wasn't sure if jumping in with his own research at that point, assuming that a living creature could be revived without damage, was the best plan, and he decided to adopt a different strategy.

At first, all he needed to know was whether the brain of a mammal could still function after being frozen. If not, the rest of the process was, to his mind, useless, and he quickly devised an experiment that would be a first step in that direction. His method was simple, though regulations governing laboratory animal research might have made it impossible today. He gave a cat a general anesthetic, slowly reduced its temperature, and, to protect its cells from damage, circulated artificial blood through its body. He then removed the brain entirely, soaking and permeating it with a glycerol solution in the hope that this "cryoprotector" would reach as many of the delicate cells as possible. That done, he began chilling the brain, slowly lowering the temperature to just below zero degrees Fahrenheit.

Six weeks later he began to reverse the procedure. The brain was warmed slowly and more of the glycerol blood substitute was injected. When he determined that the brain was completely defrosted and as close to its original condition as possible, he attached standard EEG terminals.

The tiny needles began moving.

Before freezing the brain, Suda had made several electroencephalograph tapes to have baseline data for later comparison. Comparing them to the data he was receiving, he thought they looked similar. When he compared hard copies, the results were more than similar; they were nearly identical. Suda had picked up brain waves, specific patterns, from a frozen and thawed brain.

Were these results an aberration or would they prove consistent? Would time be a factor or could the tissue be frozen indefinitely? Suda repeated the procedure at least a dozen times, increasing the freezing time and varying other conditions. Even brains stored for seven months produced brain waves after being warmed, though some dissolution of the patterns was apparent.

Suda's paper on the project was accepted, in 1966, by *Nature,* a peer-reviewed journal not open to publication of spurious claims. Convinced that, with better conditions and a clearer understanding of the chemistry behind his experiment, it might be possible to extend the frozen period, Suda left some remaining tissues in the freezer while he worked on theoretical concepts. Seven years later, a brain from the original experiment was thawed and observed. It too showed signs of activity. Conductivity tests revealed that cells deep in the cerebellar culmen were still active.

This research is, to use an X-ism, "disturbing on many levels." What exactly were the implications of Suda's experiment? Brain death is one of the ways we separate the dead from the living. Could a disembodied brain be alive? Suda's findings cast suspicion on whether or not we could determine death beyond a reasonable doubt. Even if a brain could have been appropriately termed "dead" while it was frozen, what term would describe it once it was warmed? Conscious? The function of a brain is to think, to experience, to feel. Was this warmed organ capable of any of those functions?

Perhaps we aren't ready to answer those questions just yet. Even Suda has ceased his experiments for now. The enthusiastic rush in dozens of labs worldwide has slowed—not because of a lack of progress, not because an ethics committee has forbidden further projects, but because the field itself seems to feel a need to step back and evaluate where this science could take us. The discipline that was once ridiculed and hyperbolized in fiction has, in fact, shown a remarkable sense of dignity and responsibility, a willingness to wait for the ethics to catch up with the science. The only subjects being frozen today are already deceased.

CRYONIC SUSPENSION

Cryonic suspension is the practice of freezing a terminally ill patient in the expectation that future medical technologies will be

Easy Stuff: Give yourself 1 point for each correct answer.

1. What is Roland's girl-friend's name?
2. What is Roland's job?
3. What was it about Scully's blouse that caught Roland's attention?
4. What classic joke did Arthur Grable and the others pull on a smug professor?
5. What happened to Arthur Grable's brain after his death?

Getting Tougher: Give yourself 2 points for each correct answer.

6. Where did Roland work?
7. What was the official name of the propulsion program?
8. Both of the murdered scientists died in unusually grisly ways. What were they?
9. Where did Mulder find the access code 15626 for Dr. Grable's computerized files?
10. Roland Fuller and Arthur Grable, being twins, shared the same birthday. What was it?

able to (a) reverse the injury caused by freezing and (b) restore the patient to health.

Current law prevents cryonic suspension of a patient until after legal death. It is worth noting that under favorable circumstances a patient can be declared legally dead and cryonic suspension can be started at a point in time when the patient could in fact be revived, even if only briefly. An example might be a terminally ill cancer patient who had rejected heroic measures. Changes in the law, which would increase the autonomy of the terminally ill patient, could, in the future, allow cryonic suspension to be started shortly before legal death. However, once frozen, under whatever circumstances, most medical practitioners today would view a frozen person as dead.

The rationale for cryonic suspension is the belief that current legal and medical standards are grossly in error in the criteria used to determine death, and the expectation that future medical technologies will be as superior to current practice as current practice is superior to medieval practices.

The concept that conventional medical wisdom is infallible is not supported by history. To consider but one example: A doctor named Ignza Semmelweis demonstrated clinically in the 1840s that washing your hands was a good idea. For his efforts, he was widely ridiculed and his advice largely ignored for several decades. Millions of preventable deaths occurred.

The principles of cryonics currently are being applied in many useful ways. Low-temperature surgery is a necessity for heart transplants and other delicate procedures. The same low-temperature procedures reduce bleeding during cosmetic surgery. The freezing of a cornea allows for it to be reshaped to permanently cure far- and nearsightedness. The cryonics process makes it possible for organs to be transferred safely between donors and recipients. While it may be some time before cryonics brings people back from the dead, procedures like these develop skills that can be applied later—and also help cryonics shake its sci-fi image.

THE COST OF TAKING IT WITH YOU

This is a representative cost analysis for the cryonics option. The neuro option shows the cost involved in freezing a brain and spinal stump.

	Whole Body	Neuro
Remote Transport	$14,050	$14,050
Cryoprotective Perfusion	$13,400	$11,500
Laboratory Evaluations	$ 950	$ 950
Temperature Descent	$ 8,350	$ 1,750
Total	$36,750	$28,250
Annual Liquid Nitrogen	$ 850	$ 50
Storage Costs	$ 1,700	$ 150

After the suspension costs, there must be sufficient funds to pay interest on the annual liquid nitrogen costs (conservatively estimated as 2 percent in inflation-adjusted dollars). The current fees are approximately $42,000 for neuro and $140,000 for whole body. Bear in mind that the above costs do not include having someone monitor your container in the event it defrosts prematurely, *or* the cost of defrosting you should that become possible, which can be quite expensive.

PSEUDO-SCIENCE

- In "Ice," the dog passes the worms in its stools. If the worms had attached themselves to glands deep in the brain, how did they turn up in the dog's digestive tract?

- The wind-tunnel deaths in "Roland" were visually fascinating and inventive, but at wind speeds that high, no one should have been able to cling to the protective screen. Not to mention that breathing in that environment would have been impossible. The best the victims could have hoped for was to pass out and still be unconscious when they hit the fan. The idea that they could have been yelling at Roland was a good story, bad science.

- While the full-color images shown on the microscope screen in "The Erlenmeyer Flask" look terrific, SEMs (Scanning Electron Microscopes) don't work in color, just black and white.

- In "The Erlenmeyer Flask," Scully tells Mulder that chloroplasts are plant cells instead of saying that chloroplasts are *part* of *some* plant cells.

- In "Firewalker," the organism identified as a fungus is indeed a fungus, Pilobolus, the shotgun fungus. However, its home environment is usually dung—not the insides of volcanoes or humans.

- If we assume Trepkos did sabotage Firewalker, there's something seriously wrong with the temperatures given. Perhaps it's an error in converting to and from Canada's Celsius system. While 130 degrees Fahrenheit would be just extremely unpleasant to a human, 130 degrees Celsius would be absolutely unbearable.

- "Firewalker" also takes some liberties with the periodic table. Hydrogen sulfide converting to silicon dioxide is simply impossible. Sulfur and silicon are elements, and, short of nuclear activity, one can't become the other. If an element could be changed that way, lead would become gold more often.

- Regarding Scully's test tube technique: 1) Test tubes are never held upright over flames, they would "blurp." 2) Test tubes are never left unattended over flames for the same reason. And 3) test tubes over a Bunsen burner would never get hot enough to simulate the inside of a volcano.

- In "Die Hand Die Verletzt," though Mrs. Paddock seemed to have mastered dissection, she had some trouble identifying her pigs. They were *Artiodactyla,* but the name means "even-toed," not "creatures with hooves." This separates them from "odd-toed" things, *Perissodactyla,* like horses.

- No anaconda in its right mind eats *preserved* pigs. It would also have some difficulty eating Mr. Ausbury from the foot up, especially when it reached the crotch and still had another leg to deal with. Anacondas and other constrictor-type snakes consume their food head first.

Code Name: "The Erlenmeyer Flask"

If you tip it and see "Purity Control" on the bottom, you're on your own.

CASE SUMMARY

When a tip from Deep Throat leads Mulder to a secret project using alien DNA in its gene therapy, the X-Files team has never been closer to the truth—or to one of the myriad of aliens haunting them so far. But the truth is an expensive item. Even as they race to gather evidence, witnesses are disappearing. With a government black squad working against them, and other lives at stake, can they afford to push their official limits?

A Rainbow of Aliens

DEEP BACKGROUND

Deep Throat's assurance to Mulder that "they" had been with us for a very long time could have been a little more specific. Based on the reports of contactees and abductees, a multitude of alien "races" have been identified. Inconvenient as that might be for those trying to keep a scorecard, it's a boon for *The X-Files*. With dozens of races to choose from, each with their own general appearances, motivations, and contact methods, it's unlikely the crew will be running out of story possibilities soon.

We've already been presented with a number of different alien flavors. The aliens of "Fearful Symmetry" who stole the offspring of zoo

EYEWITNESS STATEMENT

The man we met yesterday kept this place looking like he was waiting for the people from *Good Housekeeping* to show up. I would never have pegged him as one to do all this—or do a Greg Louganis out the window.

—Mulder, "The Erlenmeyer Flask"

Deep Throat's murder
shook Scully's
increasingly fragile
belief in the integrity
of the justice system.
For Mulder—hardly a
political innocent—
the loss of his mentor,
source, and almost-
friend, starkly illus-
trated the fate of those
who bent the rules.
It was Deep Throat's
real-life fans, however,
who protested his
death most vocally.
After a full season of
being titillated by this
enigmatic character,
it's hardly surprising
that viewers screamed
"Foul!" at his abrupt
departure.

animals, the Gregors, and the aliens surrounding Duane Barry's bed in his horrifying nightmares, all seemed different. Perhaps you can identify those we've seen in the list below.

ALIEN TYPE 1:

THE GRAYS. Though there are several subtypes, all are grayish in color.

- Gray Type A: The most common aliens, also known as Zeta Reticulans. According to contactees, they're a military society whose motivation is universal conquest. Standing about four and a half feet tall with large heads and wraparound eyes, a slit mouth and no visible nose, they claim to have evolved beyond a need for reproductive or digestive systems and to have been subtly altering human genetics for thousands of years in order to be able to produce a "mixed race" of themselves and humans. These grays have their primary bases in New Mexico and Nevada but are also based in many other countries.
- Gray Type B: Tall Grays, about seven to eight feet, with facial features similar to Type A Grays. They appear less militaristic than their cousins, but should still be considered hostile. Based in the Aleutian Islands, they intend to gain control of the Earth through political controls and agreements with major governments.
- Gray Type C: The shortest of the Grays, Type C's stand only three and a half feet tall, miniature versions of their larger cousins. Of all the Grays, these are the most dangerous to humans, willing to destroy their victims if they can't intimidate them into submission.

ALIEN TYPE 2:

THE REPTILIANS. Genetically akin to reptiles, Type 2 aliens are of an advanced culture who view humans as a totally inferior race. They think of us as cattle and are reputed to consider some human organs as delicacies. Supposedly, they have a powered asteroid due to arrive in our system in the mid 1990s if all goes according to plan. They believe Earth is their own ancient outpost and expect to have complete control when they arrive after deserting their own dying planet. Some people believe the Type A Grays are the slaves of the Reptilians.

ALIEN TYPE 3:

HUMAN-TYPE ALIENS. Those aliens who can walk unrecognized among us.

- Human Type A: Of normal height, with human features reminiscent of the Scandinavian region, they're also known as "Blonds." These aliens were abducted by the Grays and fitted with devices to control their actions before being released.
- Human Type B: Similar in appearance to Type A, these are Pleiadeans. Unlike the Blonds, this type is highly evolved in a spiritual sense. They have benevolent feelings toward humans and are the only aliens we should trust. They once offered their assistance to human governments but were refused, so they're now making overtures to individuals instead. They claim to be the forefathers of the entire human race, but don't spend much time on Earth due to problems at home.
- Human Type C: Very little is known, but they're apparently another of the highly evolved, benevolent, spiritual type. They appear human but their skins are pale, approaching blue, and they hail from Sirius. They are apparently aware of our danger from other aliens.

From the Headlines: Green Blood Rising

On February 19, 1994, a mystery worthy of *The X-Files* began in Riverside, California, where Gloria Ramirez was admitted to hospital. Only thirty-one years old, Ramirez was dying. Though she was known to have cervical cancer, her symptoms were atypical: difficult breathing, low blood pressure, and dementia. Treating the symptoms while trying to locate the source of the woman's sudden deterioration, the trauma staff began with a standard range of drugs that they hoped would stabilize her condition.

When she failed to respond, the staff took more drastic action and the peculiar nature of the case became evident. As Ramirez's heartbeat faltered and staff tore off her clothes to apply shock paddles, they discovered an oil that covered most of her body. Her breath, when the air bag was removed from her mouth, smelled vaguely of fruit . . . or perhaps garlic. The blood drawn from her arm contained pale flakes of something and it reeked of chemicals. Before long, a similar odor rose from her body. When a nurse leaned forward to

Easy Stuff: Give yourself 1 point for each correct answer.

1. What sort of animals did Dr. Berube have in his lab?
2. What was written on the bottom of the Erlenmeyer flask found in Dr. Berube's lab?
3. What happened when the ambulance attendants attempted to treat Dr. Secare?
4. What happened to Dr. Anne Carpenter?
5. What does Scully retrieve from the High Containment Facility in Fort Marlene, Maryland?

Getting Tougher: Give yourself 2 points for each correct answer.

6. What was unique about the opening credits for this episode?
7. What was odd about the DNA of the "bacteria" found in the Erlenmeyer flask?
8. Where did Mulder find the experimental subjects?
9. What life-threatening condition did Dr. Secare have prior to the experiment?
10. What happened to the package Scully retrieved from Fort Marlene?

ANSWERS

1. Monkeys.
2. "Purity Control."
3. A noxious gas was released from inside his chest.
4. She and her family were killed in a car accident.
5. What appears to be an alien frozen in liquid nitrogen.
6. Instead of the usual "The Truth Is Out There," "Trust No One" flashed on the screen.
7. They had more than the usual four base pairs. They had a fifth and sixth nucleotide.
8. Floating in tanks at Zeus Storage, 1616 Pandora Street.
9. Cancer.
10. It was stored in the Pentagon basement —with more of the same.

YOUR SCORE: 13

identify the source of the smell—and continued to fall forward onto Ramirez's chest—she became the first to succumb to the mysterious forces at work inside Gloria Ramirez.

In the first hour of Ramirez's treatment, three more staff members collapsed. Eight others developed lesser but equally disturbing symptoms: Tremors and spasms, severe eye irritation, and even partial paralysis assailed those trying to save Ramirez's life. When Ramirez died an hour later, no one knew any more about what had killed her than they had when she was brought in. Something mysterious had knocked out most of a well-seasoned trauma staff.

If the staff would later appear defensive to investigators, they had good reason. Simply put, no one believed their version of events. When they described the ammonia scent from the blood, it was suggested that methane, swamp gas, might have seeped up from a sewer. When they pointed to their colleagues, some of whom were hospitalized for weeks after the incident, they were forced to defend themselves against charges of mass hysteria. Their tale of toxic blood and gases caught the public's imagination, but only undermined their reputations among their colleagues. While the public was content to speculate over coffee, and writers (including *The X-Files* crew) used the case as a jumping-off point for their fiction, the hospital staff wanted answers.

Those answers were slow in coming. The samples a moon-suited autopsy team removed from the Ramirez body would pass through many hands before even the thinnest theory was developed. Even now there are those who can't believe the fantastic chain of events that would be required to support the best-guess hypothesis of the nation's premiere investigators—that Ramirez's body had produced its own version of nerve gas.

The human body, everything within the fragile covering of the skin, is a delicate ecosystem where organs and systems exist discretely. The pH of the stomach, ranging anywhere from two to four, is equal to that of HCl_2, hydrochloric acid, an acid that would literally eat away any other part of the body. In Ramirez's case, that neatly compartmentalized system broke down and her body became the flask for an exotic chemical cocktail that included codeine, Tylenol, lidocaine, Tigan, and the toxic materials employed in chemotherapy. Even that combination mightn't have killed her without the addition of a trio of odd chemicals: an ammonia derivative, nicotinamide, and dimethyl sulfone. It was those factors that eventually gave researchers the clues they needed.

While all the agents involved in Ramirez's official treatment had been accounted for, Ramirez, a very sick woman, undergoing all sorts of medical treatment, had resorted to folk remedies as well. She had rubbed into her skin a gel used by athletes containing dimethyl sulfoxide. This resulted in the oily substance the staff had noticed. The same gel would eventually combine with the other chemicals floating through her system. She might still have survived, but for the addition of oxygen—highly concentrated oxygen from a face mask. Then the dimethyl sulfoxide formed dimethyl sulfone that, as Ramirez's body cooled, broke down into dimethyl sulfate—nerve gas. The flecks in the blood vial, which had stumped early investigators, could finally be explained. The volatile and heat-sensitive dimethyl sulfate compound, on being removed from the heat of Ramirez's body, had cooled swiftly when passed through the narrow syringe needle. The flecks in the syringe were cooled dimethyl sulfone.

The mystery, at least as far as most were concerned, was solved; the answer came just a few months after "The Erlenmeyer Flask" aired and the "toxic fumes" were made part of *The X-Files*'s own lore.

Mitch Pileggi (AKA Walter Skinner) A Brief Filmography

Dangerous Touch, 1994
Pointman, 1994
Trouble Shooters: Trapped Beneath the Earth, 1993
Basic Instinct, 1992
Night Visions, 1990
Brothers in Arms, 1989
Shocker, 1989
Return of the Living Dead, Part II, 1988
Death Wish 4: The Crackdown, 1987
Three O'Clock High, 1987
Three on a Match, 1987

BEYOND DEEP THROAT

Code Name:
"Little Green Men"

CASE SUMMARY

The X-Files are closed. Scully's at Quantico. Mulder's doing grunt work any wet-behind-the-ears new agent could handle. Little wonder that when Mulder jumps on the slimmest of leads and hightails it to Puerto Rico, it doesn't take long for Scully to follow in his footsteps.

**DEEP
BACKGROUND**

The *Voyager* Message

For those who have seen this episode, the opening montage of many evocative images and sounds is difficult to forget. And those with even a little poet in them probably noted the irony of beginning this episode—the first after the closure of the X-Files division (and with it, Mulder's hopes)—with a monologue set against what was perhaps the grandest symbol of hope ever produced on this planet—the *Voyager* message.

When *Voyager 1* and *Voyager 2* were launched in 1977, each carried a gold-coated copper record encased in a durable aluminum jacket. They were the tiniest of bottles tossed into the vastest ocean, expressing a wish that has since become the object of much ridicule: that we are not the only creatures in the universe gazing at the stars in wonder and curiosity.

And what did we send in that bottle? As much of Earth's history and culture as we could cram onto it. On a bit of metal only 12 inches across, Dr. Carl Sagan and his committee organized the first multimedia presentation designed to carry our message to

EYEWITNESS STATEMENT

I wanted to believe. . . . But the tools have been taken away.

—Mulder, "Little Green Men"

the stars, a once in a lifetime opportunity to claim a bit of immortality.

Over a hundred pictures not only provide a detailed road map to our planet, but as complete a tour guide as possible in the available space. Certainly no other travel brochure could plop the Taj Mahal next door to the Sydney Opera House or the UN Building, permit deserts to abut mountains, or allow an elderly man from Turkey to become neighbors to an American astronaut. Seen all at once, the images provide a startlingly intimate picture of the planet, a picture that invokes the same dizziness felt on staring deep into the sky on a clear night.

Vision isn't the only sense this particular recording reaches. Though Kurt Waldheim, past-president of the United Nations, has delivered some thousand speeches during his term of offices, none is as brief or as enduring as the one he sent into space in 1977:

> *I send greetings on behalf of the people of our planet. We step out of our solar system, into the universe, seeking only peaceful contact.*

Fifty-four human languages, from every corner of every continent, send greetings to whoever may encounter our little bottle. The fifty-fifth language on the recording, that of the humpback whale, provides a haunting reminder that while we search outward for intelligent life, we've yet to discover all there is to be known of our own planet.

As all these voices fade away, replaced by sounds so intrinsic to our environment that we seldom even hear them, it's easy to close your eyes and wonder what an alien civilization might make of them. Would they recognize the crackle of flames, rain pattering on a roof, or the lonesome wail of the wind? Perhaps the random noises would be meaningless, but music has been called the universal language, and ninety minutes of music are the final installment on this "message in a bottle."

VOYAGER'S SONG

Bach Brandenburg Concerto Number Two, First Movement
"Kinds of Flowers," Javanese Court Gamelan
Senegalese percussion
Pygmy girls initiation song
Australian Horn and Totem song

Easy Stuff: Give yourself 1 point for each correct answer.

1. When discovered in Mulder's apartment, what was Scully's explanation for her presence?
2. What show did Mulder enjoy as a kid?
3. What piece of music does Senator Matheson play for Mulder?
4. What is the password, which Scully correctly guesses, for Mulder's computer?
5. What secretive method of communication did Scully use to contact Mulder?

Getting Tougher: Give yourself 2 points for each correct answer.

6. Scully and Mulder met in the basement of which hotel?
7. Where was Deep Throat buried?
8. What board game were Mulder and Samantha playing in the flashback of the 1973 night when Samantha disappeared?
9. Who was featured on TV during the flashback?
10. What is the number of the wiretap Mulder is working on at the beginning of this episode?

"El Cascabel," Lorenzo Barcelata
"Johnny B. Goode," Chuck Berry
New Guinea Men's House Chant
"Depicting the Cranes in Their Nest"
Bach Partita Number Three for Violin; Gavotte et Rondeaus
Mozart Magic Flute, Queen of the Night (Aria Number 14)
Chakrulo
Peruvian Pan Pipes
Melancholy Blues
Azerbaijan Two Flutes
Stravinsky, Rites of Spring, Conclusion
Bach Prelude and Fugue Number One in C Major from the "Well Tempered Clavier, Book Two"
Beethoven's Fifth Symphony, First Movement
Bulgarian Shepherdess Song "Izlel Delyo Hajdutin"
Navajo Indian Night Chant
The Fairie Round from Pavans, Galliards, Almains
Melanesian Pan Pipes
Peruvian Woman's Wedding Song
"Flowing Streams," Chinese Ch'in music
"Jaat Kahan Ho," Indian Raga
"Dark Was the Night"
Beethoven String Quartet Number 13 "Cavatina"

LANGUAGES ON THE *VOYAGER* RECORD

Sumerian	Thai	Turkish	Armenian
Aramaic	Burmese	Italian	Kannada
Russian	Dutch	Sotho	Ukrainian
French	Hindi	Korean	Serbian
Kechua	Sinhalese	Mandarin	Amoy (Min
Urdu	Latin	Swedish	dialect)
Welsh	Punjabi	Hebrew	Telugu
Nguni	Netali	Cantonese	Hungarian
Wu	Nyanja	Rumanian	Persian
Polish	Hittite	Indonesian	Luganada
Gujoratilla	Portuguese	Bengali	Rajasthani
(Zambia)	Arabic	Vietnamese	Oriya
Akkadian	Spanish	Greek	Czech
English	German	Japanese	Marathi

SOUNDS OF EARTH ON THE *VOYAGER* RECORD

Whales	Rocket	Volcanoes
Mud pots	Planets (music)	Surf
Crickets, frogs	Rain	Hyena
Elephant	Birds	Wild dog
Footsteps and heartbeats	Chimpanzee	Fire
Tools	Laughter	Herding sheep
Blacksmith shop	Dogs, domestic	Riveter
Tractor	Sawing	Morse code
Truck	Kiss	Auto gears
Ships	Baby	Life signs—EEG, EKG
Horse and cart	Jet	Horse and carriage
Lift-off *Saturn 5*	Pulsar	Train whistle

VOYAGER RECORD PHOTOGRAPH INDEX

Calibration circle
Mathematical definitions
Solar system parameters
Solar spectrum
Mars
Earth
Chemical definitions
DNA structure magnified
Anatomy of eight animals
Diagram of conception
Fertilized ovum
Fetus
Nursing mother
Group of children
Family portrait
Structure of Earth
Seashore
Sand dunes
Forest scene with mushrooms
Fallen leaves
Snowflake
Flying insect with flowers
Seashell (Xancidae)
School of fish

Solar location map
Physical unit definitions
The sun
Mercury
Jupiter
Egypt, Red Sea, Sinai Peninsula/Nile
DNA structure
Cells and cell division
Human sex organs
Conception
Fetus diagram
Diagram of male and female
Father and daughter (Malaysia)
Diagram of family ages
Diagram of continental drift
Heron Island (Great Barrier Reef of Australia)
Snake River and Grand Tetons
Monument Valley
Leaf
Sequoia
Tree with daffodils
Diagram of vertebrate evolution
Dolphins
Tree toad

Crocodile

Waterhole

Sketch of Bushmen

Man from Guatemala

Andean girls

Elephant

Old man with dog and flowers

Cathy Rigby

Schoolroom

Cotton harvest

Supermarket

Fishing boat with nets

Chinese dinner party

Great Wall of China

Construction scene (Amish country)

House (New England)

House interior with artist and fire

Taj Mahal

Boston

UN Building, night

Artisan with drill

Museum

Woman with microscope

Rush-hour traffic, India

Golden Gate Bridge

Airplane in flight

Antarctic expedition

Radio telescope (Arecibo)

Astronaut in space

Sunset with birds

Eagle

Jane Goodall and chimps

Bushmen hunters

Dancer from Bali

Thailand craftsman

Old man with beard and glasses (Turkey)

Mountain climber

Sprinters

Children with globe

Grape picker

Underwater scene with diver and fish

Cooking fish

Demonstration of licking, eating, and drinking

House construction (African)

House (Africa)

Modern house (Cloudcroft, New Mexico)

Violin with music score (Cavatina)

English city (Oxford)

UN Building, day

Sydney Opera House

Factory interior

X-ray of hand

Street scene, Asia (Pakistan)

Modern highway (Ithaca)

Train

Airport (Toronto)

Radio telescope (Westerbork, Netherlands)

Page of Newton's book, *System of the World*

Titan Centaur launch

String quartet (Quartetto Italiano)

THE ARECIBO OBSERVATORY AND SETI

Unlike the deserted, mothballed station portrayed in "Little Green Men," the Arecibo station on Puerto Rico is a thriving observatory that welcomes more than 200 scientists each year—in addition to its 140 regular employees. It's the main facility of Cornell University's National Astronomy and Ionosphere Center, one of three national centers for research operated by the National Science Foundation, and home to the largest radar-radio telescope in the world, which is some 1,000 feet across.

What *The X-Files* did get right was the important role the Arecibo facility has played in the Search for Extraterrestrial Intelligence (SETI) project. SETI, which theoretically began in 1959, was the first organized effort to use microwave radio signals to search the skies for signs of intelligent life. Throughout the 1960s the Soviet Union, as SETI's driving force, aimed dozens of omnidirectional antennae at the distant stars. They found nothing. In 1988, the Arecibo facility began scanning. It was the dawn of the world's most ambitious astronomical project—to map the entire sky, and anyone who might be out there.

One year later, Congress stopped all funding.

Today, Arecibo functions as a premier research facility.

123

Code Name: "The Host"

CASE SUMMARY

Mulder, disgusted by the shutdown of the X-Files, is ready to brush off a New Jersey murder as just another gangland-style hit. Luckily for him, Scully—handling her reassignment a little more professionally—finds the parasite that leads to a frightening mutant killer imported from radiation-blasted Chernobyl.

DEEP BACKGROUND

What Came Out of Chernobyl

Before April 1986, Chernobyl wasn't a word that sprang to the tip of Western tongues. Even in the Soviet Union, familiarity with the town was confined to the part of Ukraine where the Pripiat River flowed and the V. I. Lenin Nuclear Power Plant stood in the heart of a sleepy agricultural region. There was simply nothing extraordinary about Chernobyl until 1:21 A.M. on April 26, when a nuclear reactor exploded and all hell broke loose.

The name of this community would become notorious, though details of the explosion traveled more slowly than the deadly radiation drifting across Europe. Despite the fact that the Chernobyl meltdown had released thirty-five times more radiation than the bombs dropped over Nagasaki and Hiroshima, the Soviet government wasn't talking. It wasn't until an abnormal reading was taken at a Swedish nuclear station that the world began to grasp the full impact of the situation.

Thirty-one people died the morning of the explosion in an attempt to douse a nuclear fire; some 250 more contracted severe radiation poisoning and died more

EYEWITNESS STATEMENT

Nature didn't make that thing, Mulder, we did.

—Scully, "The Host"

124

slowly. Hundreds of farm animals dropped dead in the next weeks. Hundreds of thousands of residents would be relocated out of the thirty-kilometer "extreme contamination zone," but the 2 million citizens who lived in the direct fallout zone are still living on the contaminated land that once fed most of the Soviet Union. In Lapland, the *Cladonia,* or reindeer, moss concentrated the fallout, and, years later, whole herds of reindeer, the backbone of an entire way of life, would have to be slaughtered.

How could it have happened?

It began with an unauthorized experiment in which operators, in order to learn more about the plant's operation, knowingly and deliberately circumvented the safety system. Reactor 4 overheated before anyone could regain control of operations. Its heavy water "flashed" into steam. As oxygen and hydrogen split, the gaseous hydrogen reacted violently with the graphite moderator. The explosions blew a thousand-ton "lid" off the reactor and forced radioactive debris high into the atmosphere. There was no containment building to stop it. Fully 10 percent of the core, including the radioactive isotope cesium-137, sailed out into the sky.

Though Europeans didn't know it until days later, nearly the entire continent would be affected. From Scandinavia in the north to the southern tip of Greece, from the steppes of Russia to the United Kingdom, the deadly fallout was spread by uneven wind patterns. Significant amounts of the radioactive material would be found up to 1,300 miles from the site of the explosion.

Even the worst of the prior nuclear accidents all rolled into one doesn't come to even 5 percent of the radiation released at Chernobyl (50 to 100 million curies), so estimating the eventual damage is difficult. However, from direct observation and indirect inference, *conservative* estimates suggest that 28,000 to 100,000 human deaths from cancers and genetic defects directly attributable to the meltdown will occur in the next fifty years.

While *The X-Files* went over the top in creating the latex half-human-half-fluke that would infest New Jersey sewers and Porta Potties, in reality the mutations and deaths still appearing around Chernobyl, though perhaps more subtle, are equally terrifying. Lethal mutations have given rise to mouthless fish that die in droves on release from their eggs and supporting yolk sacs. Adult birds have died of starvation sitting atop eggs that would never hatch because the embryos they contained were so deformed.

For many of these poisoned creatures, death must seem a blessing. The spring following the accident saw the manifestation of hun-

Easy Stuff: Give yourself 1 point for each correct answer.

1. What did the sanitation worker think had attacked him?
2. What did Scully find on the arm of her autopsy subject?
3. Who assigned Mulder to this case?
4. To what position was Scully assigned after the X-Files were closed?
5. How did Scully make the connection between the incident aboard the Russian vessel and her John Doe?

Getting Tougher: Give yourself 2 points for each correct answer.

6. Which wiretap is Mulder working on this time?
7. To which part of the body did the fluke larva attach?
8. After escaping from the ambulance, where did the Flukeman hide?
9. How did the fluke exit Frank's body?
10. Where was the Flukeman briefly incarcerated?

dreds of nonfatal but painful conditions. A nest of kittens without eyelids was found mewling pitifully by one team of researchers; an elderly woman who refused to leave the land she was born on died of a cancer so virulent it wasn't even detectable in her system four months previously. Worst of all, newborn children exhibited deformities directly attributable to irradiation, and there were some 15,000 pregnant women in the fallout path.

Though some fans found this episode a tad melodramatic, it's hard to find fault in any script that vividly recalls dangers we've been quick to shrug off— *and* gives us a rousing good story at the same time.

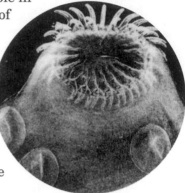

From little parasites, mighty Flukemen grow.

_____

RADIATION REVERSAL

If there's no cloud without a silver lining, then what good there is to come from the Chernobyl incident is undoubtedly the push given to research on how to treat and possibly cure victims of nuclear radiation poisoning. Miraculously, some progress is being made:

1. Not particularly helpful to the victims of Chernobyl, but a possible blessing for power plant workers, are the number of substances now found to provide some protection against radiation injury when administered prior to irradiation. Many of them apparently act by out-competing radiation-produced radicals for nutrients and oxygen.

2. Experiments with rats suggest that the hormone thyroxine, a normal secretion of the thyroid gland, can aid in the healing process. If such naturally occurring substances are indeed effective, then it may be possible to treat radiation victims without introducing yet more foreign substances.

3. Radiosensitivity is also under genetic control to some degree: Susceptibility varies among different inbred mice—as does resistance. Transgenic solutions (i.e., injecting people with mouse cells), normally challenged on ethical grounds, may offer the single best hope for irradiation victims.

4. Not all radiation disease is irreversible. Bone-marrow transfusions are effective if administered early. While it's too late for many of the victims of Chernobyl, use of this method has been helpful to some, especially the young.

FLASHBACK: ASSISTANT DIRECTOR WALTER S. SKINNER

Assistant Director Walter Skinner once told Mulder that Skinner himself stood squarely on the professional and ethical line that Mulder habitually crossed. In some circles that might be called fence sitting; in others it would be termed principled. Which description best fits Walter Skinner and his relationship to the X-Files team?

Without a doubt, the chain of command places Skinner a notch or two above his two stubborn—and successful—agents. He can grant Scully and Mulder's most peculiar cases official sanction as easily as he can undermine their best efforts on cases that fall well *within* the normal boundaries of FBI jurisdiction. Trying to anticipate where his support will or won't land seems impossible. He refused to officially proceed on the deaths of eighteen people in "F. Emasculata," yet he showed no reluctance to take unofficial action in "One Breath." Whatever his motivations, they aren't as simple as adhering to the strict letter of the law.

The limits of his office are equally unclear. When the X-Files were temporarily shut down, Skinner informed Mulder that the order came from higher up, that there was nothing he could have done to prevent it. Yet, within months, on nothing more than Skinner's say-so, Scully and Mulder are returned to their previous assignment. Had all the opposition to their investigations suddenly evaporated? Or was it *Skinner* who had shut down the office in the first place? Was he protecting two agents who'd stumbled onto something bigger than they realized? Or was he protecting something or someone else altogether?

And what *was* his relationship to the mysterious figures that floated just outside the Bureau itself? In "One Breath," it seemed to Mulder that Skinner had been able to locate The Smoking Man with surprisingly little difficulty. Yet Mr. X, the other covert influence following the X-File agents, appeared to be as much a mystery to Skinner as to Scully. The implication that there are separate people behind these two powerful men is hard to avoid.

For Mulder and Scully, already working in the dark on almost every front, Skinner's sweeping statement that everyone takes orders from somewhere could have been just one more uncertainty in their complex equations. In a scenario where colleagues, superiors, and even outside agents have more information than they do themselves, Mulder and Scully might have no choice but to follow Deep Throat's final advice and trust no one, even those they'd believed trustworthy.

Darin Morgan, brother of Glen Morgan (another *X-Files* writer), and writer of episodes like "Humbug," actually made his debut on the show as the Flukeman in this episode. The latex suit was reportedly one of "the most God-awful creations ever to be deliberately wrapped around a human body."

Code Name: "Blood"

CASE SUMMARY

Faced with their own artificially heightened phobias, the residents of a small town will do anything—even kill—to free themselves of their terror. Mulder and Scully, confronted with conflicting theories—several of which implicate government authorities from the municipal to the federal level—have to sift through the smallest of clues before finding the culprits. Those culprits are both new and all too familiar.

DEEP BACKGROUND

Phobias: Fear to the *N*th Degree

While few phobics go so far as to kill others to assuage their fears, a phobia can certainly be destructive. Unfortunately, it is too often self-destructive. In 1985, Maria Consuella Dablos was found dead in her New York City apartment. The official cause of death was starvation, yet she lived above a deli, in a city where food is sold on every street corner. She wasn't poor; nearly $600 was found in her purse and apartment. She wasn't physically disabled. She was a twenty-seven-year-old woman who appeared to be in perfect health. At the time of her autopsy, the coroner found "no underlying cause to anticipate early death." The case passed nearly unnoticed in the bustling city, until six years later, when a behavioral psychologist named Marcia Blake added a notation to the Dablos case: "Though physical death was caused by starvation, the underlying pathology responsible for the death was agoraphobia." Maria Consuella Dablos had starved to death rather

EYEWITNESS STATEMENT

Forty-two-year-old real estate agent murders four people with his bare hands? That's not supposed to happen anywhere.

—Mulder, "Blood"

than face the overwhelming panic she felt whenever she left the confinement of her apartment.

People who are afraid of spiders usually swat them with a paper, step on them, or just jump away. But phobias are a different story. Charles Vares, whose phobic fear of spiders became evident at an early age, was sixteen when a group of schoolmates dumped a bucket of them on him before football practice. The young halfback had a heart attack that took him off the field for the rest of the season and ultimately led to his dropping out of school.

Technically, a phobia is defined as an extreme, irrational fear of a specific object or situation. To be further labeled as a disorder, a phobia must interfere with or significantly alter a patient's lifestyle in a negative manner. While not everyone with a phobia starves to death, the degree to which people adjust to avoid a specific frightening situation can be extreme. One army colonel turned down a promotion three times to avoid serving in an underground bunker.

Most psychologists believe that phobias are a learned response. The person who fears enclosed spaces might associate tight spaces with traps, might connect them with a completely different event that happened to occur in a small space, or, some think, might have experienced a birth anxiety.

Phobias can continue to exist by a transferral process long after the original object or event that caused the fear is itself forgotten. Claire Bolt's phobia of water was traced by psychologists to a single event, an accidental burn by hot water. Bolt's original childhood fear had been of hot things. As she grew older, she found herself perfectly comfortable around open flames, stoves, curling irons, anything hot, but increasingly afraid of her own shower. Her inability to understand her fear made it even more frightening. Why should a glass of water, a sink of dishes, or the sight of the ocean scare her? Like many phobics, she was reluctant to seek help for her problem. Unfortunately, without proper treatment phobias will, in 70 percent of cases, become worse.

At first Bolt was able to force herself to handle water. She was an impeccably tidy person, certainly not the type to skip showers or leave dishes about for several days. With each passing day, however, Bolt's physical symptoms of anxiety grew worse. She found herself hyperventilating when she drove by a beach, and unable to cross over a bridge to go to work. She finally sought help when her personal hygiene fell off, when she'd been reprimanded a dozen times for lateness to work, when her kitchen was about to be declared a health hazard, when she needed to be rescued on a fine, sunny day,

Easy Stuff: Give yourself 1 point for each correct answer.

1. Name two of the machines whose displays seemed to send messages.
2. What baseball position did Mulder play as a boy?
3. What was the postal employee's phobia?
4. What was the postal employee's name?
5. How many Lone Gunmen do we see in this episode?

Getting Tougher: Give yourself 2 points for each correct answer.

6. What surveillance device did The Lone Gunmen describe as being attached to the back of a fly?
7. What magazine did Mulder say kept him from reading the August edition of *The Lone Gunman*?
8. What item of equipment did Mulder borrow from The Lone Gunmen?
9. What is displayed on Mulder's own cellular phone?
10. How much money did the postal worker's coworkers raise for him?

stranded in the dead center of a bridge. Not only was Bolt afraid of water, she was afraid of her physical reaction to her own fear.

As fear of fear is such a large part of phobic responses, behavior therapy is often successful in overcoming phobias. With behavior therapy, patients are exposed gradually to the feared item, all the time knowing they can make the fear go away at will. They confront their fears in a "safe" way. Gradually the fear of the fear abates and the patient/psychologist team can deal with the object or event itself. If the fear is transferred from something else, as in Claire Bolt's case, then the transitional fear is dealt with as well. In this way, the strong associative links between the feared situation, the person's experience of anxiety, and his or her subsequent avoidance of that situation are broken and are replaced by a less-maladaptive set of responses.

The Other Side of the Coin: Philias

The notion that nature abhors a vacuum but loves balance is borne out in the existence of philias. Like phobias, they are intense reactions to items or circumstances—but positive ones. The biophiliac, for example, has an intense love of living things. While that may not sound serious, or problematic, it can be for hundreds of people.

Carrie Benoit spent eight years being hired and fired from dozens of jobs before landing the ideal position, at least for her, in a plant nursery. "I didn't realize how terribly unhappy I was without something green around me." Carrie is now capable of seeing that in the past she would deliberately, if subconsciously, arrange situations that would get her fired. She was perfectly happy at her local unemployment office—which had recently been "greened" to perk up its flat, institutional feel.

Code Name: "Sleepless"

CASE SUMMARY

Investigating a deep-penetration squad whose members never needed to sleep and whose kill rate in Vietnam exceeded all other squads put together, Mulder discovers that one of the team members is out for vengeance. While his new (and unwanted) partner, Alex Krycek, is willing to follow him that far, Krycek balks at the rest of Mulder's theory—that the man effects his killings with his thoughts alone. Will Mulder have to open the mind of yet another partner before they can catch a killer?

Get Those ZZZZZZs

DEEP BACKGROUND

Left to our own devices, we'd sleep about one-third of our lives away. If we can't, we get grumpy. While not quite as inclined to nap as, say, the sloth, who sleeps about twenty hours a day, we seem to suffer more, and more quickly, from a lack of sleep. When deprived of sleep, we begin to yearn for it in a physical sense. So overwhelming can the compulsion be that we're powerless to control it and we just drop off. Most of us are sleep deprived to a greater or lesser extent. Are you? If you need an alarm clock to shorten your usual sleep pattern, if you find yourself nodding off in the afternoon, if you fall asleep as soon as you crawl into bed, or if you find yourself short of breath without extraneous activity, the answer is probably yes. Most sleep studies suggest adult humans need

EYEWITNESS STATEMENT

The autopsy revealed forty-three separate internal hemorrhages and skeletal fragments which just don't happen spontaneously! Not without some corresponding external trauma.

—Alex Krycek, "Sleepless"

131

closer to nine than eight hours per night. Over a week, those extra minutes add up, and a big snooze on Sunday morning isn't the ideal way to catch up.

If we need so much sleep, there must be a reason. It would seem easy to find out why: Just keep people awake for several days and note how they deteriorate. By monitoring the change in their mind and body states, it should be possible to isolate the effect of sleep on our overall health and welfare.

Naturally, that's been done.

That sleep deprivation causes physical and emotional changes goes without saying, but the larger question remains unanswered: Can lack of sleep actually hurt us? Will it disorient us to the point of intellectual or emotional damage? Could our biochemistry become so unbalanced that our bodies would be hurt? Could we actually be *poisoned* by a lack of sleep?

Fatigue is an obvious first symptom of sleep deprivation, one frequently found in city dwellers who, because of constant light sources, appear to sleep less well than their rural counterparts. Other symptoms are subtle, some dangerously so: impaired creativity and concentration, diminished immunity to disease, hand tremors, irritability, occasional misperceptions in performing tasks. With some tasks, such as driving a truck and controlling air traffic, these symptoms can be devastating. The Exxon *Valdez* oil spill, the Three Mile Island nuclear accident, in fact, some 70 percent of all manmade disasters have occurred after midnight when operators were likely to be drowsiest.

On short, highly motivating tasks, however, sleep deprivation has little effect. When seventeen-year-old Randy Gardner made his way into the *Guinness Book of World Records* by staying awake for eleven straight days, he had to keep moving at all times to stay awake. Nevertheless, during his final night of sleeplessness, Gardner managed to beat a researcher 100 straight times in a pinball game. He then slept fifteen hours and awoke feeling fine.

In rare cases, brain-diseased people have lost their ability to sleep, with disastrous results. One fifty-two-year-old man gradually became severely fatigued, shaky, disoriented, and incontinent. He would lapse into a dreamlike stupor from time to time, but without exhibiting the brain waves of sleep. Nine months after the sleep difficulty began, he died.

Why, then, must we sleep? We have few answers, but we think sleep probably helps to restore body tissues, especially those of the brain that are frequently damaged by everyday activities. Of the entire body, only the brain is incapable of feeling pain or fatigue—and the brain can become as chemically fatigued as a muscle.

Sleep may also play a role in the growth process. During deep sleep, the pituitary gland releases a growth hormone. As adults grow older, they release less of this hormone, and they spend less time in deep sleep. In addition, the sleeper's lowered body temperature conserves energy for the daytime hours.

If there's a truly frightening aspect to "Sleepless," it's the way it recalls how, time and again, testing or the lack of testing has endangered military servicemen without their knowledge. From Agent Orange to the Gulf War Syndrome, the fear that signing up is signing yourself over as a do-with-me-as-you-please lab creature is a very real one.

A CADRE OF NIGHTMARES

Frightening experiences associated with sleep are grouped together as nightmares. But professional sleep therapists recognize nightmares by specific types:

Incubus: The classic nightmare of adult years. Consists of arousal from deep sleep with a sense of heaviness over the chest and diffuse anxiety, but little or no dream recall.

Night terrors (pavor nocturnus): Disorder of early childhood. Delta-sleep is suddenly interrupted with a scream; the child may sit up in apparent terror and be incoherent and inconsolable. After a period of minutes, he or she returns to sleep, often without ever having been fully alert or awake. Dream recall generally is absent, and the entire episode may be forgotten in the morning.

Anxiety dreams: Most often associated with spontaneous arousals from REM sleep. These are the dreams we remember, the type that have us searching for the light switch and avoiding a return to sleep on the chance of falling back into the same dream. Anxiety dreams aren't limited to anxious people but appear to occur spontaneously. Sleep specialists suggest that dreaming is a necessary release, even among calm, well-adjusted individuals.

Easy Stuff: Give yourself 1 point for each correct answer.

1. What did Mulder find in his newspaper?
2. What was the name of Mulder's unwanted new partner?
3. All members of Cole's unit had a distinctive scar. Where?
4. By what nickname was Augustus Cole known?
5. How did the two cops die in the motel?

Getting Tougher: Give yourself 2 points for each correct answer.

6. Where did Salvatore Matola work?
7. What chemical, produced during sleep, was Cole deficient in?
8. How many people had Cole's squad killed?
9. What was the designation number of Cole's Recon Squad?
10. What was Dr. Grissom's address?

DREAM SYMBOLS

Some sleep specialists see dreams as universally symbolic representations of our deepest fears and desires. The vast majority of dream symbols involve animals or mythical creatures. Symbols are fun to play with, and here are some of the most common associations:

Birds:	Dreaming
Bulls:	Sex
Cats:	Hidden things
Crows:	Omen of evil
Dragons:	Power, magic, eternity
Flowers:	A marriage
Gardens:	Birth of a baby
Hornets:	Repercussions
Horses:	Sex
Monsters:	Fears
Spiders:	Wisdom
Toads:	Transmutation, change
Wolves:	Death

The ancient Babylonians were perhaps the most organized dreamers of all. They categorized and indexed their dreams according to type and content, often keeping a record of them for their entire lives. In Babylonian tradition there were five base types of sleep experiences that children were taught along with their numbers and letters.

Dream:	Figurative, mysterious, requiring interpretation.
Vision:	An exact account of a future event.
Oracular Dream:	A message about something to come.
Insomnium:	An ordinary dream, of no account.
Phantasm:	A type of nightmare, often supernatural.

Code Name: "Duane Barry"

When an ex-FBI agent with an intriguing medical history escapes from a mental hospital (holding his doctor and three others hostage in a travel agency while claiming to be an abductee), Mulder, resident expert on crazies, is called in. Despite warnings from the hostage team, it's not long before Mulder is "buying into Duane Barry's fantasies." But it's Scully, still assigned to Quantico, who thinks she's found the key to Barry's bizarre behavior in the 150-year-old case of Phineas Gage.

CASE SUMMARY

The Strange Case of Phineas Gage

DEEP BACKGROUND

With the exception of work done during World War II under less than humane conditions, the progress of human brain studies has been slow. Even today, head injuries like Duane Barry's gunshot wound are medical mysteries. Because many experiments required to answer even basic questions would ensure that the test subject became a vegetable, they simply can't be done. So, when a case like that of Phineas Gage comes along, neurosurgeons offer their best wishes for a full recovery, but are, frankly, more interested in observing the outcome.

One afternoon in 1848, twenty-five-year-old Gage, a railroad worker, was working for the Rutland and Burlington Railroad in Cavendish, Vermont. He was packing gunpowder into a rock with a tamping rod when a spark ignited, precipitating an explosion. The rod he was using shot upward through his left cheek, and out the top of his skull. The rod was 3-feet, 7-inches long and more than an inch in diameter. The left

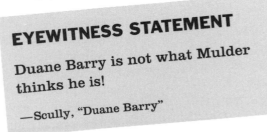

EYEWITNESS STATEMENT

Duane Barry is not what Mulder thinks he is!

—Scully, "Duane Barry"

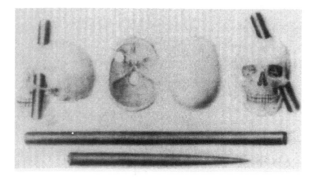

The rod Gage carried in his head until death.

frontal lobe of his brain was massively damaged.

To everyone's amazement, though a portion of the rod remained in his head for the rest of his life, Gage was still able to sit up and speak, and after the wound healed, he returned to work. He suffered absolutely no physical impairment, no sensory impairment. Even his mental abilities and memories were intact. His personality, however, was not. The affable, soft-spoken Phineas Gage was now an irritable, profane, capricious person who lost his job and ended up earning his living as a fairground exhibit. This person, said his friends, was "no more Phineas Gage than Phineas Gage was God himself."

Dr. Harlow, the attending physician, described how the injury later affected Gage's behavior:

> *His physical health is good, and I am inclined to say he has recovered. Has no pain in head, but says it has a queer feeling which he is not able to describe. . . . He is fitful, irreverent, indulging at times in the grossest profanity . . . manifesting but little deference for his fellows, impatient of restraint or advice when it conflicts with his desires, at times pertinaciously obstinate, yet capricious and vacillating, devising many plans for future operations, which are no sooner arranged than they are abandoned in turn for others.*

A Brief History of the CIA

The Central Intelligence Agency began its existence in 1947, as a stepchild of the Office of Strategic Services (OSS), which had been active during the war, but which was seen as inappropriate during peacetime. It was intended to be the principal intelligence-counterintelligence agency of the United States government.

The "central" portion of the agency name was considered the most important. Both before and during the war, intelligence efforts had come under the auspices of no less than *fourteen* different agencies, including the Army, Navy, and FBI, and those were only the agencies of which the public might be aware. Needless to say, with so many distinct groups attempting to gather information, there was bound to be duplication of effort. A bit more surprising perhaps was the level of competition between agencies and the lack of communication between them. It was a literal case of the right hand not knowing what the left hand was doing. From time to time, quasi-embarrassing situations arose where one agency's operative found himself mistakenly investigating the operatives of another agency.

Roosevelt had created the OSS in 1942 to gather up the fragmented information under the supervision of a single agency, and named William J. (Wild Bill) Donovan its head. For the next three years the OSS collected and analyzed foreign intelligence wherever the U.S. military was operating. The OSS obtained intelligence through secret agents in enemy territory, it carried out counter-propaganda and disinformation activities, and it staged special operations behind enemy lines involving sabotage, demolition, and the supplying and direction of resistance fighters.

Donovan's rather eccentric personality never appeared to interfere with his ability to run the OSS. In fact, it seemed to be a critical factor in allowing the organization to quickly overcome the inexperience of its own operatives. Under Donovan's capable hand, the organization would eventually employ some 12,000 agents.

It was Truman who eliminated the OSS in 1945 in favor of a more coordinated intelligence service. The following year, he established the Central Intelligence Group and the National Intelligence Agency, employing many of the OSS's former agents, but the armed forces continued to operate separately from even these new organizations.

Just a year later, Congress created the National Security Council (NSC) and, under its direction, the Central Intelligence Agency, which would carry out such national security functions as the NSC might direct. Though no CIA director was as flamboyant as Donovan or as autocratical as the FBI's Hoover, they've been a diverse group. Some have been career military men, others diplomats, and a few have even been career CIA men.

The CIA is organized into four major directorates:

1. Intelligence analyzes and organizes information from overt sources as well as covert activities that can include espionage, aerial and satellite photography (which services have also been used by outside scientific interests), and interception of radio, telephone, and other forms of communication. This information is circulated as bulletins, reports, and exhaustive surveys.

2. Operations is directly responsible for all covert operations, including, but not limited to, clandestine collection of intelligence (that is, espionage) and special covert activities.

TRIVIA BUSTER 29

Easy Stuff: Give yourself 1 point for each correct answer.

1. Why was Mulder assigned to this case?
2. What did Agent Lucy Kazdin ask Krycek to get?
3. Where did Duane Barry hold his hostages?
4. What was Duane Barry's occupation before he was institutionalized?
5. What did Duane claim the aliens had done to his teeth?

Getting Tougher: Give yourself 2 points for each correct answer.

6. Where was Duane Barry being held and treated?
7. What was the name of the psychiatrist Duane kidnapped?
8. How many hostages did Duane have when Mulder arrived?
9. To what famous medical subject did Scully compare Duane Barry?
10. What intelligence equipment did Mulder take into the hostage situation?

3. Science and Technology, sometimes compared to Q of James Bond fame, is charged with keeping up with scientific and technological advances, developing technical gadgets for use by the agency, and providing technical and scientific support to agency operations.

4. Administration handles the agency's administrative matters, and includes the Office of Security, which is responsible for the security of personnel, facilities, information (internal security), and such varied material as dossiers on defectors from other governments.

Covert activities can be truly secretive or, as is often the case, performed almost openly as part of the "diplomatic" function assumed by almost all intelligence services, or under the guise of corporations that the CIA acquires or creates out of nothing. The agency also debriefs traveling businessmen, tourists, and journalists who agree to be questioned and who are returning from destinations of interest to the CIA.

Some of the CIA's operations have been more successful than others. The CIA restored to power the Shah of Iran and ousted Mohammad Mosaddeq in the process. The agency destabilized the unfriendly Guatemalan government, which quickly gave way to one more amenable to American policies. The Cuban Bay of Pigs affair, however, was an unmitigated disaster. And the CIA's involvement in the Watergate scandal did little to boost the popularity of the U.S. government.

Unlike the Soviet KGB, the CIA is limited by its own inaugural legislation to intelligence and counterintelligence activities on *foreign* soil, while the KGB had numerous *domestic* intelligence-gathering and police functions. Those are qualities the CIA has occasionally coveted. Obviously, espionage and counterespionage operations require a certain amount of secrecy if they are to be successful, and, from time to time, the CIA has attempted to step outside its legal limits under cover of "security." In an open society, though, such brief sorties frequently come to light. Between an observant public and press and the watchful eye of a government unwilling to lose control of its own creation, the CIA has generally stayed within its boundaries.

Code Name: "Ascension"

CASE SUMMARY

Every agent's nightmare: A fellow officer is in trouble and there's not a damn thing that can be done about it. It's even worse for Mulder, whose trust is so hard to earn. Scully's missing, and who can help him find her? His new partner? His superiors, who have agendas of their own? His outside contacts? As Mulder is about to discover, sometimes all you have is yourself.

Stunts: A Cut in the Action

DEEP BACKGROUND

If every actor were physically—and mentally—capable of performing all his own stunts, the work of a dozen different people would be dramatically easier. No more duplicate setups, one for the actor, one for the stunt double. No more hours of meticulous editing to ensure a smooth transition between two different film sequences. No more squinting to ensure that embarrassing continuity errors have been eliminated.

But few actors have the skills of a trained stunt double, and only a small percentage consider themselves qualified to perform the numerous stunts that even a single script can demand. So why would actors risk injury attempting to incorporate an entirely new and difficult set of skills into their performances? Reasons vary. Kurt Russell, for example, is a natural athlete who finds stunt work challenging. Then again, just as some actors come to acting to overcome innate shyness, others take on stunt work to overcome specific fears. Buster Keaton, Sylvester Stallone, and Alexander Gudonov, all accomplished stuntmen as

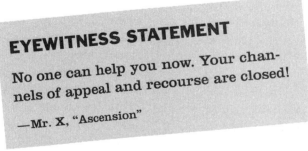

EYEWITNESS STATEMENT

No one can help you now. Your channels of appeal and recourse are closed!

—Mr. X, "Ascension"

Easy Stuff: Give yourself 1 point for each correct answer.

1. Where did Scully's cross and chain come from? ✓
2. Where did the piece of metal Scully was carrying at the time of her abduction come from? ✓
3. Where was Scully when Duane was stopped by the trooper? ✓
4. What was Duane Barry's "official" cause of death? ✓
5. What song did Krycek claim Duane was whistling? ✓

Getting Tougher: Give yourself 2 points for each correct answer.

6. What unique message, instead of "The Truth Is Out There," flashed on the screen during the credits? ✓
7. On what route was the trooper killed? ✓
8. Name the resort where Mulder and Krycek catch up with Barry. ✓
9. What does Mulder find in the trunk of Duane's car? ✓
10. What forensic evidence did Mulder see on Duane's medical bracelet? ✓ —1

well as actors, have each confessed to some fear of heights, fires, or falling.

When questioned about *his* reasons for doing his own stunts, David Duchovny cited artistic integrity and a desire to give his audience as honest a portrayal as possible. The stunts he performed for "Ascension," for instance, would no doubt be considered above and beyond the call of duty.

We're not talking here about a simple short fall into an inflatable bag. Or a safely-behind-glass encounter with zoo animals. Or a run-of-the-mill diving roll across a train station platform. No, the stunts called for in "Ascension" were as ambitious as any of those a trained stuntman could ever be expected to take on. Dangling from a swaying gondola, dozens of feet in the air, with nothing but a restraint strap to keep him from tumbling down the side of a British Columbia ski slope, David Duchovny was certainly giving his audience that "honest" performance. A morning-after of sore muscles was the likely result of three intense fight scenes, a high-platform balancing act, and a gut-wrenching climb up a smooth metal surface.

THE FALLS

A big fall can signal the highest dramatic point of a script, the physical point of no return. On *The X-Files,* the fall that will stay with fans the longest is most likely that of Samantha Mulder and the mysterious pilot in "Endgame." As the two topple off a bridge—a result of all Mulder's choices up to that moment—the audience can clearly see this as a decisive instant in his life.

Less outwardly dramatic, perhaps, was Scully's drop from the ceiling after being telekinetically pinned there in "The Calusari." Though Mulder had seen the similar fall of the nurse in "Excelsis Dei," and watched an intruder at Lauren Kyte's home dangle eerily in midair, this was Scully's first such experience.

But the most punishing fall of all is definitely Mulder's in "Colony." Mulder's fall from a moving car was preceded by a bounce off its windshield.

THE BIG STUNTS

Like big falls, the *big* stunts require something extra, in scope, meaning, or execution, from all those involved. Used too often, even the most exotic stunts lose their impact; used selectively, they push a story forward and stay with an audience long after the credits roll. And the big stunts aren't the exclusive property of the guys.

Few fans were breathing easily as Dana Scully careened down the stairwell in the final moments of "Irresistible," relating the chaotic path of her body with a deeper meaning. A terrified flight from a horror only she could fully understand, Scully's desperate attempt to escape said as much about her courage as her fear.

Occasionally, a stunt, near-subconscious symbolism, and dramatic visual impact come together not only to deliver a stunning screen experience but to broaden the audience's understanding of the moment. Such was the case in "Excelsis Dei," when a torrent of water, long accepted in the literary world as symbolic of cleansing and change, burst loose inside the convalescent home, washing over our two favorite agents—who'd been struggling with a breach in their usual rapport.

ONE ON ONE

Much of *The X-Files'* dramatic tension comes from the understated reactions of its leads, magnifying the impact of those rare moments when the normally reserved characters finally let loose and get physical. In those rare instances when tightly focused rage has been allowed expression, it's usually in the form of that Hollywood classic, the brawl scene.

To date, Scully has avoided catfights and bar brawls, leaving the choreographed stunts to Mulder, Mr. X, and Skinner—all of whom at one time or another have gone head to head.

ANSWERS

1. It was a gift from her mother for her fifteenth birthday.
2. Duane Barry's abdomen.
3. In the trunk of the car.
4. Strangulation.
5. *Stairway to Heaven.*
6. Deny Everything.
7. Route 229, just off the Blue Ridge Parkway.
8. Skyland Resort.
9. Scully's necklace, a gold chain with a cross.
10. Blood and several strands of bright red hair.

YOUR SCORE: 14

Code Name: "3"

CASE SUMMARY Scully's missing and there's no one Mulder can trust. He retreats to the work that has sustained him for so many years, hot on the trail of a group of serial killers. He's ready for anything the job can throw at him—anything but a beautiful vampire-fetishist. Kristen, whether criminal or victim, is no one to be trifled with.

DEEP BACKGROUND

Vampyres! The Erotic Subculture

Sexual. Intense. Dangerous. Powerful. The vampire legend tempts human imagination with the lure of the forbidden, sweet promises of immortality, and the thrill of power. That legend, as any X-Phile knows, also falls squarely within the realm of an X-File. With the rising popularity of Anne Rice's *Interview With the Vampire,* the classic elegance of Bram Stoker's *Dracula*, and the cult-driven impetus of television's *Forever Knight* already evident, the challenge to the crew of *The X-Files* was clear—create an episode dripping with the genre's sensual elegance without resorting to trite imitation.

Breaking completely new ground, *The X-Files* delved into a tantalizing fringe element of the club scene, the vampire subculture: a completely *human* construct in which to build their own chilling tale and introduce an unholy trinity of characters. In the darker shadows of nearly every club scene are people for whom the trappings of vampirism have become the ideal. At night they indulge a love of gothically styled clothes, sip dark red wine, and exchange long, languid looks with their lovers. Then they go home, put out the

EYEWITNESS STATEMENT

It's not who you are. It doesn't make you happy.

—Mulder, "3"

garbage, and find work clothes for the following morning. At least the vast majority of them do.

Some few, very few, unable or unwilling to disentangle themselves from their nightly fantasy, follow a different path. They exchange "love-nips" as others exchange kisses, include the taste of blood on their list of sensual delights, shun the sunlit hours, and truly come to *believe*.

It's not hard to understand the appeal of vampires. While details differ, near-heroic attributes are always part of the package. Physical strength, mental dexterity, incredible senses of smell, hearing, and sight, make human beings appear puny by comparison. The ability to fly, shapeshift, control the minds of animals and humans, or call fog from a clear night are certainly beyond our scope. It's the vampire's tendency to see humans as food that has made their names anathema through the centuries.

Fortunately, their tremendous strengths have always been balanced, at least in myth, by equally striking vulnerabilities. The Ch'ing Shih, a Chinese vampire with poisonous breath in addition to the usual phalanx of supernatural abilities, should in theory rule the night. Not so. Should the hunting Ch'ing Shih happen across a pile of rice, it's compelled to stop, break off its hunt, and count every grain before it can pass. While it's counting, it's easy prey for normal weapons or ordinary sunlight.

Perhaps the most traditional way to permanently dispose of a vampire is to hang it in the sun for a few minutes, but, as was accurately reflected in the script's depiction by writers Glen Morgan and Jim Wong, there's more to that idea than meets the eye. Dracula, the most famous vampire, only gradually gained an aversion to daylight in film and television. In the original 1937 film, Dracula, like many others of his ilk, found light uncomfortable, but hardly a lethal impediment. Early guides for the vampire hunter stressed *belief* above alchemy, faith above science, a theme that resonates through all the X-Files, not just this episode where a vampire who'd been killed by exposure to sun later walks through it without harm. In fact, in a rare turnaround for *The X-Files,* and certainly counter to any expectations fans may have held before viewing "3," this episode's climactic scene takes place not in a foggy, damp night scene adjacent to sewers or tunnels or cemeteries, but in a brilliantly lit home without a wisp of fog to be seen.

Belief plays a large role in other methods of vampiric execution, whether by crosses or holy water, though it's never clear *whose* belief

If you didn't catch it the first time through, the reference written on a wall by the vampires read as follows: "He who eats of my flesh and drinks of my blood shall have eternal life, and I shall raise them up on the last day."

This was the only episode Gillian Anderson missed as a result of her pregnancy.

143

is being tested. Is it the vampire's belief or the wielder's that makes these weapons so potent in popular literature? Would the Ch'ing Shih, perhaps a Confucian in its previous life, fear such a weapon? If it's the wielder's faith at issue in this contest, why would any symbol be necessary?

Of course, less esoteric means of killing or escaping from vampires do exist. A stake through the heart of ash, maple, or hawthorn is held to be nearly universally effective, as is decapitation with a gravedigger's shovel, drowning in saltwater, or burning.

Then again, few humans could survive that sort of treatment either.

ON BECOMING A VAMPYRE

For nearly 300 years, Eastern Europeans practiced preventive medicine that was concerned with warding off vampirism and lycanthropy in addition to the diseases of the day. In fact, in A.D. 909, one Brother Constantine of Bavaria painstakingly compiled the definitive list of vampire medications—a list some 1,100 items long. It was no simple task to avoid becoming a vampire, and death was one of the most common ways this transformation took place. There was a right way and a wrong way to die. Sick relatives were often confined to their beds long before it was physically necessary, simply to keep them from doing anything that could make them a vampire, including:

1. Dying excommunicate.
2. Dying unbaptized.
3. Dying apostate.
4. Dying while recovering from being a werewolf. This diagnosis could be avoided by isolation for at least two full cycles of the moon and close observation for signs of sprouting hair or canines.
5. Dying while under curse from one's parents.
6. Dying by suicide. The sick were often bound and gagged to prevent them from taking their own lives to end the misery of their illness.
7. Dying in a fall from the left side of one's wagon. While this originally stemmed from Moorish and Islamic peoples who observed the custom of using the right hand to eat and the left for private bodily functions, it quickly became a mainstream belief.

Were you unfortunate enough to die under any of those conditions, your family would have to sit watching you until you were well rotted and thus safe to bury.

Even if you took great pains to avoid vampirism at death, such a fate was, for some, unavoidable. Signs of eventual vampirism were detectable at birth, and included the following:

1. Being born with a tooth already erupted.
2. Being born with red hair.
3. Being born the seventh son of a seventh son.
4. Being born the child of a mother who'd slept with demons.
5. Being born with the placenta still over one's head.

Finally, if you turned out all right at birth, and knew what to avoid doing at the end of your days, you had a pretty good chance of avoiding the wrong kind of eternal life. Between birth and death, you simply had to avoid the following:

1. Being promiscuous.
2. Unknowingly drinking the blood of a vampire.
3. Being bitten by a vampire.

THE ETHNIC VAMPIRE

Vampires exist in many traditions, among them:

Asanbosam (African): The Asanbosam have hooked feet and prefer the victim's thumb to neck.

Bajang (Malaysian): The Bajang often appear as polecats. When not under the sway of sorcerers, they often preyed on the same family for generations.

Baobhan Sith (Scottish): The baobhan sith always appeared as beautiful women who would dance with young men until they became too weak to put up a fight.

Empusa (Mediterranean): Related to the incubi and succubi, these female vampires appear as beautiful women when they hunt, and hags when they've finished.

Jaracara (Brazilian Basin): These snakelike creatures enjoy a more varied diet than their European counterparts. In addition to blood, they steal the breast milk of sleeping women.

Krvopijac (Bulgaria): Noted for their one nostril, the Krvopijac require precise disposal. Only a magician can catch the vampire's spirit in a bottle and burn it.

Easy Stuff: Give yourself 1 point for each correct answer.

1. What did Mulder find in the whirlpool plumbing?
2. Where did John work?
3. How did John "die"?
4. What was the name of the club where Mulder met Kristen?
5. How did the female vampire die?

Getting Tougher: Give yourself 2 points for each correct answer.

6. Name one of the two unusual items in Kristen's purse.
7. What was the name of the restaurant to which Mulder followed Kristen?
8. What's Kristen's full name?
9. What unusual items are found in Kristen's home?
10. What verse was written in blood on the wall?

1. A hypodermic needle.
2. A blood bank.
3. He burned to death in the sun.
4. Club Tepes.
5. She was impaled on a wooden coat rack.
6. Hypodermic needles and a compact without a mirror.
7. Ra (named for the Egyptian sun god).
8. Kristen Kilar.
9. Veterinary needles, part of a snake bite kit, and a loaf of bread filled with blood.
10. John 52:54, which doesn't even exist.

YOUR SCORE: __13__

Mulo (Serbia): Defying the notion that vampires are nocturnal, the Mulo travel the roads day and night looking for victims from which to eat the flesh as well as drain the blood.

Nosferatu (widespread in Central and Eastern Europe): The vampire on whom the Dracula legend was born. Elegant, charismatic, and refined, if a little pale.

Wampir (Russian): Wampiri appear human and walk abroad in daylight. With a stinger under their tongue instead of fangs, they must be burned under special circumstances to be destroyed.

And a few others to watch out for:

Austrian—dracul	American Indian—kwakiytl
Wallachian—murony	Bohemian—ogolgen
Romanian—strigoi	Tibetan—khadro/dakini

THE VAMPIRE DISEASE

Porphyria, an unusual genetic condition that interferes with the metabolism of iron, a major component of blood, has been called Vampire's Disease since 1985 when David Dolphin presented it as a plausible explanation for the vampire mythos.

Some porphyria patients certainly exhibit strange and eclectic symptoms, including extreme sensitivity to light, a reddish brown discoloration of teeth and urine, heavy growth of body hair, severe anemia, and congenital defects of the face and fingers, with several patients possessing the "pointed ears" traditionally associated with devils, demons, and vampires.

But porphyrics have no cravings to drink blood, human or otherwise. They also fail to exhibit an aversion to holy symbols, garlic, or any of the traditional banes.

Perrey Reeves: A Brief Filmography

"The Return of Ironside," 1993
Child's Play 3, 1992
"Homefront," 1992
"Plymouth," 1991
"Mothers, Daughters and Lovers," 1990
"The Preppie Murder," 1989

Real-life significant other to David Duchovny, actress Perrey Reeves was featured as Kristen in the second season *X-Files* episode "3." And you wondered why they smoldered on-screen?

Code Name: "One Breath"

CASE SUMMARY

Poisoned with a mutated form of her own DNA, Dana Scully hovers precariously in the misty world between life and death, while her partner, the only one not to have given up on her, must stand aside and let her family make life and death decisions. The only avenue left open to him is to find her assailant. His failure, against players who exist almost as shadows, is preordained, but he finds something more important in the process of trying.

Near-Death Experiences

DEEP BACKGROUND

A man . . . hears himself pronounced dead by his doctor. He begins to hear an uncomfortable noise, a loud ringing or buzzing, and at the same time feels himself moving very rapidly through a long dark tunnel. After this, he suddenly finds himself outside of his own physical body . . . and sees his own body from a distance, as though he is a spectator. . . . Soon other things begin to happen. Others come to meet and to help him. He glimpses the spirits of relatives and friends who have already died, and a loving, warm spirit of a kind he has never encountered before—a being of light —appears before him. . . . He is overwhelmed by intense feelings of joy, love, and peace. Despite his attitude, though, he somehow reunites with his physical body and lives.

EYEWITNESS STATEMENT

I don't have to be psychic to see that you are in a very dark place. Much darker than where my sister is. Willingly walking deeper into the darkness cannot help her at all.

—Melissa Scully, "One Breath"

147

Easy Stuff: Give yourself 1 point for each correct answer.

1. What is Scully's sister's name?
2. Who signed as a witness to Dana's Living Will?
3. How does Mulder signal to X that he wants a meeting?
4. What happened to the man who stole Scully's blood vial?
5. What did Mulder find in a pack of cigarettes?

Getting Tougher: Give yourself 2 points for each correct answer.

6. Which of The Lone Gunmen comes to visit Scully and bring her flowers?
7. Who is the new, unseen member of The Lone Gunmen?
8. What famous person do The Lone Gunmen have as a background on their computer screens?
9. Which nurse stood on the shore of Scully's lake and watched over her?
10. What verse is on Dana Scully's headstone?

Now *there's* an experience Dana Scully could relate to! While *The X-Files* skipped the seeing-your-own-body-from-above-scenes, the rest closely parallels Scully's experience in this episode. This passage from Raymond Moody's best-selling book, *Life After Life,* is a composite description of a *near-death experience.* Because reports of these experiences are nearly always positive, they are devoured by those eager for proof that there is happiness after death. (Only one report in a thousand is of having gone to hell.)

What should we make of these reports? Do they prove that we can look forward to bliss on the other side of death? Do they confirm Plato's doctrine that mind—or soul—is separable from body? Do such flights of mind reliably occur to those who face death?

Near-death experiences are more common than you might suspect. Each of several investigators interviewed a hundred or more people who had come close to death through such physical traumas as cardiac arrest. Thirty to 40 percent of those interviewed recalled some sort of near-death experience. When George Gallup, Jr., interviewed a national sample of Americans, in 1982 and 1986, 15 percent reported having experienced a close brush with death. One-third of these people—representing some 8 million individuals by Gallup's estimate—reported an accompanying mystical experience. Some of these people claimed to recall things said by others while they lay unconscious and near death (but then, some anesthetized patients undergoing major surgery later display similar recall of operating room conversation).

Did Moody's description of the complete near-death experience sound familiar? The parallels between it and descriptions of the typical hallucinogenic experience are striking: replay of old memories, out-of-body sensations, and visions of tunnels or funnels and bright lights or beings of light. In short, the content of the near-death experience is just what one would expect from a hallucination. Moreover, oxygen deprivation—like that associated with cardiac arrest—and other insults to the brain are known to produce hallucinations.

Perhaps, then, the brain under stress manufactures the near-death experience. Patients who experience temporal lobe seizures often report similarly profound mystical experiences, as have solitary sailors and polar explorers while enduring severe monotony, isolation, and cold. Even the twilight state between waking and sleeping may produce sensations of floating up off the bed. Fantasy-prone persons are especially susceptible—perhaps we should say *open*—to near-death and other out-of-body experiences.

One study concludes that the near-death experience is best understood "as a dissociative hallucinatory activity of the brain." When external input dims, the brain's own interior activity becomes perceptible. To illustrate by analogy: When gazing out a window at dusk, we begin to see the reflected interior of the room as if it were outside, either because the light from outside is dimming (as in the near-death experience) or because the inside light is being amplified (as with hallucinogenic drugs like LSD). When projected on our perceptual window, our mind's internal images appear real. Those having a near-death experience, like those on an LSD trip, explore "the beyond within."

Some investigators of near-death experiences object. People who have experienced both hallucinations and the near-death phenomenon often deny their similarity. Moreover, a near-death experience often changes people in ways that a drug trip doesn't. They become kinder, more spiritual, more likely to believe in life after death. Skeptics reply that these effects stem from the simple realization of mortality.

The controversy over interpreting near-death experiences raises a basic mind-body issue: Is the mind immaterial? Can it exist separate from the body? *Dualists* answer yes. They believe that the mind and body are two distinct entities—the mind nonphysical, the body physical—that somehow interact with each other. As Socrates says in Plato's *Phaedo,* "Does not death mean that the body comes to exist by itself, separated from the soul, and that the soul exists by herself, separated from the body? What is death but that?" For Socrates, as for those today who believe that near-death experiences are proof of immortality, death is not really the death of the person. Death is merely a person's liberation from the bodily prison, an occasion for rejoicing. (Carried to its extreme, this dualist view has given rise to glorification of the afterlife trip under such titles as "The Thrill of Dying" and "The Wonderful World of Death.")

Monists answer no to the separation of mind and body. They contend that mind and body are different aspects of the same thing. Whether they are scientists who assume the inseparability of mind and body or theologians who hold to an afterlife that involves some form of bodily resurrection, monists generally believe that death is real and that without bodies we truly are nobodies.

Gillian Anderson was unusually pale in this episode because of the cesarean section she underwent less than a week earlier. The picture of a swollen tummy in "Ascension" led some to believe an alien baby scenario was about to unfold.

Case #: X-2.09-111894

Code Name: "Firewalker"

CASE SUMMARY

When a volcanic research team suddenly goes silent and a robot's image of a dead man becomes the outside world's only view into the remote camp, the base team turns to Mulder and Scully for help. Despite Mulder's evident concern, a newly recovered Scully is determined to return to her normal workload. When they arrive, her presence turns out to be vital in identifying the bizarre infection that has overrun the camp.

DEEP BACKGROUND

Volcanoes, Silicon Life, and the Rest

Like so many episodes of *The X-Files,* "Firewalker" took a host of ideas, some proven and others highly theoretical, and set them next to one another, arranging them in a new way to make us question some of our stauncher beliefs.

Could life exist in a volcano?

Most people's swift response would be a resounding "No!"

By combining the smallest nuggets of scientific information, though, the X-crew makes us reconsider that response.

EYEWITNESS STATEMENT

We're not exactly "proper channels."

—Mulder, "Firewalker"

VOLCANIC LIFE

It does exist. Just not in the way we usually imagine: clinging precariously to the inner walls of a land-based volcano.

In 1977, an American deep-sea research ship was investigating underwater volcanoes erupting from a ridge south of the Galapagos Islands. Three kilometers below the surface of the ocean they found vents on the sea floor that were spouting hot, chemically rich water into the sea. In these jets, and in the crevices of the rocks around the vents, the scientists discovered great concentrations of bacteria consuming the chemicals. The bacteria, in turn, were being fed upon by immense worms, 3 to 5 meters long and up to 10 centimeters in circumference. They were unlike any other worms previously encountered by science, for they had neither mouth nor gut and they fed by absorbing the bacteria through the thin skin of feathery tentacles, rich in blood vessels, that sprouted from their tip.

Since these organisms live in the black depths of the ocean, they're unable to tap the energy of sunlight directly. Nor can the worms obtain energy secondhand from the falling fragments of dead animals drifting down from above—remember, they have no mouths. Their food comes entirely from the bacteria that derive their sustenance from the volcanic waters. Indeed, the worms may well be the only large animals anywhere that draw their energy entirely from volcanoes, which then would form the base of a complex food web.

Alongside the worms lay huge clams 30 centimeters long, that also feed on the bacteria. Rising jets of hot water created other currents that flowed toward the vents across the sea floor, bringing with them organic fragments that are eaten by other organisms— strange, hitherto unknown fish and blind white crabs—clustering around the clams and the worms. So in these submarine volcanic springs, a dense and varied colony of creatures flourished in the darkness.

Nor is the phenomenon completely foreign to terrestrial environments. Hot springs dot much of the Earth's surface. The water they produce, which originates partly from sources far below and partly from rainwater that has permeated deep into the ground, has been heated by a lava chamber and forced back up through cracks in the rocks. Water accumulates in small subterranean chambers, becoming superheated under pressure until finally it flashes into steam and spouts to the surface as a geyser.

In other cases the upward flow is regular, slower, gentler, and the water forms a deep, perpetually brimming pool. Even in these scalding waters, bacteria flourish, and along with them are more advanced organisms like blue-green algae. The algae add an important element to the system—chlorophyll, the nearly magical substance that enables plants to use the energy of the sun to convert chemical substances into living tissue.

Such organisms are found in the hot springs of Yellowstone Park in North America. There the algae and bacteria grow together to form slimy green or brown mats. Nothing else is known to survive in the hottest parts of the pools occupied by these mats, but where the pools spill over, the water cools the few degrees necessary for other creatures to live. The algal mats provide a rich source of food that is eaten voraciously by everything from brine flies to raccoons.

ABOUT SILICON LIFE . . .

Could the silicon-based life-form Mulder theorizes in "Firewalker" actually exist somewhere in the universe? There are two schools of thought on that and they're not mutually exclusive.

Those who speculate that life needn't be based on carbon, as Earth life is, are usually found eyeing the Periodic Table of the Elements because the table groups elements by their *properties,* their similarities.

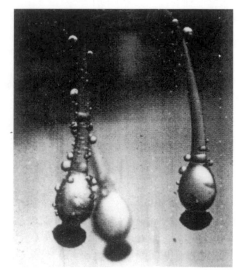

Pilobolus: the supposed silicon-based life form.

For example, carbon (C) and silicon (Si) both sit happily in column IV-A because they react similarly with other elements, share the same number of valence electrons, and form compounds that react alike. By combining carbon and oxygen during human respiration, a compound CO_2 is formed; theoretically at least, a silicon-based organism could go through its own version of respiration and produce SiO_2, a compound that does indeed exist. We call it silica—sand—and it is the material found inside the victims in "Firewalker."

The problem, according to the other camp, isn't the metabolic processes, but the ability to form long molecules, like DNA, from silicon. Attempts to create long silicon-based chains haven't been successful, and, without those huge molecules, silicon life would be limited to the simplest of organisms.

Then again . . . how complex are fungi?

JOURNEY TO THE CENTER OF THE EARTH

As children, we were introduced to natural science, which was supposed to tell us about the world we lived in. More or less, we were told the truth as it was known at the time. What we weren't told, then or since, unless we followed science as a career, was that those early science lessons were frequently "best-fit science," theories that could explain *most* known phenomena, but that were tacitly acknowledged to be incomplete. But that was okay because most people are content to turn on a lightbulb without understanding *how* it works.

The problem with best-fit science is that, while it's practical on a day-to-day basis, it inspires no curiosity about the world. Everything in best-fit science has already been explained. There's nothing left to question or discover. For example, every child who has read his or her textbook's chapter on volcanoes (and likely the parents who'll help build those foaming models as well) is told that the Earth has a nickel-iron core in a magma form and that's the end of the discussion. While that's true, at least as far as we know, it's only *part* of the truth. Actually, 90 percent of that core is nickel and iron. We haven't a clue about the other 10 percent. Well, we didn't until recently. The most significant insight into this long-standing mystery came from lab experiments involving materials under extremely high pressure and temperature. Geophysicists Yingwei Fei and Ho-kwang Mao of the National Science Foundation (NSF) Science and Technology Center (STC) for High-Pressure Research described experimental results strongly supporting the idea that the core's missing component is oxygen, or perhaps a combination of oxygen and sulfur.

To conduct their research, Fei and Mao used a new version of the diamond-anvil cell, an instrument in which tiny samples are mechanically squeezed between two facing diamonds. External heating is used to achieve high temperatures and pressures that approximate those of Earth's core-mantle boundary.

If Fei and Mao's work stands up, the next generation of science fiction might revolve around oxygen-breathing organisms capable of withstanding the heat and pressure of a planet's inner core instead of the gravity fluctuations and cold of outer space.

Dante: Firewalker's Big Brother

Firewalker, the arachnoidlike robot investigating the Cascade Mountains in the episode named for it, is a fictional incarnation of a series of robots being developed by NASA for use on planetary exploration missions and being tested on the most inhospitable surfaces of good old Earth.

One of the most effective prototypes is Dante II, a tethered robot developed at the CMU Field Robotics Center. Though the hope is that Dante will eventually walk the surface of distant planets, it's already won the hearts of volcanologists after its exploration of Alaska's Mt. Spurr in July 1994. During the previous year, eight scientists had died trying to accomplish tasks similar to Dante's: the

Easy Stuff: Give yourself 1 point for each correct answer.

1. What is the name of the firewalking robot?
2. Where did Mulder find the words "NEW LIFE-FORM" written?
3. What did Scully find in Tanaka's lungs?
4. How many people died from the fungus infection?
5. How long are Scully and Mulder supposed to be quarantined?

Getting Tougher: Give yourself 2 points for each correct answer.

6. Where was Daniel Pierce's body stored?
7. What drug was Trepkos supposed to be taking?
8. How did Trepkos dispose of Jason Ludwig?
9. What did Ludwig attack Mulder with?
10. What was Ludwig's profession?

collection of high-temperature fumarole gases from inside the volcano. A tethered robotic unit like Dante II enables scientists to conduct their research at something a little safer than arm's length. Securely fastened to the crater rim, Dante II can rappel up and down sheer walls to obtain samples from the volcano's floor.

To ease the relationship between human scientists and the mechanical hands and eyes of the probes, the Intelligent Mechanisms Group (IMG) has been developing advanced telepresence and virtual environment-based operator interfaces since 1991. While useful to earthbound operators who, if forced to, could physically follow the robot, the advanced interfaces are essential to the planned interplanetary missions that would be 100 percent dependent on telemetry. In late 1993, the IMG demonstrated its new interfaces in a radically different environment when a field test of the Telepresence Remotely Operated Vehicle (TROV) sent it deep under the sea ice near McMurdo Science Station in Antarctica, where it performed flawlessly.

The IMG has now turned its expert eye on Dante II with the intention of providing it with virtual environment and visual simulation tools. These additions would provide vehicle configuration and terrain visualization to operators and scientific observers. Additionally, the IMG is using the teleoperations expertise it obtained from TROV to implement live stereo video (similar to Firewalker's feedback, but more detailed) on Dante II and enabling the interaction of multiple observation sites. It's going to be one hot machine.

Code Name: "Red Museum"

CASE SUMMARY

When Wisconsin teens start staggering out of the woods with mysterious messages scrawled on their naked backs, Mulder and Scully head into the heart of America's cattle country. What they find—a vegetarian sect, a Peeping Tom, and an old enemy playing with bioengineered cows—is so entangled they'll have to work fast to identify the culprits before the evidence disappears.

What's in Our Cows? Frankenfood?

DEEP BACKGROUND

The battle over bioengineered foods is giving people another reason to choose vegetarianism—and sanitation workers in the nation's capital quite a mess to clean up. When the U.S. patent office started handing out licensing rights for everything from the Flavr Savr Tomato to designer bacteria, all protestors could do was wave signs. But they're beginning to have something to throw. In a demonstration at the Food and Drug Administration (FDA), farmers, parents, and environmentalists poured the milk of bovine growth hormone-treated cows—hundreds of gallons of it—across the street and into storm sewers. In the aftermath, Ben & Jerry's Ice Cream Parlors quietly ordered new lids for their products with the words "Not from treated cows" prominently displayed.

Though humans have genetically manipulated food since Mendel decided to keep track of his pea plants, the ability to *recombine* genetic material has brought agriculture to a new level and into a media circus. Blue roses were cute, but when pigs started bleeding human hemoglobin, things got real

EYEWITNESS STATEMENT

You know, for a holy man, you've got quite a knack for pissing people off.

—Mulder, "Red Museum"

Scientists and consumer groups argue over the need to use chemicals to increase milk production, but the United States has had a milk *surplus* since the 1980s.

Before CBS and Fox nixed the idea, writers on *The X-Files* and *Picket Fences* had been working on a crossover story that would allow Fox Mulder to continue his investigation of the events of "Red Museums" in *Picket Fences'* Rome, Wisconsin. The basic storyline did go ahead and Rome residents discovered odd things in their cows as well, but it was another agent, not Mulder, who arrived to investigate.

serious real fast and the lay public, which had the uncomfortable feeling it had missed something, started asking a lot of questions. Two groups were there with answers—and two completely different versions of the truth.

According to officials from the FDA and American Medical Association (AMA), the public furor over BGH, a cattle hormone artificially produced by genetically altered bacteria, was a fuss over nothing. Their assurances that *all* cows made BGH, that injections of the hormone only boosted an already existing and perfectly natural process, eased some concern. But according to groups like the Pure Food Campaign (PFC), it was a very short step from having bacteria produce your bovine hormones to adding human genetic material to cows to encourage the production of leaner beef. The cannibalistic themes evoked by such images were impossible for many consumers to ignore.

This was unfortunate for those still trying to get their products past the FDA. Lobby groups like the Consumers' Union, the Environmental Defense Fund, and the National Wildlife Federation had stepped in, striking not at faraway producers, but at retailers. Soon restaurants were refusing to purchase treated milk, schools were pressuring milk producers to lay off the BGH, and picketers were parked in front of prestigious hotels. Scientists found themselves in the unusual position of having to defend themselves on a street level instead of in front of the FDA.

Groups like Jeremy Rifkin's PFC addressed the key issues: Could the artificial freshness of the genetically engineered food hide deadly bacteria? Would antibiotics used to tag altered genes provoke unexpected reactions or create antibiotic resistance in those ingesting artificially enhanced foods? And what about cross-pollination with native flora? The FDA, which hadn't conducted any long-term testing before granting licenses for bioengineered food, was in a tough position. Valid concerns were being raised, and the FDA had to come up with some answers.

GENETIC MARKERS

There's no easy way to observe whether new genes have been successfully inserted in a cell. So to tell successfully altered cells apart from failures, geneticists will join the new gene to an antibiotic gene that *is* relatively easy to test for. While simple and effective, this does raise the question of whether there's any difference between ingesting the antibiotic in a pill or in a tomato. And what about the gene itself? If genes from a peanut were inserted into a tomato, how would someone allergic to peanuts react to a salad made from such a tomato?

Scientists say the proteins can't survive oral ingestion or gastral digestion. The PFC wants proof—long-term proof.

It appears that the FDA is having second thoughts as well. They've required all known allergenic-bearing foods to be appropriately labeled until testing has proven the items safe. Perhaps their hesitation has something to do with the fact that people are now developing a resistance to the antibiotic kanamycin, which is used to treat childhood pinkeye and is also the genetic tag found in tomatoes.

CROSS-POLLINATION

Anyone who's ever tried to get rid of the common dandelion knows that plants don't always behave as we'd like them to. Groups like the National Wildlife Federation want to know exactly how new biogenetically engineered plants will be contained and what we might expect if they were to be accidentally or deliberately introduced into natural habitats.

While the FDA has allowed outdoor testing of engineered plants for nearly ten years, Steve Vanderpan, spokesman for the Flavr Savr tomato, has addressed this issue with complete honesty and in public. He admitted in the *New Yorker* that his company had no idea what might happen in cross-pollination situations, and that unwanted mutants wouldn't be a surprise.

While the FDA is being more cautious now than it was a few years ago, neither the PFC nor any other group has ever put forward a single case of a bioengineered food directly linked to any harm to humans. But remember, the FDA also allowed disasters like silicone breast implants, DDT, and thalidomide.

Scientists claim the media have misrepresented the case for altered foods, being too quick to publish the sensational and ignoring the daily work done in hundreds of labs. Protestors, however, believe that their efforts are the only way to get the truth from huge corporations or the government. There's likely some truth in both positions. And whether we end up eating engineered tomatoes or not, one change, for the better, has certainly come out of the controversy. While science training for technicians once ignored the communication skills emphasized by the humanities, scientists have learned they must be able to relate to the layperson in a common language instead of multisyllabic techno-Latin and Greek.

TRIVIA BUSTER 34

Easy Stuff: Give yourself 1 point for each correct answer.

1. What was written across Gary Kane's back?
2. What was found behind the mirror in the Kane home?
3. How did Beth's husband die?
4. Where did the Church of the Red Museum members come from?
5. What were the children actually being injected with?

Getting Tougher: Give yourself 2 points for each correct answer.

6. What was the name of the slaughterhouse?
7. What pizza topping did Beth Kane decide to pass on?
8. How were the children being tracked?
9. What did the doctor claim to be giving the children?
10. What was Richard Odin's previous name?

MIBs

The Men In Black, one of whom Scully kills in this episode, are as much a part of UFO legends as conspiracy theories and time loss. They came on the scene accompanied by a sensational story and haven't really left the stage since. Dressed in black, driving big black cars or flying equally black helicopters, and wearing sunglasses even at midnight, they were mystery personified.

Unlike most things in the field of UFOlogy, the origin of the MIB can been traced to a single, well-recorded incident. In 1953, Albert K. Bender ran an organization called the International Flying Saucer Bureau (IFSB) and published a limited-circulation magazine, *Space Review*. The 'zine covered the usual sightings, essays, and speculation on UFOs, nothing particularly controversial—until the October 1953 issue when an unexpected announcement stunned readers.

Bender claimed to have discovered the secrets behind UFOs, hinted at a powerful force that prevented him from revealing it, and warned readers to be careful in the future. He then quickly stopped publication and dissolved his organization. He later revealed that he'd been visited by three Men In Black who'd "advised" against his continued involvement with UFO studies.

Over the intervening years, other, similar reports have appeared, but the basic plot remains the same: *Ordinary person learns something about UFOs or is contacted or is abducted. Person receives a visit from a Man (occasionally a Woman) or several Men In Black who know more than they should.* The MIB make threats, usually vague, usually directed at family or friends instead of at the person. The person senses that he or she is being followed. The phone makes odd noises or rings for no particular reason; home electronic equipment acts strangely. When the person stops whatever he or she was doing, the weird happenings cease. There are variations, of course, but the general theme of vague terror remains.

Code Name: "Excelsis Dei"

When Scully brings in a case of her own involving the "entity rape" of a nurse in a home for the aged, Mulder is skeptical. But whether the cause is ghosts or magic mushrooms, a crime has been committed and Scully is determined to solve it. No one is more surprised than Mulder when Scully's intuitions prove accurate.

CASE SUMMARY

Kombucha: The Miracle Mushroom

DEEP BACKGROUND

After the 1960s, when flower children sampled every exotic fungus to be found, we thought we understood what Magic Mushroom meant. *The X-Files* gave us a new definition. What else could you call a mushroom that cures Alzheimer's, allows elderly men to outrun twenty-year-old orderlies, and conjures up spirits the likes of which even flower children have never seen?

The Magic Mushroom of the 1990s is a whole different ball of wax. Hailed as a fountain of youth, athletic tonic, and cure for whatever ails you, including AIDS, the Kombucha mushroom is also called, by some, the snake oil of this decade.

This time it's not traveling salesmen who are peddling the wonder cure. Neighbors, convinced of the tonic's value, share the "babies" of their living colonies with friends. Health food stores display it floating serenely in its tea and sugar bath. Alternative medicine magazines have beautiful ads for it scattered through their pages. And, everywhere the mushroom springs up, so do testimonials about its miraculous abilities.

Kombucha, aka Manchurian tea, has been said to shrink prostates, restore youth to skin

EYEWITNESS STATEMENT

I put it back in that drawer—with all those other videos that aren't yours.

—Scully, "Excelsis Dei"

and hair, eradicate PMS, eliminate flatulence, even fade those pesky freckles. It seems that all you have to do is identify your problems and start your Kombucha culture to solve them. Some observers of the sudden upsurge of interest in the product have called it a "living pet rock," pointing to the tendency among Kombucha lovers to name their colony. Others, listening to the increasing claims that, among its other wonders, Kombucha can halt the progress of AIDS, find it frightening. For them, it's all too easy to remember the last folk remedy to sweep through California, the one that had desperate AIDS patients slugging poisonous hydrogen peroxide.

And what is a Kombucha? It's a symbiotic colony of yeast and bacteria with the yeast giving it some claim to being a fungus. Kombucha, however, bears no resemblance to any mushroom. The colony, all the organisms together, actually looks like a big, clear jellyfish and reproduces itself every eight days.

Depending on who you ask, Kombucha is an ancient Egyptian, Russian, Chinese, Japanese, or Korean remedy; some even claim it originated in Atlantis. Commercial dealers often attribute its use to famous individuals, especially long-lived celebrities. Some admit to using the tonic, others stare blankly, but, in 1994 alone, it's estimated that 1 million ordinary people either purchased a Kombucha or received one as a gift.

But growing your own Kombucha isn't as easy as popping a pill. Kombucha lovers hover protectively over their little microbrewery awaiting the results of a recipe started more than a week before. To start the production of the tonic, a medium of three quarts of boiling water is mixed with a cup of raw sugar and moved to a sterile glass bowl. Once the sugar has dissolved, four bags of tea (Chinese or black), are steeped in the sweetened water. It's this tea, once cooled, that becomes home to the Kombucha culture.

The glass bowl, Kombucha inside, is covered with a clean, breathable cotton towel and stored in a warm, barely lit spot for a week. During the week, a natural fermentation (similar to that of wine) takes place. The result: a sharp, ciderish, sometimes bubbly drink— and a second culture, the baby, which can be given to a friend. Considering that the going price for a brand new culture is about $50, it's a fairly thoughtful gift.

The majority of physicians concentrating on AIDS cases have few compunctions about alternative treatments. Most have long suspected that it will take more than a single agent to defeat it. What does worry them is that the Kombucha treatment has its own special problems.

1. Kombucha is a vigorous organism, capable of regenerating from even the smallest smear. It can't be disposed of down sink drains because it's as likely to take up residence in the trap as be washed away. If it does set up house, the Kombucha is the perfect home for other, less pleasant guests.

2. While adverse reactions to the tonic have been few and far between, they do occur. Hives, rashes, headaches, and nausea are all standard reactions to allergies to fungi.

3. Kombucha tonic contains no artificial chemicals, but it does contain sugar, and a fair amount at that. For AIDS patients, who often suffer from pancreatitis, that sugar can be dangerous. For diabetics looking for an all-natural drink, after a week it's easy to forget there's sugar in the tea.

4. Contamination is a distinct possibility. Anything left sitting at room temperature for a week can become a breeding ground for molds and even bug larvae.

Kombucha may indeed prove to have benefits as a drug, but, like aspirin and Valium, which also began life as folk remedies, its effectiveness can't be harmed by unbiased scientific study. An understanding of how the Kombucha operates in the human body might lead to even greater benefits.

Water, Water Everywhere: More SFX Files

Any time filming requires the introduction of water, in any form, to a set, the difficulties of getting that film "in the can" increase by a factor of at least a hundred. Water and electricity are one obvious incompatibility, but that's actually one of the easier and more obvious problems to work around.

Underwater shots, as in "Excelsis Dei" and "Død Kalm," present unique difficulties for set managers, cameramen, the actors, lighting crews, everyone. And, as usual, anything that can go wrong, does. Water is a living environment for many creatures, including green algae that thrive under the nurturing light and heat of studio lamps. Without regular chemical treatments, these tiny aquatic plants can contaminate a filming tank or pool, creating a ghoulish green cast to the underwater scene while impairing the clarity of the image. As the algal growth cycle progresses, continuity becomes a serious concern. Film shot at different times in the growth cycle will vary in color. In the event that portions of a scene must be reshot, lighting conditions become nearly impossible to duplicate.

Easy Stuff: Give yourself 1 point for each correct answer.

1. Who decided to take on this case?
2. What was Leo's previous occupation?
3. From what disease did most of the patients at the nursing home suffer?
4. Dorothy sees something hanging around Scully. What?
5. What were Hal and Stan trying to watch when Nurse Charters confiscated their remote control?

Getting Tougher: Give yourself 2 points for each correct answer.

6. What, besides mushrooms, did Mulder find in the mushroom beds that Gung maintained in the basement?
7. Under what conditions did this case become an FBI matter?
8. How many stitches did it take to close the cut on Nurse Charters's lip?
9. Who did Nurse Charters think raped her?
10. What is Leo drawing as the episode comes to a close?

The chlorine-based chemicals that might control algal growths are generally ineffective if used at typical pool concentrations. The more intense studio lighting requires a chemical concentration nearly double that of a public pool, and that can leave actors with red, irritated eyes. In addition to personal concern for the people involved, the producers and directors are acutely aware of a schedule that allows eight days or less to get an episode filmed. Any time lost to illness, especially preventable conditions like chlorine-induced eye irritations, is an expensive disruption.

Time, even without algal blooms, is difficult to manage during underwater shoots. *Everything* entering a water environment has the potential to carry dust or dirt, minuscule specks that will require hours to precipitate out or be mechanically removed. To help avoid delays, set and prop managers initiate special procedures. Props are carefully washed. Shoes an actor must wear in water require similar treatment. Anything that could float across the shot at an inconvenient time is weighted or wired in place. Fabrics from wardrobe are tested for transparency before the cameras start filming and, if necessary, skirts are weighted at the hem to prevent unintentional ratings violations.

Water, a fluid medium with different optical properties than air, provides a challenge for filmmakers. All objects, including actors, look thinner and foreshortened under water. Walls appear to tip toward one another, floors seem to slope. Without careful attention to perspective, distances become flattened and motion is nearly impossible to judge. The "depth" and "texture" normally gained by using film instead of video tape is lost. In "Excelsis Dei," clearly marked corners, an abundance of straight lines, and a scarcity of full-view shots in the submerged bathroom set (constructed in a tank), narrowed viewers' attention to specific actions and helped alleviate the one-dimensional effect.

WATER BY ANY OTHER NAME: ICE, FROST, RAIN, SNOW, FOG

In "End Game" and "Ice," falling snow was an essential scene setter, but, for an effect lasting less than a full minute per episode, a trip to the high Arctic is clearly out of the question. Studio effects allow two basic approaches for providing the snow seen at the beginning of "Ice." The first is to film a storm of polystyrene granules inside a small black box for later superimposition over a base film of an illuminated Arctic ice station model. For scenes in which an actor is moving across the landscape, superimposition is still a possibility, but a snow machine and fan may be more efficient, especially if a snow or ice set has already been erected for other scenes, and a shot, as in "Ice," is being done indoors.

Some of the most artistic water work done by special effects technicians includes delicately frosted window patterns of methylated spirits and finely powdered chalk; polystyrene and wax icicles; and water-filled blocks of warped acrylic plastic that simulate ice. For examples of all these techniques, watch the windows in "Ice," and the scene in the same episode where Scully disposes of the handgun.

ASTROLOGICALLY SPEAKING . . .

Mulder is a Libra—theoretically a natural born diplomat. Maybe someone should have done a chart for him—*before* he ticked off all his superiors.

LIBRA

QUALITY: Cardinal.

ELEMENT: Air.

KEY PHRASE: I provide balance.

DESCRIPTION:

Librans value peace above all. They are frequently willing to overlook the flaws in others in order to avoid dissent, and are capable of bringing harmony to the antagonistic elements around them.

POSITIVE CHARACTERISTICS:
Cooperative, diplomatic, socially comfortable, suave, judicious, persuasive.

NEGATIVE CHARACTERISTICS:
Lover of intrigue, indecisive, easily deterred, often appears fickle and incapable of settling on a personal code of ethics or honor.

Code Name: "Aubrey"

CASE SUMMARY

When a small-town cop finds the bones of an FBI agent who'd been missing for nearly half a century—and can't explain how she did it— Mulder suspects it was more than blind luck. Both Mulder's Jungian background and Scully's broader, intuitive view are needed to separate dream from reality, memory from history, and present from past.

DEEP BACKGROUND

Blood Evidence: Here a Spot, There a Spot

DNA TESTING

If Scully and Mulder were waiting in their Aubrey motel room for the results of DNA testing, we can only hope they liked to play cards. The tests Scully mentions take weeks, even months, to return significant results. While the timing was off, however, the importance of toxicological evidence, especially blood evidence, can't be understated. It's swiftly becoming the darling of law enforcement agencies everywhere and will soon be as commonly admitted in evidence as fingerprints and other physical evidence.

Forensic scientists have been chipping away at the unique factors in blood for decades. First simple groupings (A, B, O, or AB) were identified, then the Rh, Lewis, and Kell factors further separated samples. Advances in serology now permit the isolation and identification of additional blood factors, including histocompatibility antigens, blood enzymes, and serum proteins that may soon allow for the individualizing of other body fluids.

Some of the more common blood tests now include:

RFLP. RFLP testing, a technology that came to prominence in 1980 when it was used in linkage studies, was made famous in 1982 when it became part of a diagnostic test for sickle-cell anemia. It depends on the ability to identify several factors along a strand of DNA, then calculate the probability of the same sequence turning up in that particular order in two unrelated samples; in other words, the frequency. RFLP testing requires thousands of good cells to return significant results, but it has a higher percentage of accuracy than PCR.

PCR. An alternative to RFLP, PCR amplification is further divided by the particular section of code being investigated. The DQ-alpha testing mentioned by Scully depends on the synthesizing of the second exon on human leukocyte antigen, HLA-DQ-alpha, and is only one of three families of genes of the sixth human chromosome. PCR requires a minuscule fraction of the genetic material used in RFLP testing.

In civilian use, DNA testing, especially in commercial labs, is most frequently used to *include* individuals in a test group, because DNA is still used primarily in the determination of paternity. In criminal use, however, the purpose is often to *exclude* suspects, as in a 1986 case where a man being held on two rape-murder charges swore his innocence. Without his exclusion from the list of suspects, police might have had no reason to look any further. Unlike fingerprinting, which can match an individual to a particular print, as in "Tooms," DNA fingerprints aren't and never have been assumed to be unique.

While both PCR and RFLP testing are dependent on the use of nuclear DNA, found only in the nucleus of cells, future test development will be focusing on mitochondrial DNA, a more plentiful supply, and may change the face of criminal forensics yet again.

PHYSICAL SIGNS

The blood spots that are a natural result of violent crime were the subject of police investigations even before the microscopic art of DNA testing became common.

The shape, position, and extent of bloodstains often give valuable information about the circumstances surrounding the commission of a crime. The height from which a blood drop fell can be inferred by the shape of the splatter. The angle at which the blood struck a par-

Easy Stuff: Give yourself 1 point for each correct answer.

1. Who else in the Mulder family likes sunflower seeds?
2. What word(s) were carved on the victims' chests?
3. What did B. J. smash into Mulder's head?
4. What did Detective Morrow originally claim led her to the body in the field?
5. What did B. J. Morrow find in the Cimarron County Catalog 4756 of 1942?

Getting Tougher: Give yourself 2 points for each correct answer.

6. What was B. J. Morrow's relationship to Harry Cokely?
7. What disturbing phrase did Cokely use to refer to Scully?
8. Name the motel where Detective Morrow was to have met Lieutenant Brian Tillman to discuss the pregnancy.
9. What name did the press give Cokely before he was captured?
10. In what community does Mrs. Linda Thibedeaux live?

1. Mulder's father.
2. "Sister" on the women, "Brother" on the men.
3. An oxygen cylinder.
4. A dog digging at the site.
5. A mugshot of a young Harry Cokely.
6. She was his granddaughter.
7. "Little sister."
8. Motel Black.
9. The Slash Killer.
10. Edmond, Nebraska (238 N. Fifty-fourth Street).

YOUR SCORE: 15

ticular surface can also be determined. Rough estimates can even be made as to the age of bloodstains by physical examination.

Given the height, angle, and approximate age of the sample, an experienced investigator can begin to re-create a crime scene, and, hopefully, use the details discovered there to ensure the capture of the *right* criminal. One British case that is often quoted to new criminalists explains how physical evidence remains an important tool in the investigation of crime.

Twin brothers, with DNA so similar as to defy even new technologies, were involved in a robbery gone bad when one of them killed a store owner. To make matters more confusing, both brothers had been injured in the struggle and their blood was mixed all over the scene. By comparing the height from which the blood must have fallen with the position of each man's injuries, it was quickly determined that only the one with a cut to his upper arm could possibly have committed the murder.

Whether by gross examination or delicate, cell-by-cell testing, blood continues to be one of the investigator's most cherished components of evidence.

Code Name: "Irresistible"

Mulder and Scully are called in to profile and catch a disturbed man with more fetishes than fingers. Tracing the convoluted swirls of the man's mind gets personal for Scully who, unlike her experienced partner, has never been involved in a sexual-deviance case. When the killer fixates on her, kidnaps her, and seems set to make her his next victim, even Mulder is shaken.

CASE SUMMARY

The Fetishist

While mutants and aliens as portrayed by *The X-Files* are scary, the show's forays into the depths of the human mind can be particularly terrifying. Episodes like "Beyond the Sea" and "Miracle Man" should have been accompanied by a warning for the psychologically squeamish, but nothing could prepare a viewer for the evil that oozed across the screen in "Irresistible." Donnie Pfaster, the fetishist, may have been human, but barely. Though fetishes aren't that uncommon, killing to satisfy them, objectifying the victims, choosing victims on the basis of their *nail polish,* is beyond most people's comprehension. Luckily for society as a whole, most fetishism never progresses to that point.

DEEP BACKGROUND

DEFINING THE FETISHIST

Many people find silk underwear or sheets, lace teddies, or leopard-skin boxer shorts add a lit-

EYEWITNESS STATEMENT

It is somehow easier to believe, as Agent Bocks does, in aliens and UFOs, than in the kind of inhuman, cold-blooded monster who could prey on the living to scavenge from the dead.

—Scully, "Irresistible"

tle something to their sex lives, but these people aren't fetishists—not unless the sheets or shorts become more important than their partner or essential to the completion of their own fulfillment.

Mixing other paraphilias, of which fetishism is one, into the mental makeup, however, can make diagnosis more difficult. Common paraphilias associated with fetishism can, and have, included transvestism, zoophilia, pedophilia, exhibitionism, voyeurism, sexual masochism, sexual sadism, coprophilia, frotteurism, or necrophilia.

A fetishist, almost always a male, is sexually enthralled by some inanimate object or some specific nongenital part of a person. His disorder of *fetishism* takes the form of using nonliving objects (fetishes) as a repeatedly preferred or exclusive method of achieving sexual excitement.

In Practice

Beautiful shoes, stockings, gloves, toilet articles, fur garments, and especially underwear are common sources of arousal for fetishists. While some carry on their fetishism in private by fondling, kissing, smelling, or staring at the adored object as they masturbate, others bring their fetish into their reciprocal sexual encounters, asking their partners to don the fetish before or during sex.

Some fetishists are collectors, more interested in amassing examples of their desired object than in seeking unusual sexual encounters directly associated with the object. For them, fantasizing about the collection while engaged in sexual activity is often sufficient, though they'll occasionally become professional criminals, burgling week after week to add to their hoard.

For other individuals, specific parts of the female body become the fetish (though few combine this aspect of fetishism with collecting, as Pfaster did). Locks of hair, feet, ankles, hands, fingernails, delicately shaped ears, and large breasts may be the narrowed focus of all passion. To secure contact with his fetish, the fetishist may engage in rather extraordinary maneuvering—such as working as a shoe salesman, even though he could qualify for a better-paying position—and may even commit assault.

Subjectively, the attraction felt by the fetishist toward the object or part of the body is

FETISHISM: The term "fetishism" was actually borrowed from anthropological writings in which "fetish" (also spelled *fetich*) referred to a charm thought to contain magical or spiritual powers.

involuntary—and irresistible. Because it has such a strong, compulsive quality, the fetishism may be a dominant force in the man's life. The degree of the erotic focalization distinguishes fetishisms from the ordinary attraction that high heels and net stockings may hold for heterosexual men and from their normal appreciation of beautiful hair, bosoms, and ankles.

Psychoanalytic theorists generally consider that fetishisms and the other paraphilias serve some sort of defensive function, warding off anxiety about normal sexual contacts. Learning theorists usually invoke some kind of classical conditioning in the person's social-sexual history. For example, a young man in his early sexual experiences might masturbate to pictures of women dressed in black leather, and then develop a fetish for black leather. Indeed, one experiment lent some mild support to learning propositions. Male subjects were repeatedly shown slides of nude and alluring females interspersed with slides of women's boots. The subjects were eventually aroused by the boots alone. The "fetishistic attraction" induced, however, was weak and transient.

It appears instead that, just as some people are "prepared" to learn to become phobic to certain objects, others are prepared to learn to be sexually stimulated by certain classes of stimuli. However, if simple association were at work, as with Pavlov's dogs, ceilings and pillows would be high on the list of fetishes. Without more evidence, the classical conditioning model is unlikely to be adopted by psychotherapists.

How then to explain the Pfasters of the world? At this point, we really can't. What is an eccentricity in some can, under specific circumstances, turn deadly. And there's precious little to give us warning.

Getting Technical: Paint Sampling

When Pfaster runs Scully's car into a ditch, he leaves behind valuable evidence—paint from his own vehicle. Under some circumstances, paint evidence really can, through a mix of physical and chemical investigation, be matched to a single automobile.

If both the suspect's car and a paint chip are available, the first step would certainly be a physical exam. A jagged edge from the paint fleck, matched with the edges of the matrix from which it came, is a basis to connect the car with the crime scene. Multilayered paint, as was the case in "Irresistible," can isolate manufactur-

TRIVIA BUSTER 37

Easy Stuff: Give yourself 1 point for each correct answer.

1. Where was Donald Pfaster working as this episode opened?
2. What did Agent Bocks suggest was responsible for the disturbed graves?
3. What did the hooker find so disturbing about Pfaster's bedroom?
4. What was Pfaster's full name?
5. How does Mulder suggest Pfaster be described in official communications?

Getting Tougher: Give yourself 2 points for each correct answer.

6. What was Pfaster studying?
7. What program does Scully take advantage of during her trip to Washington?
8. What does Agent Bocks find in the frozen peas?
9. Where did Pfaster take Scully after running her off the road?
10. How many older sisters did Pfaster have?

ers, years of production, even the make of vehicle, if the discrete layers possess sufficient individuality. Otherwise, the paint would fall into the category of class, rather than physical, evidence.

Examination of paint for class characteristics involves the use of chemical tests to determine constituency, as well as examination with instruments such as the infrared spectrophotometer, emission spectrograph, or electron microprobe.

Like most FBI collections, the paint collections are extensive, including house paint, artists' paint, and even street paints as well as those for vehicles.

WHAT WILL SHE WEAR NOW?

It's about time Dana Scully got a new trenchcoat. Her old one, which took her through The *X-Files'* first two seasons, was recently auctioned off at an AIDS benefit event. Dozens of other *X-Files* objects were sold to the highest bidder, and the show's total contribution was over $42,000.

SOME ITEMS SOLD:	COST
Autographed clip-on I.D. tags #1	$615.00
Autographed clip-on I.D. tags #2	951.00
Autographed T-shirt #1	255.00
Autographed T-shirt #2	207.00
Autographed T-shirt #3	331.00
Autographed T-shirt #4	319.00
Comics, *X-Files*, #1–3	311.00
Leather badges (autographed set #1)	2,123.00
Leather badges (autographed set #2)	10,200.00
Scully's trenchcoat (autographed lining)	5,175.00
Autographed posters	4,010.00
Autographed scripts (set of 3)	4,550.00
Ties (autographed by David Duchovny)	8,000.00
Autographed set of comics	5,300.00

Code Name: "Die Hand Die Verletzt"

CASE SUMMARY

Ritualistic murder brings Scully and Mulder to a small town where frogs fall and water runs backward on a daily basis—or at least whenever the two agents consider leaving. While the locals whisper about strange things happening at woodland altars, Scully investigates the substitute teacher no one remembers hiring and Mulder begins tracking cultists.

A Fall of Frogs

DEEP BACKGROUND

"Mulder, toads just fell on us!"

Although the image of two power-suited FBI agents huddling under umbrellas as frogs plop down around them left viewers caught between laughter and incredulity, wondering how the pair would explain this one, it's old hat to meteorologists. They'd have been the first to support Scully's waterspout theory for the bizarre downpour in "Die Hand Die Verletzt."

As long ago as the spring of 1666, a priest in Kent, England, reported:

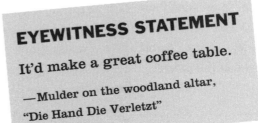

EYEWITNESS STATEMENT

It'd make a great coffee table.

—Mulder on the woodland altar, "Die Hand Die Verletzt"

> *About Easter . . . in a pasture field in this parish, which is a considerable distance from the sea or any branch of it, and a place where there are no fish ponds but a scarcity of water, was scattered over with small fish, in quantity about a bushel, supposed to have been rained down from a cloud, there having been at that time a great tempest of thunder, hail, wind, etc. These fish were about the size of a man's little finger . . . and were shown publically in Maidstone and Dartford.*

The title from this episode is taken from the prayer in which "die hand die verletzt" is translated as "the hand that wounds."

This show's opening credits feature James "Chargers" Wong and Glen "Bolts, Baby!" Morgan, references to the name and logo of the San Diego Chargers who, during the week this episode aired, were playing in the Super Bowl.

Mulder's assertion that the town's water is running backward (or clockwise) because of the Coriolis force isn't entirely true. The Coriolis force only affects large systems like hurricanes and currents. The water in drinking fountains and toilet bowls is usually directed by the shape of the fixture.

The high school in "Die Hand Die Verletzt" was called Crowley High School, an allusion to Alistair Crowley, who was influential in founding modern Wicca.

Similar records, meticulously maintained, indicate that although fish are the most common creatures raining down on the countryside, they're by no means the only species.

A Bournemouth youth reported in 1891:

One day we had a violent thunderstorm. Having no shelter, I was wet to the skin in a few minutes, and saw small yellow frogs, about the size of a florin or half-crown, dashed on the ground all around me. I ran to shelter under a larger mortar-pan, and, after the storm was over, found in this pan hundreds of these small frogs. . . . Thousands were impaled on the furze bushes on the common close by.

Even birds, supposedly at home in the air, have fallen out of it *en masse*. On the night of March 13, 1904, some 750,000 longspurs fell within a few square miles of Minnesota. So many blackbirds fell over Shreveport in 1941 that military police were called to assist in removing them. A soldier reported whole flocks "just plopping to the ground."

Molluscs have fallen in France; a full-grown salamander, nearly 11-inches long, fell in Nashville, Tennessee; and live lizards showered Montreal in 1857. The residents of Guam were stunned to have *tinca tinca,* a European freshwater fish, scattered over their island. Strange as all these events must have been, the oddest case of all belongs to Dubuque, Iowa, where, after a violent hailstorm, ice pellets melted to reveal tiny, still-living frogs.

Naturally, such events drew attention, including the interest of scientists who, like Agent Scully, immediately put aside any suggestion of supernatural causes. In many cases, the theory of tornadoes or waterspouts scooping the creatures up and later hurling them to the ground was easily accepted. As in the cases above, the vast majority of these "falls" are connected to violent weather. Witnesses frequently gave descriptions similar to that of a man from Steyl-Teegelen, Holland, who saw a waterspout form, then retract into a low-level cloud that, to the accompaniment of several loud detonations, flew apart and dumped a huge quantity of water and fish over the town.

Many scientists, however, are reluctant to close the books on these incidents. Frogs live in densely inhabited environments shared by insects, fish, birds, and snails, not to mention plants, small stones, mud, and other detritus. Lakes seldom contain a single type of fish. Yet in only a handful of cases have more than one type of creature been dropped at any location. In August 1894, residents of Bath were pelted by thousands of jellyfish, but not a single scaled fish. To further compound the case, all these jellyfish were, within fractions of an inch, the same size. As no smaller or larger specimens were found anywhere in the surrounding area, an argument for size separation by centrifugal action is difficult to support.

Another puzzling aspect is the condition of the specimens found. Fish are, without question, water breathers, but live specimens are often found deposited miles from the nearest source of water. A five-and-a-half-pound turtle, unarguably heavier than many of the stones, plants, or other creatures in its usual vicinity, crashes through a window unaccompanied by any of those other objects. Jellyfish, with their delicate tissues, fall uninjured while sand eels, frozen solid, shatter on impact with the ground.

Last, and perhaps most curious, are those rare cases when, without any visible signs of unusual weather, *thousands* of specimens fall from clear skies. On October 23, 1947, an employee of the Department of Wild Life and Fisheries, considered an impeccable observer of this particular type of phenomenon, submitted a report that challenged even the accepted conventions of a fish fall. Thousands of fish, totaling several tons and covering an area 75 to 80 feet wide and over 1,000 feet long, fell in gardens, atop roofs, even in cisterns —and all from a clear, if misty, sky.

No unusual weather fronts were reported within a 100 mile radius. No rain fell in association with the event. No thunderclaps or other anomalous noises were reported. The fish, like the toads in "Die Hand Die Verletzt," simply fell.

Wicca: New Age Religion from Old Sources

As Mulder is quick to tell Scully, Wicca has nothing in common with demon worship, or the cultist they're hunting in this episode. A modern interpretation of early pagan religions, Wicca is an Earth religion and Wiccans (also known as Witches or Practitioners of the Craft) are well known for their reverence of the Earth. In general, Wiccans revere both the male and the female, and believe that human will, properly directed, can have tangible results.

Wiccans are a subset of pagans, though they define pagans as "country-dwellers" not as those without religion. They have a creed, the Wiccan Rede, by which most members abide. In a much-shortened version, the Rede states "An it harm none, do what thou wilt." The interpretation of what can cause harm is for the Wiccan to

Easy Stuff: Give yourself 1 point for each correct answer.

1. What musical did the students want to perform?
2. What animals made an unexpected appearance at the woodland altar?
3. What were the students expected to dissect as part of their final exam?
4. How many children did Shannon Ausbury claim to have had?
5. What animals fell on Mulder and Scully's umbrellas?

Getting Tougher: Give yourself 2 points for each correct answer.

6. What body parts were missing from Jerry Stevens's body?
7. How many babies did Chignon claim to have had?
8. What personal item did Paddock steal from Scully?
9. What did Mulder and Scully find written on the blackboard?
10. Name the library book the kids borrowed to use in preparing for their ritual.

contemplate, and Wiccans are expected to expend a considerable amount of time arriving at a set of personal ethics rather than sim-ply accepting those enforceable by law. When Wiccans form congre-gations, also called covens, they are usually small groups. Wiccans take a personal interest in the welfare of each group member. The guiding force for Wiccans, whether as part of a coven or individually, is usually the Charge of the Goddess, "All acts of love and pleasure are My rituals." There is also a Charge of the God, but it tends to vary between covens.

Wicca is not a mainstream religion, but neither is it a violent sect that endorses the human sacrifice and torture in "Die Hand Die Verletzt."

Necrotizing fasciitis, aka the "flesh-eating disease," which took out the teacher who preceded Ms. Paddock, is thought to affect only one person in a million. The virulent bacterial infection can be horribly disfiguring in as few as twelve hours, and deadly in less than forty-eight.

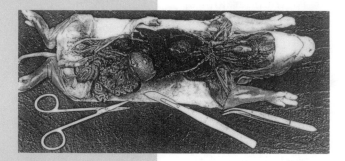

The actress portraying Ms. Paddock portrays another biology teacher for a Butterfinger commercial.

Code Name: "Fresh Bones"

CASE SUMMARY

While investigating the apparent suicides of two Marines at a camp for Haitian refugees in Norfolk, Virginia, Mulder and Scully grapple with claims of military brutality, "voodoo" curses, and zombie soldiers rising from their graves. Separating truth from reality becomes increasingly difficult as the agents themselves are drawn into the imprisoned Haitians' imported culture and experience Haiti's magic for themselves.

Wade Davis, the Zombie Project and Ethnobiology

DEEP BACKGROUND

On April 30, 1962, Clairvius Narcisse arrived at Haiti's famous Albert Schweitzer Hospital. On May 2, two experienced doctors signed his death certificate and expressed their condolences to his sister. After identifying the body, Marie Narcisse added her thumbprint to that certificate. The body was stored on ice overnight and was released the next day to Marie and younger sister Angeline for burial. As is customary on many tropical islands, services were almost immediate—in this case within eight hours. Friends and relations grieved and, ten days later, covered the grave with a slab marker.

In 1980, Clairvius Narcisse, very much alive, walked into his family home.

Even in mysterious Haiti, his return caused an uproar. The Narcisse case, unlike dozens of similar incidents reported—and ignored—each year, came with a solid medical record, Scotland Yard's approval on a fingerprint comparison, and the Narcisse family's testimony.

EYEWITNESS STATEMENT

Fresh bones, they pay good, but I go there for the frogs. You find the best frogs at the cemetery.

—Chester Bonaparte, "Fresh Bones"

175

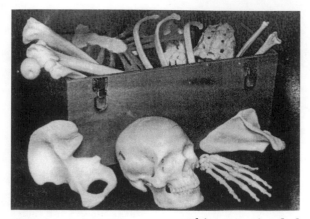

It's not nice to peek in other people's footlockers.

Clairvius's return from death was the first case documented in ways non-Haitians could understand, and that was one reason it became of great interest to an investigator named Wade Davis and the Zombie Project he started in 1982. The vodun zombie had stepped from Haiti's mystical past, through the sensationalism of film and popular fiction, and into the sterile arena of modern medicine. Unfortunately, though Narcisse was alive, the zombification process remained a mystery and the complex society producing zombies remained closed and misunderstood by outsiders. The Zombie Project study team began its work by reviewing the existent zombie research. Within days, serious recording problems came to light. Though Haiti resembled one huge plantation for much of its early history, and most inhabitants had shared a common experience under a handful of overseers, its early *written* history had come from minority landowners and urbanites. A few paintings, verbal folklore, and a scant number of testimonials written in an as-told-to format by non-Haitians was the extent of traditional reference material. Reports gathered from French Catholic towns had little relevance in light of the worldview of the rural regions where 80 percent of the population lived, where vodun was the religion, and Creole was the language.

Wading through a hodgepodge of information, Davis couldn't help wondering if it was gathered for the denigration of Haitians instead of for practical study. With few exceptions, non-natives preferred tales of decapitated chickens and voodoo dolls to the richer cultural tapestry of religion, music, folklore, and art that might provide a real historic context for zombification. The most intense research done in Haiti was by *Hollywood*—hardly a solid, unbiased starting point. Hollywood gave us walking mummies, chicken-shakers, and crones sticking pins in dolls. Nowhere in the "B" movies and dime-store novels was Haiti's incredible history revealed.

The Zombie Project began with a commitment to tackle zombification without prejudging its culture. It brought together talented chemists, doctors, art historians and artists, even theologians, all willing to view Haiti from a Haitian's viewpoint—or at least acknowledge zombification as but one part of a diverse way of life. In this eclectic academic arena, ethnobiology (a multidisciplinary field merging pharmacology, botany, biology, and anthropology) was the science that built bridges between these disparate fields of knowledge. In some ways, Davis's approach was standard scientific procedure: describe the problem, develop a hypothesis, identify variables, test, evaluate, and, if necessary, begin again. However, in one crucial way, his work was unique. Davis asked more than *how* zombies were created or what drug combinations might explain the phenomena, he asked *why*.

The discovery process began with an acknowledgment unusual for scientists—that bokor, or priests, respected members of Haitian society, were experts whose assistance had an intrinsic monetary value. Rather than assume the bokor must submit to researchers' questions, that researchers held some right to study valuable products *gratis,* or that any bokor *needed* an opportunity to justify his profession, Davis, like locals, negotiated for the items and information he needed.

As Davis observed the lengthy zombification process, moved among residents, and reported to the rest of the team, he absorbed the *context* of each part of the ritual, as well as the techniques involved. Many aspects of the process, and of the Narcisse case in particular, were troubling. During Davis's study under Haiti's bokor and houngan, he sensed sadness, even reluctance, during their preparation of powders. From the Narcisse family and Clairvius came hints that *Clairvius* had brought his death upon himself. Instead of celebrating his return, his family barely tolerated him.

Davis had to suspect Clairvius's crime related to his family life. Through reports from Narcisse's neighbors, Davis discovered that, in a society where sexual freedoms and responsibilities are clearly defined, where a half-dozen types of male-female relationships are respected, Clairvius had impregnated five women and refused to acknowledge their children. Attempts by the women's families to negotiate a settlement were rebuffed. His response was intolerable, a disgrace to a family already smarting under his antisocial behavior. Clairvius's brother, who under Haitian law co-owned the family farm, was refused a family loan without reason. Clairvius's personal home was one of a dozen in a family compound, but the only one re-roofed. He had his hand on the family income and refused to distribute it, even to feed his own children, or improve the farm. Desperate, the family appealed to the houngan to impress upon Clairvius the damage his greed brought the entire group.

But Clairvius continued to ignore any needs but his own. While his children lived under another's roof, their mothers shamed by his actions, he spent family money when and where he chose. Products

The Serpent and the Rainbow, a film by Wes Craven, is based on Davis's first book about his experiences in Haiti. As a tribute to the work done by Davis, the final scene of "Fresh Bones," from inside the coffin, echoes the final scene of the Craven movie. Some viewers even claim to have seen a rainbow during the episode. Did you?

from his farm were shunned in the market. Still he did nothing.

Eventually, under Davis's prodding, Clairvius admitted to receiving warning visits from the houngan and also from a Bizango society, the vodun church's judicial arm. His societal transgressions had been enumerated, he'd been given a chance to respond to the accusations made against him, and, with his likely punishment fully articulated, Clairvius was given three years to address his crimes. Instead, he became only more tyrannical.

When he fell ill and suspected that his long-delayed judgment had been imposed, he appealed to the houngan for an antidote. The houngan couldn't have found a reason to delay judgment, even if he'd wanted to. Narcisse's entrance into the Schweitzer Hospital, an organization completely outside the vodun medical, social, and religious community, was his last-ditch effort to avoid a punishment richly deserved under his own culture's laws.

THE MAKING OF A ZOMBIE

To Haitians, the creation of a zombie requires more than the right combination of ingredients. While the herbs, powders, and ritual are important, it's the strength of the individual bokor and his connection to the loa (spirit aspects of the one God) that determine the power of his zombie powders and antidotes.

At a careful distance from human habitation, the bokor directs the amounts and condition of various components while invoking the loa. If the bokor has been successful, then the victim soon "dies," and even the most talented physician would be hard pressed to distinguish the newly made zombie from a real cadaver.

Here are some sample ingredients in a bokor's zombie powder. Some ingredients are intended to protect the vodunist or ensure physical delivery of the powder to the victim's system. Colored talcs create protective patterns on the floor around ritual areas. Talcs, multihued sands, and dyes produce vé-vé like those on the tree in "Fresh Bones." Powdered glass, coated thorns, or the spiny stem of a raspberry cane are just a few ways powders can be introduced into victims.

- *Puffer fish,* containing the powerful sedative tetrodotoxin mentioned in "Fresh Bones," are obtained fresh, sun-dried whole for two to five days, and ground into a fine powder which the vodunist carefully avoids inhaling.

- *Toads or lizards,* in the absence of puffer, can be used. However, as toads produce less powerful results, they're confined in a jar overnight with a sea worm to bring out their essence. The worm, resembling a snake, scares the toads, causing their paratoid glands to produce vast quantities of active chemicals. Bufotenin, bufogenin, and bufotoxin are all produced by *Bufo marinus,* perhaps the most prized of the Haitian toads. In the morning, toad and worm are killed, sun-dried, and ground. A local bokor can be a financial boon for local children who, like Chester Bonaparte, make decent money chasing down toads. To date, no Haitian lizard seems capable of producing the "zombie chemicals." It's possible that use of lizards is a holdover from the African branches of Haitian society.
- *Gunpowder,* as an ingredient and also an aural element of the ritual, is the most unusual item on the bokor's list.
- *Dried gallbladders* of mules or men.
- *Plants,* all local, perform many functions for the skilled vodunist. Some, like *Mucuna puriens,* have tiny hairs on their seedpods or stems that provoke itching. When the intended victim scratches, as Scully did, tiny breaks are produced in the skin and compounds like tetrodotoxin gain access.
- *Human remains,* preferably fresh, retrieved from graveyards and reburied at the practitioner's home for forty-eight hours, are considered powerful ingredients. Skin, anointed with herbal oils, is dried and ground. Bones are scraped on graters or pounded into dust with mortar and pestle. The body part of a child is considered more potent as it brings birth and death, the living and dead, closer together.

There are two equally probable theories as to how the victims are revived. For one, most medicinal ingredients, whether in poisons or cures, remain active in the body for a fixed time. In places where swift burial is a health concern, a bokor could be reasonably sure the body would be in the ground when the powder wore off in twelve to twenty-four hours. The other theory, supported by the jars of liquid often found in opened coffins, suggests an antidote as part of the revivification.

Antidotes, like zombie powders, are often unique to single practitioners and locales. Though the ingredients differ, some consistent rules seem to govern their production.

Ideally, an antidote is made at the same time as the poison it is

Easy Stuff: Give yourself 1 point for each correct answer.

1. What did Private Jack McAlpin see in his cereal bowl?
2. What does Chester Bonaparte sell to Mulder for $5?
3. What did Mulder and Scully discover in Chester's sack?
4. Why didn't Scully and Mulder autopsy the body of the first victim, Manuel Guttierez?
5. What was found in the morgue instead of Jack McAlpin?

Getting Tougher: Give yourself 2 points for each correct answer.

6. Private McAlpin's car crashed into a tree with a chalk symbol on its trunk. Name one of the other places where this symbol was seen.
7. Where was Private Harry Dunham's hometown?
8. What chemical is found in McAlpin's bloodwork?
9. What does Mulder find on the dock instead of Chester?
10. What playing card was found in Mulder's room?

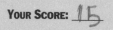

YOUR SCORE: 15

meant to counteract. Unlike powder preparation, where a houngan or bokor may direct activity without actually handling the physical elements, antidote production is a personal, hands-on activity. The ritual preparation and use of antidotes takes place in public view within the community's temple, often involving the participation of several spiritual leaders. (The poisoning of a victim is normally handled by the secretive societies that are associated with a particular houngan or bokor.) All antidotes are aromatic. Common ingredients include mothballs, ammonia, and perfumes.

The purpose of an antidote isn't to revive the dead. Instead, antidotes protect those who might be exposed to zombification—like the houngan's aides and victims who haven't "died" yet. A newly made zombie, extracted from its grave, seldom fully recovers from the experience. The theory that the brain areas most sensitive to the oxygen deprivation of underground confinement include those governing personality and independent thought is supported, but fails to explain zombies who "awaken" from their lassitude when their bokor dies.

Finally, unlike poisons, with their chemically identifiable ingredients, antidotes appear to be pharmacologically inert. While there is evidence that pH-specific treatments, including ammonia, could denature tetrodotoxin, the vodunist's claim is that only the bokor's power, and the loa working through him is the *real* "active ingredient."

A VODUN GLOSSARY

Arrêt: Magical force invoked by the houngan for the protection of a household.

Bokor: One who practices sorcery and black magic as a respected profession.

Buga: Local name for the toad *Bufo marinus*.

Garde: A personal protection against malicious magic. The one Mulder buys from Chester would have been of the type that protects only one person at a time, not an arrêt.

Hounfour: The vodun temple, not only the physical structure but the people (hounsis) as well.

Houngan: The vodun priest.

Loa: Aspect(s) of God. Contrary to popular representation, the hounsis don't worship a pantheon of gods. Instead, they recognize various faces of one God and some individuals feel a particular affinity for one aspect over another. In practice, the loa are similar to the Trinity (Father, Son, and Holy Ghost) recognized by the Christian church.

Placage: A socially sanctioned relationship that establishes the sexual and economic ties between a man and woman. Many types exist. Titles include: *Femme caille,* a woman who shares a man's house; *Maman petite,* a woman who's borne a man's child without living in his house; *Femme placée,* a mistress who doesn't share the same house as her mate and has yet to bear him children; *Bien avec,* a woman with whom a man has frequent, but not exclusive sexual contact. A *placage honnête* is a monogamous relationship, rare for both men and women in rural Haiti.

Servi loa: The term used by vodun followers to describe their religion—not voodoo. It translates rather literally as "to serve the loa."

Vé-vé: Symbolic design drawn with flour, talc, or ashes, and intended to invoke a particular loa. There are as many forms of vé-vé as there are loa.

Vodun: The theological principles and practices of traditional Haitian society.

Wanga: Magical charms used for evil purposes. The service records of McAlpin and Guttierez, impaled with chicken feet, would be an example.

Zombi: A general term for the living dead. More specifically: *Zombi astral,* a spirit zombi; *Zombi cadavre,* a physical zombie; *Zombi jardin,* a working zombie; *Zombi savanne,* an oddity occurring when a zombie (like Narcisse) returns to a normal state of living.

The actress portraying Robin McAlpin in this episode played Peggy in the pilot.

Code Name: "Colony"

CASE SUMMARY

When a group of identical doctors with identical jobs are killed up and down the northeastern states by identical means, it comes to the attention of Mulder and Scully via a series of anonymous notes dropped into their e-mail. Their investigation takes on a whole new cast when the doctors turn out to be clones and a woman claiming to be Samantha Mulder turns up at the home of Mulder's father.

DEEP BACKGROUND

Fact and Fiction: The Case for Clones

Cloning, which comes from the Greek word for twig, has different meanings depending on whether you're talking to a scientist or a moviegoer. The term was first used in agriculture to describe the naturally occurring process of budding. Now, among those same scientists, it's generally accepted as meaning the artificial creation of genetically identical individuals from a single cell. For moviegoers, especially those who've indulged a liking for science fiction, the definition is a little looser. Scientists refer only to cloning from embryonic cells; writers of fiction can allow cloning to proceed from *any* cell, even adult body cells that have nothing to do with reproduction.

It's this more fanciful vision of cloning that allows replicas of adults or identical eight-year-old girls to exist on *The X-Files*. The reality is a little different.

Embryonic cells—those taken from the earliest divisions of a newly fertilized egg—are fundamentally different from mature body cells. When an embryo begins its existence, all of its cells are basically the same;

EYEWITNESS STATEMENT

The certainty . . . becomes a comfort that allows you to move on. We bury our memories so deep after all that has been destroyed.

—Bill Mulder, "Colony"

only later will they begin to differentiate (to take on specific tasks). After the first two cell divisions, when the brand-new embryo consists of only four cells, there's no way to determine which of the four will end up as a nerve cell or which will become a bone cell. A cell able to become anything is referred to as being *totipotent*.

Totipotentiality doesn't last forever. Among humans, it seems to be lost by the time the miniature embryo reaches thirty-two cells. Up until that point, the cells could be separated, the nuclei dropped into thirty-two different cells and, in the fullness of time, result in thirty-two new, identical individuals. After that point, however, the cells will not divide properly and will not survive. By the time a human being is born, after thousands of cell divisions, there isn't a single cell in its body that doesn't have a set task, that hasn't lost its totipotentiality.

The cellular change that results in the loss of totipotency is yet to be identified, making it clearly impossible to reverse the procedure for any one cell and reduce it to a state where it might be cloned. This is the problem—and the challenge—facing geneticists. And they're not about to give up.

If scientists were to gain a complete understanding of the differentiation process, it would open up a world stranger than science fiction. The same aging process that causes cells to differentiate, that counts each cell division, also counts the number of times a cell is replaced when mature. Science suspects that we were made and designed to begin to "break down" shortly after our reproductive value is expended. If we learned how to reverse the process, we'd have discovered how to avoid cancer, reverse malignant tumors, and ultimately halt the aging process altogether.

Until then, reproductive specialists are still interested in the type of cloning that is within the scope of modern science: embryonic cloning. With even the best *in vitro* fertilization program returning only a 15 percent success rate, embryonic cloning has an immediate application. It offers obvious benefits to infertile couples: Couples who have generated only a single embryo for transfer could, through embryonic cloning, give themselves many more opportunities for impregnation. For women who have difficulty producing eggs, such technologies would be invaluable.

Infertile couples often find the costs of advanced technologies in the reproductive field prohibitively expensive. A patient's hormone level must be monitored; ovaries examined by ultrasound; a surgical procedure requiring anesthesia employed to retrieve the eggs. Embryonic cloning would allow a couple to avoid repeated proce-

Easy Stuff: Give yourself 1 point for each correct answer.

1. How did the pilot "disguise" himself?
2. In which regional office of the Bureau did Weiss work?
3. How were the obituaries of the three doctors sent to Mulder?
4. What was the name of the CIA agent who offered to work with them?
5. What happened to Scully's shoes?

Getting Tougher: Give yourself 2 points for each correct answer.

6. What code name did the CIA agent give the clones?
7. Name the clone who jumped from his apartment window.
8. Where does Mulder's father live?
9. At what hotel did Scully stay?
10. Where did the clones have their laboratory?

dures to gather eggs, bringing the entire process closer to the financial reach of more couples.

Since naturally occurring identical twins cause the legal field no difficulty whatsoever, it's entirely possible that these "artificial" twins would be just as easily accepted and that the scientific process of cloning would become better understood and more easily separated from fiction.

THE STORYTELLERS

Ep-#	Title	Writer(s)
1.01	Pilot: "The X-Files"	Chris Carter
1.02	"Deep Throat"	Chris Carter
1.03	"Squeeze"	Glen Morgan and James Wong
1.04	"Conduit"	Alex Gansa and Howard Gordon
1.05	"The Jersey Devil"	Chris Carter
1.06	"Shadows"	Glen Morgan and James Wong
1.07	"Ghost in the Machine"	Alex Gansa and Howard Gordon
1.08	"Ice"	Glen Morgan and James Wong
1.09	"Space"	Chris Carter
1.10	"Fallen Angel"	Howard Gordon and Alex Gansa
1.11	"Eve"	Kenneth Biller and Chris Brancato
1.12	"Fire"	Chris Carter
1.13	"Beyond the Sea"	Glen Morgan and James Wong
1.14	"GenderBender"	Larry Barber and Paul Barber
1.15	"Lazarus"	Alex Gansa and Howard Gordon
1.16	"Young at Heart"	Scott Kaufer and Chris Carter
1.17	"E.B.E."	Glen Morgan and James Wong
1.18	"Miracle Man"	Howard Gordon and Chris Carter
1.19	"Shapes"	Marilyn Osborn
1.20	"Darkness Falls"	Chris Carter
1.21	"Tooms"	Glen Morgan and James Wong
1.22	"Born Again"	Howard Gordon and Alex Gansa
1.23	"Roland"	Chris Ruppenthal
1.24	"The Erlenmeyer Flask"	Chris Carter
2.01	"Little Green Men"	Glen Morgan and James Wong
2.02	"The Host"	Chris Carter
2.03	"Blood"	Glen Morgan and James Wong
2.04	"Sleepless"	Howard Gordon
2.05	"Duane Barry"	Chris Carter
2.06	"Ascension"	Paul Brown

2.07	"3"	Glen Morgan and James Wong
		(original script: Chris Ruppenthal)
2.08	"One Breath"	Glen Morgan and James Wong
2.09	"Firewalker"	Howard Gordon
2.10	"Red Museum"	Chris Carter
2.11	"Excelsis Dei"	Paul Brown
2.12	"Aubrey"	Sara B. Charno
2.13	"Irresistible"	Chris Carter
2.14	"Die Hand Die Verletzt"	Glen Morgan and James Wong
2.15	"Fresh Bones"	Howard Gordon
2.16	"Colony"	Chris Carter
		(story by: Chris Carter and David Duchovny)
2.17	"End Game"	Frank Spotnitz
2.18	"Fearful Symmetry"	Steve DeJarnatt
2.19	"Død Kalm"	Howard Gordon and Alex Gansa
		(story by: Howard Gordon)
2.20	"Humbug"	Darin Morgan
2.21	"The Calusari"	Sara B. Charno
2.22	"F. Emasculata"	Chris Carter and Howard Gordon
2.23	"Soft Light"	Vince Gilligan
2.24	"Our Town"	Frank Spotnitz
2.25	"Anasazi"	Chris Carter
		(story by: Chris Carter and David Duchovny)

Germantown, where Scully discovered the genetics lab of the cloned Gregors, is also the home of Cellmark Diagnostics, famed for its work with DNA evidence.

Megan Leitch
A Brief Filmography

The spooky environs of *The X-Files* world shouldn't bother Megan Leitch (Samantha Mulder); she's worked on some of the most physically and psychologically frightening projects of recent times.

No Child of Mine, 1993
Knight Moves, 1992
The Resurrected, 1992
Omen IV: The Awakening, 1991
Stephen King's It, 1990

Code Name: "End Game"

CASE SUMMARY

With his sister as the only acceptable ransom for his kidnapped partner, Mulder lays a desperate plan that quickly goes wrong. Alone in the Arctic, he finds himself in the all-too-familiar position of trying to catch up with ideas and people he barely understands. Scully, in the meantime, has found at least part of his answer—in the bodies of her kidnapper's other victims.

DEEP BACKGROUND

And the Dead Speak

Forensic pathology, Scully's chosen specialty, attracts an unusual cadre of practitioners, all of whom go to work each morning with the full knowledge that they've no patients to save, that they'll likely spend most of the day in less than pleasant surroundings, and that, when their job is done, they could face a lawyer who'll spend hours trying to compromise everything they've touched. One other thing they share is a belief that the work they do has value.

Forensic pathology goes beyond the mere cause of death; it must establish *all* the facts, lethal and nonlethal, that might assist in the courts. The cause of death is not automatically revealed when a body is opened; it is not isolated and tangible but rather is a theory to explain as many clues as possible—and it's certainly subject to interpretation and human error. Because of that, legal autopsy requires meticulously detailed descriptions, measurements, and documentation.

Nothing beats experience in the investigation of a crime scene, and the experienced forensics examiner can often add together clues from the body with physical evidence from the scene to

EYEWITNESS STATEMENT

WHERE IS SHE?!

—Mulder, "End Game"

establish the mode of death. For example, suicide victims often remove their glasses before jumping; accident victims don't. An autopsy alone can't determine intent, but the scene and the circumstances may contribute unmistakable evidence.

A legal autopsy must be complete if only to rule out any other potential contributory cause of death. All autopsy reports, but especially forensic reports, must be dictated to a stenographer or into a recording instrument during the actual performance of the procedure. That record often becomes legal evidence.

Every autopsy plays an important part in exposing mistakes, delimiting new diseases and new patterns of disease, and guiding future studies. Morbidity and mortality statistics acquire accuracy and significance when based on careful autopsies; they also often give the first indication of contagion and epidemics. In medical education, the autopsy is the focal point at which the profession first learns to assess and to apply medical knowledge. In addition to determining the cause of death, most autopsies have a larger purpose. It's that purpose that keeps most pathologists working in a thankless job.

Propping Up the Set

We get to know fictional characters through the little things they leave lying on their dressers, the things we glimpse in their car's glove compartment, the pictures they put on their walls, and the munchies in their cupboards. To create an entire fictional history for Scully and Mulder required dozens of props to add just the right touches to sets that are, in reality, as cozy and intimate as the middle of a concert stage.

Mulder's apartment, the ultimate bachelor's digs, gives hints about his character with each new camera angle. A fish tank with no fish, a nearly empty refrigerator, a basketball shoved under an end table, a seemingly endless supply of wacky ties, and a couch well dented from being slept on—all of this gives us as many clues about Mulder the person as his cramped and colorful little office—though it would be hard to top the "I WANT TO BELIEVE" poster over his desk. (That poster, which fans fruitlessly try to find for sale, is a case in point, reminding us of how deliberately everything on these sets has been added. The poster is a one-of-a-kind item commissioned by the prop and design staffs.)

Scully's home, like Mulder's, is also a revealing source of character detail. But her apartment is a pleasant surprise: the tailored,

TRIVIA BUSTER 40

Easy Stuff: Give yourself 1 point for each correct answer.

1. What was the name of the submarine?
2. How could the retrovirus be rendered inactive?
3. What was Agent Weiss's official cause of death?
4. How many Samanthas did we see in this episode?
5. From what bridge did the pilot and Samantha fall?

Getting Tougher: Give yourself 2 points for each correct answer.

6. What method did Samantha tell Mulder to use to kill the pilot?
7. Why did the clones work in abortion clinics?
8. What is Mulder's apartment number?
9. What was the number on the keycard Samantha left for Mulder?
10. How does Scully attempt to contact Mulder's source?

ultra-professional Scully has a softer side in private. A deep antique tub is accessorized with thick, oversized towels. Bath salts and bubbles decorate the shelves. Candles abound in every room. The books in Scully's home, all convincingly tattered or dog-eared, aren't on display in her living room, but are tucked into her bedroom within easy reach of a bed covered in a deep quilt. While Mulder's cramped apartment seems almost an extension of his office, Scully's is more of a refuge.

That same attention to detail in the established sets is seen in every new space we're shown. Tooms's first victim didn't die in any old office, he died in an office complete with personal mementos that made us sorry he died before we could find out what those knick-knacks meant to him. Max Fenig's trailer with its sixties decor, the quasi-military precision of each item's placement in The Lone Gunmen's digs, and the tidy but sparse rooms of Bill Mulder's Martha's Vineyard home convey information to us on the most subtle level.

Whereas basketballs, candlesticks, and other character-building props aren't that hard to come by, other prop requests have tested the resourcefulness of the stage crew. Woodland altars, papier-mâché nests for liver-sucking mutants, frozen alien fetuses, and swarms of locusts aren't exactly stock items. Neither are human organs, elephants, or loaves of blood-filled bread, though the blood-filled bread was an improvement over the other vampire-avoiding options. A ring of running water or living rose bushes would have been difficult to set up in the middle of any modern kitchen.

Props have also been used to great effect on *The X-Files* to evoke memories of specific people or events with individual items. Scully's little cross, which Mulder carried for so many months throughout his search for her, is a potent symbol of hope. The smoldering "Morley" cigarettes, with their cloying smoke, have become so firmly associated with conspiracies and evil that some X-Philes have expressed a growing desire to either switch their brand of a similar name or quit. While *The X-Files* is without a doubt a genre series, the symbolism that runs from episode to episode proves that "literary" strategies also work on prime time.

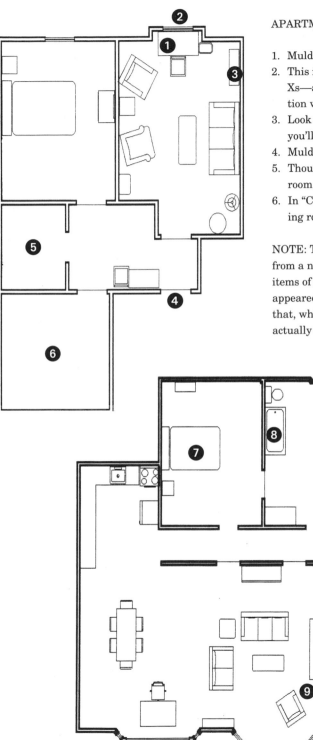

APARTMENT OF FOX MULDER

1. Mulder's computer.
2. This is the window where Mulder posts the masking tape Xs—and shines his blue light bulbs—to initiate communication with his mysterious contacts.
3. Look closely at Mulder's fish tank during "End Game" and you'll notice something missing—the fish!
4. Mulder's apartment number is 42.
5. Though we've never seen it, we assume he does have a bathroom.
6. In "Colony," Mulder's kitchen is clearly visible from the living room—which puts it roughly in the hallway.

NOTE: These floor plans are a compilation of information from a number of episodes. From show to show, particular items of furniture, windows, doors, and even whole rooms have appeared, moved, and disappeared. Just another reminder that, while the rooms here appear as a continuous unit, they're actually a number of sets.

APARTMENT OF DANA SCULLY

7. Mulder *did* end up in Scully's bed once, though the circumstances in "Anasazi" weren't what romantic viewers might have wished for.
8. Scully gave Tooms the opportunity to admire her antique tub when she handcuffed him to it in "Squeeze."
9. Ambrose Chapel made himself pretty cozy here in "Colony."
10. Duane Barry seemed to have a problem with doors. He came through this window in "Duane Barry."

NOTE: Determining the floor number of Scully's apartment is confusing. Though her utility panel says 402, which is usually the fourth floor, Duane Barry broke a first floor window to get into her apartment.

189

Code Name:
"Fearful Symmetry"

CASE SUMMARY

When invisible animals go on a rampage, killing a federal employee and destroying personal property, Mulder and Scully investigate the nearest zoo. Far from a peaceful retreat where man can commune with nature, this zoo is the nexus for pressure by animal rights groups, bean counters, and even its own employees. It's possible that the only place to find truth is within the cage of a hand-signing ape.

DEEP BACKGROUND

The title "Fearful Symmetry" is from the William Blake poem "The Tyger." If you watched carefully, you'd have seen that the building where the tiger was captured was named "Blake Towers."

EYEWITNESS STATEMENT

Bright light. Man save man.

—Sophie the Ape, "Fearful Symmetry"

Hands Talk

Though many behaviors have been identified that separate man from the rest of the animals, the most enduring is our ability to speak. But according to linguistics labs worldwide, that identification is facing a serious challenge—a challenge that creatures like *The X-Files'* fictional ape, Sophie, evoked.

While no one would argue that many species of animal can communicate (bees direct one another to flower patches without difficulty), a human-type "language" has a more narrow definition. For humans, the connection between a word and its referent is arbitrary and must be learned by anyone wishing to speak the language. For example, a cow is only a cow to English speakers, and a native speaker of Urdu must first learn the word "cow" before he can discuss that particular animal. Some referents aren't even obviously connectable to their words. But abstractions such as "love," while they can't be touched or manipulated, are as easily learned by human children as "rock" or "sun."

Human language is flexible. We can discuss events and situations we've never experienced, and impossibilities. Through allusions and metaphor, we can expand our range of descriptions. Our language has syntax and grammar, rules for how words go together. Some examples of this feature are obvious: "Bob tickle Koko" and "Koko tickle Bob" have different meanings. Other examples are less clear: We say, "I have a big, red balloon." We don't say, "I have a red, big balloon."

These are features that we've yet to identify in the existing communication systems of other animals, though many attempts have been made to *impose* them. Between 1910 and 1945, dozens of linguists and scientists tried to teach human speech to chimpanzees, our closest biological relative. All failed. We now know it would have been impossible for them to succeed. Chimpanzee physiology simply doesn't allow chimps to reproduce human-style sounds.

Since that discovery, efforts have moved from vocal languages to nonvocal ones. The sign language used by the deaf and hard of hearing, as well as pictograms and speech boards, have all been used and proven successful to one degree or another. Many apes appear capable of adopting a 50-word vocabulary. A significant number have 100- to 200-word vocabularies.

Washoe, a female chimpanzee who was trained by Beatrice and Allan Gardner, readily adopted more than 150 signs that were of value to her. She learned nouns at an incredible rate, swiftly including her trainers, favorite foods, and special objects like toys in her repertoire. Verblike words were acquired more slowly once "please," "hurry," and "more" were mastered, though true verbs such as "come," "go," "tickle," and "eat" were added regularly.

Sarah, a chimpanzee trained to use plastic tokens instead of signs to represent words, had a broader (but not significantly larger) vocabulary. In addition to nouns and verbs, Sarah learned many adjectives (colors, shapes, and sizes in particular) as well as prepositions like "in" and "under."

With the question of whether nonhuman animals could assign arbitrary symbols appearing to be answered, linguists and behavioral biologists were able to evaluate *how* those arbitrary symbols were being used. Did the signs and tokens really function as words? Or was the ape simply obeying its trainer's instructions? Did Sarah or Washoe or the others actually understand the meaning of their words? Was it possible the apes had simply discovered an if-then relationship? If they flashed one sign, a banana would appear; if they flashed a different token, then different food was forthcoming.

TRIVIA BUSTER 42

Easy Stuff: Give yourself 1 point for each correct answer.

1. African or Indian, which type of elephant did Meecham claim Genesia was?
2. What was the gorilla's name?
3. What language did Sophie speak?
4. What did the brown spots on the drawings signify?
5. Scully found evidence of foul play on Kyle Lang's body. What device was used on him?

Getting Tougher: Give yourself 2 points for each correct answer.

6. Mulder saw David Copperfield make a monument disappear. Which one?
7. Which organization did Kyle Lang represent?
8. From what business did the video teleconference originate?
9. Where was the tiger found?
10. How many words did Sophie understand?

It was imperative that researchers rule out the action-reward stereotype. If they didn't, a series of levers could be made into a language of a sort, though clearly one without syntax.

Early work indicated the chimps could make some important distinctions. For example, although Sarah's token for an apple was a blue triangle, when asked what color an apple was, she responded that it was red, not blue. The token wasn't the apple, it *represented* the apple. Other chimpanzees, whose symbols covered a number of foods and tools, were able to consistently separate the foods from the tools, indicating the same "grouping" mode of thinking that allows humans to include both a huge beanbag and an upholstered Queen Anne antique in our category of chairs.

Keyboard symbols were the tool of choice in another study involving a pygmy chimp named Kanzi who was unusually proficient. He didn't seem to need long training sessions with food rewards and appeared capable of inferring meaning from context—without clues from his trainers. Not only did he comprehend human communications on his speech board, he listened attentively to regular human speech and could respond to it with the board.

Humans and animals seemed to be able to share a common language, but could the apes manipulate words, compose sentences that followed the syntactic rules, choose their words to indicate relationships between things? Researchers knew apes could use more than one symbol or gesture in a row: One chimp, Lana, pressed "Please machine give Lana drink" on her speech board; Washoe and other chimpanzees trained in gestural sign language frequently produced strings like "You me go out" and "Roger tickle Washoe." Skeptics, however, have raised doubts about the significance of these strings of signs and symbols. They correctly pointed out that humans were interpreting Lana's taps on the keyboard. Wasn't it equally possible that something was going on in Lana's mind similar to "Tap here, then here, then here. Now wait for drink?" Pigeons can be trained to press four colored keys in a particular order to get a drink—even though no words have ever been assigned to the keys. Does that make the keys a sentence?

The Crusades television program by the PAWS organization prompted at least one writer/producer from *The X-Files* to gather more information. The film shown of "elephant training" was, unfortunately, actual footage shot at a major zoo.

In the case of sign language, two other questions are brought up regularly. Isn't it possible the apes learn to reflect the signs used by their trainers right back at them? If a trainer were to sign "Does Washoe want drink?" and the ape replied "Washoe want drink," it's possible that replying "Washoe tired" to "Is Washoe tired?" is patterned learning. All Washoe needs to do is drop the first sign and it appears that communication is occurring. Washoe mightn't be particularly tired or thirsty but it's unlikely that the question would be asked if a positive response wasn't anticipated.

The second problem is in deciding where a sentence begins and ends. Because the ape's vocabulary is truncated, it's possible that a series of gestures meant to be independent could be interpreted by a trainer as a sentence. There are no capital letters or periods in any of the language forms used in experimentation.

On the other hand, some apes have independently learned to produce their own strings of signs in particular order. Things like "more drink" or "give me" instead of "drink more" or "me give" hint that the placement of the symbols is important to them as well.

And what about this? A chimpanzee called Lucy was accustomed to instructing her trainer, Roger Fouts, by gesturing "Roger tickle Lucy." One day, instead of complying with this request, Fouts signed back "No, Lucy tickle Roger." Although at first nonplussed, after several similar exchanges Lucy eventually did as asked.

Language research with animals is perhaps the most difficult of any area of research and its investigators often find themselves in a Catch-22 situation. In order to evaluate progress, an outside agent must have specific criteria to look for, such as a standard set of symbols, or a word count. Therefore, in order to attract research money, researchers have to find a quantifiable way to represent their work. But language is fluid. Communication is the natural result of unstructured attempts to convey meaning. To honestly compare other primate language habits to ours, the system should be flexible enough to include symbols that arise spontaneously or informally.

Real zoo animals were used in all scenes except those with Sophie. Sophie was a suited actor provided by Rick Baker and Company, which has received an Academy Award for its portrayal of apes.

In one experiment, Lucy demonstrated a hitherto uniquely human trait—she lied! When asked about a pile of chimp doo-doo on the floor, she blamed three different culprits before finally admitting, "Lucy dirty, dirty. Sorry Lucy."

Code Name: "Død Kalm"

CASE SUMMARY

When the USS *Ardent* disappears in an area Mulder calls a second Bermuda Triangle, he's determined to find the ship that he believes is part of a modern-day Philadelphia Experiment. Scully, more concerned with the extraordinarily rapid aging of one of the ship's rescued crewmen, is equally determined, if for a different reason.

DEEP BACKGROUND

The Philadelphia Experiment

The Philadelphia Experiment wasn't actually an experiment, it was a movie based on a series of peculiar events alleged to have taken place one misty evening in October 1943. While some swear the events of *The Philadelphia Experiment* are true in every respect, others ask why it took a decade for such an incredible tale, if real, to come to light.

Until the mid-1950s the retroactively named Philadelphia Experiment hadn't made as much as a ripple in the media. Then a fat envelope landed on the desk of one Morris Ketchum Jessup. Jungle explorer, Lamont-Hussey Observatory astronomer, discoverer of double stars, photographer for Carnegie Institute archaeological expeditions, M. K. Jessup was also the author of four books on UFOs.

Among the letters forwarded to him from his publisher was one from a Carlos Miguel Allende, in which Allende wrote with great authority on levitation theory and technique. Jessup jotted a polite

Død Kalm: Norwegian for dead calm.

EYEWITNESS STATEMENT

Everything stopped. Everything. Even the sea. Even the wind. Then the ship, my ship, she began to bleed, through the hull, through the rivet seams.

—Captain Barclay, "Død Kalm"

note in response and forgot about the whole thing until he received a second letter from Allende.

This time, Allende let Jessup know that he was familiar with Jessup's public lectures suggesting that research into Einstein's Unified Field Theory could unlock the mystery of antigravity. Allende advised Jessup to abandon that line of research, as it had already been tried and it had failed horribly. He also wrote that tests in October 1943 had resulted in the complete invisibility of a ship, a destroyer, and all of the crew. According to Allende, half of the crew went insane from the experience. The experimental ship (only later would researchers identify it as the USS *Eldridge*) disappeared from its Philadelphia dock, appeared just moments later at a Norfolk dockyard, then returned safely to its berth in Philadelphia.

Not surprisingly, Jessup didn't swallow the story whole. A year later, however, he was invited to the Washington, D.C., Office of Naval Research. On arriving, Jessup discovered that the office had received a copy of his own book, *The Case for the UFO,* which had apparently been heavily annotated by three different people and sent to Admiral N. Furth. Among the details scrawled in the book's margins was the story of a Navy vessel that had disappeared and returned.

Furth had apparently thrown the book away as unimportant, but his junior officers still had questions. They had copies of the book made by the Varo Manufacturing Company of Garland, Texas. An unsigned introduction to the Varo copies was added. These few copies would eventually be known as the Varo editions.

In October 1958, fifteen years later, Jessup and a group of interested people gathered at the home of Ivan Sanderson, another prominent writer on mysterious events. Sometime during the evening, Jessup took part of the group aside and gave them the original copy of his book. Apparently in complete seriousness, he asked them to lock it up somewhere safe—just in case something happened to him.

Six months later, Jessup was found dead in his car.

He'd committed suicide.

While most people had thought the Allende letters and the notes in Jessup's book were nothing more than an elaborate hoax, his death drew new attention to the case.

Twenty years of speculation and rumor allowed the tale to grow, and eventually it resulted in the film called *The Philadelphia Experiment.* The movie (like *The X-Files,* at times) was more than willing

---

Easy Stuff: Give yourself 1 point for each correct answer.

1. Which of the two agents has a tendency to seasickness?
2. What sort of book was Scully writing in?
3. To what comedian did Mulder compare himself?
4. What did Captain Barclay mistakenly call "blood"?
5. What highly reactive chemicals did Scully suggest as a cause for their aging?

Getting Tougher: Give yourself 2 points for each correct answer.

6. What was the registration number of the USS *Ardent*?
7. What was the name of the Canadian fishing trawler that rescued the crew of the USS *Ardent*?
8. What was the name of the project that Mulder suggested was responsible for the disappearance of a Navy vessel during World War II?
9. Name two of the items Scully gathered as water sources.
10. What was Ionesco selling to the Japanese?

ANSWERS

1. Mulder.
2. The official log of the USS *Ardent.*
3. George Burns.
4. Rust.
5. Free radicals.
6. 925.
7. The *Lizette.*
8. The Philadelphia Experiment.
9. Juice of six lemons, water from a snow globe, and sardine juice.
10. Illegally captured whales.

YOUR SCORE: _15_

to sacrifice accuracy for good fiction, and some pertinent facts were lost in its interpretation. For example:

- Carlos Allende was a pseudonym.
- The rate of mental illness among the crew of the USS *Eldridge* was no higher than among the general population.
- Though the annotations in Jessup's book were written in multi-colored ink and various handwritings, "Allende" had written all the notes himself.
- Though Allende claimed the USS *Eldridge* couldn't have made the trip between Philadelphia and Norfolk that quickly, he failed to mention the channel between the two ports.

Free Radical Theory of Aging: The body and its cells are damaged by biochemical compounds called free radicals. These compounds are produced as normal waste products of cellular metabolism, are highly reactive, and are toxic to cells and DNA. As the rate of some chemical reactions increases with exposure to electricity, those seeking longevity tend to avoid living near power lines and any unnecessary exposure to electrical appliances. If the water in "Død Kalm" was acting as a battery, it might indeed have excited the activity of free radicals.

The current USS *Ardent* is an Avenger-class oceangoing minesweeper/mine-hunter carrying ship's pennant number MCM 12. The real *Ardent* was launched in 1991, though the plaque on the fictional one indicates it was *commissioned* that same year. The real *Ardent* is unlikely to rust. Like most minesweepers, it has a wooden hull and fiberglass superstructure.

The U.S. Navy stopped building Destroyer Escorts in 1975 and reclassified all DEs as "frigates." DE-925 was canceled in 1944 or 1945 along with most of the remaining World War II Evarts-class ships. It seems that DE-925 was painted across a retired *Canadian* vessel.

BLOOPERS

Whether you're watching for the first time or the tenth, look for the rare instances when something snuck by the X-crew.

- In "Deep Throat," Scully removes the magazine from her gun to reveal only one bullet. Why would anyone load only one bullet?
- Colonel Belt should not have been able to jump out of a hospital window during the episode "Space." Florida, like most states, requires hospital windows to be of the fixed type.
- How did Agent Jack Willis pass his physical tests, which presumably included blood and urine testing, without revealing his diabetes?
- When Michelle Generoo's car begins to roll in "Space," it's pouring rain, but by the time Mulder and Scully arrive to tug her out of her wrecked car—before the wheels can even stop spinning—the rain has stopped and the ground isn't even damp enough to stain the trousers of the kneeling Mulder.
- In "Colony," we listen to Mulder's answering machine several times. Curiously, his recorded greeting isn't the same each time—though he never returned home to tape a new one.
- Continuity errors can be a great deal of fun for the careful observer. Perhaps the next time you watch "Colony," you'll pay special attention to Scully's bus ride and notice how a man who started out sitting behind her was suddenly in the front of the bus.
- When Scully tells Mulder she's getting a motel room off I-90 in Germantown, Maryland, it must have been a long way off—several states, at the least. I-90 runs through New York and Massachusetts.

While Trondheim as a Norwegian surname is unusual, the *town* of Trondheim can be seen on the map in the X-File offices.

Code Name: "Humbug"

CASE SUMMARY

When a retirement community for circus performers is terrorized by the mythical Fegee Mermaid, which likes to eat its victims and leaves fin-marks instead of footprints, Scully and Mulder have to separate the truth from the humbug. In a town populated by tattooed men, bearded ladies, and people who routinely retract their testicles into their body and hammer nails into their noses, the paranormal might seem almost mundane.

**DEEP
BACKGROUND**

The Circus: A Brief History

Though most people think of the circus as an ancient entertainment, it's actually only a few hundred years old. The circuses mentioned in connection with ancient Rome weren't circuses as modern audiences visualize them. They were racetracks, for the most part, where huge spectacles, including full-scale chariot battles and even mock naval battles, could be reenacted.

Still, modern day circus performers were known even to ancient peoples. Acrobats and jugglers have been bouncing across the countryside for thousands of years. Rope dancers were popular in Greece and the Romans were fond of animal acts—especially elephants. The clown, in more forms than we currently employ, entertained both streetfolk and kings. Animal acts were big with King Alfred of England as early as A.D. 850. Later rulers showed a preference for human performers (who tended to create less mess on the hall floor) and it was around 1000–1500 that tumblers, contortionists, and dancers swept the European stages. Itinerant animal trainers worked with everything from monkeys to horses to bears, and the distinction between them and a traveling zoo was slim.

It's generally agreed that the modern form of the circus actually began in England about 1770 when a gentleman named Philip Astley, a former sergeant major turned trick rider, found that if he galloped in a circle while standing on his horse's back, centrifugal force helped him to keep his balance. The beaten circular path became the first circus ring.

Unable to make a show out of one man on one horse, Astley added clowns, musicians, and a multitude of rotating acts. As business picked up, he added a roof, benches for the audience, and a stage for productions. Astley didn't call his resulting entertainment a circus; to him, it was always "The Amphitheatre" because of the sloping benches, or the "Riding School" because the main acts continued to be equestrian.

Circuses soon became the employment of choice for performers. For the jugglers, acrobats, and others who'd once worked the fairgrounds, the circus offered a stable arena where customers came to them instead of them chasing customers. The variety offered by the circus could pull in much larger audiences, and any performer who chose to do so could put down roots.

Astley became terrifically popular in England and it didn't take long for him to realize the opportunity in traveling as the old troupes had done—if the audience was right. In 1772, Astley and company performed for the French court and discovered that France had sufficient performers of varied talent to support its own circus. Ten years later, Astley opened his next amphitheatre in Paris. Even the French Revolution, which hampered relations between France and Britain, wasn't a real problem. He simply leased the whole thing to Antonio Franconi, a colorful man, superior trick rider, and—most importantly—a capable manager. The two were partners for many years and, as Franconi's children grew up, they took over the circus in France, expanding it and establishing the circus ring at forty-two feet in diameter.

By 1900, the circus was well established from South Africa to China to Canada and competition had become a real factor. Though the common man was the intended audience and most circuses catered to his taste, the nobility and the aristocrats as well had become enchanted by the circus. The huge, permanent circus in St. Petersburg regularly perfumed the stables so as not to offend the noses of visiting aristocrats.

Easy Stuff: Give yourself 1 point for each correct answer.

1. Which picture in the menu border was Mulder unable to identify?
2. What was surprising about the tattooed man's diet?
3. What "snack" did Scully share with the tattooed man?
4. What was in the chest?
5. What did Scully and Mulder exhume from the sheriff's backyard?

Getting Tougher: Give yourself 2 points for each correct answer.

6. What did Hepcat Helm call his funhouse?
7. What is a gaff?
8. What was Sheriff Hamilton's prior occupation?
9. What was the name of Mr. Nutt's dog?
10. What was Dr. Blockhead's other name?

ANSWERS

1. The Fegee Mermaid.
2. He ate anything, including live fish.
3. Crickets, live crickets.
4. Nothing. Scully fell for one of Barnum's old tricks.
5. A potato.
6. The Tabernacle of Terror.
7. A phony, like the conjoined twins who weren't identical.
8. He was Jim-Jim, the Dog-Faced Boy.
9. Pompadour.
10. Jeffrey Swaim.

YOUR SCORE: 15

Circus "families" began to emerge strongly during the nineteenth century. Youths trained from early childhood in various skills became premier performers. There were strategic marriages among circus families, cadet lines that established new circuses, and a strict code of conduct. In Eastern Europe, where the circuses were often associated with the Rom gypsies, literal kings and queens were acknowledged. The circus was a society within a society, people brought together not only by their jobs, but their chosen lifestyle. The retirement town shown in *The X-Files* has its roots in a tradition of self-supporting, entrepreneurial, community-oriented people that produced great artists, musicians, and writers as well as sideshows.

In America, the circus and the Ringling Bros. are inseparable. Through mergers and buyouts, the Ringlings would eventually control some eleven major circuses and have a main tent that seated

THE FEGEE MERMAID

The exhibit mentioned so prominently in this episode was perhaps the most often shown of the dozens of fake mermaids floating about Europe during the 1800s. The exhibit started its European tour as the East Indian mermaid at the Turf Coffee House in St. James, England, where, for several weeks in 1822, it attracted thousands of visitors. Even after the amalgamation of monkey and salmon was revealed as a hoax, it was still capable of bringing in the lookie-loos.

P. T. Barnum saw the mermaid around 1840 and decided to continue in the United States what had obviously been a booming business. With an advertising campaign that would have done Procter & Gamble proud, the hideous creature was escorted to no less sensational a home than New York City's Concert Hall on Broadway. The mermaid would also do a tour at the American Museum in the same city before being permanently ensconced in the Museum of the Circus at Florida. Not bad for a creature Barnum described as "an ugly dried-up, black-looking, and diminutive specimen."

over 10,000 people—one of the largest in the world. The Ringling Museum of the Circus in Sarasota, Florida, is where many of their performers overwinter and retire, and where many of the original circus wagons have been restored for exhibition.

Chang and Eng: The Siamese Twins

Born joined at the waist in Meklong, Siam (now Thailand), in May 1811, Chang and Eng became so famous that all other conjoined twins, regardless of nationality, have until recently been called *Siamese* twins. While they were still just boys, Chang and Eng attained the status of celebrities in their homeland and were even invited to be guests of the King of Siam.

However, as people started coming from all over to see them, it didn't take long for someone to realize that visitors would likely pay for the privilege. In 1829, when circuses worldwide were in their heyday, Chang and Eng left Siam with a British agent and embarked on a tour that took them from Canada to Cuba and into almost every country in Europe. While their earnings as minors went to their agent, on turning twenty-one, the pair decided to take their affairs into their own hands and began to arrange tours to suit themselves. In a remarkably short time, they had amassed a small fortune and bought a plantation (complete with slaves) in Mount Airy, North Carolina. When they became naturalized citizens of the United States, they took on the surname Bunker and shortly thereafter married sisters Adelaide and Sarah Yates. While they ran the Mount Airy property together, the brothers maintained separate homes about three miles apart. They alternated houses on a three-day basis to spend time with their wives and many children.

Throughout their lives, separation surgery had been one possibility suggested to the brothers. They had, however, decided against it. There was some risk associated with the procedure, albeit small, and the men considered themselves well adapted to their circumstances. They could run, swim, and hunt, and their family situation was stable. Though they were attached by a band of skin around their waists, there was no sharing of organs and, most important, no blurring of their distinct personalities. They were complete both as a unit, and as individuals.

The brothers died in 1874, just three hours apart. Some, including the mysterious museum owner in "Humbug," suggest that Eng died of fright on awakening to find himself attached to his dead brother—although there is no proof to support this theory.

While Scully may have been taught sleight of hand as a child, Gillian Anderson wasn't. Always the trouper, she really did put that bug in her mouth, not once, but *three* times.

The performers in this episode belong to the Jim Rose Traveling Sideshow, where they actually do everything seen during the show, and a few other things too wild for even *The X-Files*. Jim Rose is personally famous for his diet of lightbulbs and almost anything else.

Code Name: "The Calusari"

CASE SUMMARY

A balloon moving against the wind may be the only clue in the death of a young child, but, on arriving to investigate, a plethora of bizarre events convinces Scully she's facing a rare form of child abuse. For his part, Mulder thinks answers may be found in a dead rooster and a group of elderly chanters called the Calusari.

DEEP BACKGROUND

Exorcism—Past and Very Much Present

In order for a group of dedicated exorcists like the Calusari to arise in a society, there must be a belief in something to exorcise.

Possession, by devils, demons, and even regular people with evil intentions, is an old and enduring religious and folk tradition. First clues to possession are extreme mood swings, unusual behavior, and personality changes. If the changes continue, it's reasonable to assume the person is under the direct control of an external supernatural power. Sure signs of spirit possession include violent movements, shrieking, groaning, and the uttering of peculiar speech. A normally pious member of a religious body may curse and blaspheme, even exhibit terror or hatred of sacred persons or objects. Even Christianity allows for the extreme possibility that *some* of these states have an evil transcendental cause.

Most scientific studies treat these symptoms as psychophysical manifestations. Some conditions historically termed demonic possession have come to be treated as epilepsy, hysteria, somnambulism, or schizophrenia.

In some traditions, the possessed individual becomes ill and is regarded by his community as

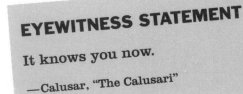

EYEWITNESS STATEMENT

It knows you now.

—Calusar, "The Calusari"

having committed some spiritual transgression; recovery is held to require expiation of his sin, often by a sacrifice. In other traditions, the possessed person is conceived of as a medium for the controlling spirit and functions as an intermediary between spirits and men. The medium's major role is to diagnose and heal other spirit-afflicted individuals. In this tradition the trance behavior of the medium is often self-induced, stimulated by drugs, drumming, or collective hysteria. In a trance, the medium appears genuinely insensible to ordinary stimuli.

Any ritual abjuration of an evil spirit to abandon an object, place, or person is, technically, an exorcism. In the Christian tradition, Jesus expelled demons by a word and stated that this act was a sign of the coming of God's Kingdom. His followers drove out demons "in His name." In the first two centuries of the Christian era, the power of exorcism was considered a special gift that might be bestowed on anyone, lay or cleric. About A.D. 250, however, there appeared a special class of the lower clergy, called exorcists (the roots of the Calusari), to whom this special function was entrusted. About the same time, exorcism became one of the ceremonies preparatory to baptism, and it has remained a symbolic part of the Roman Catholic baptismal service. The exorcism of persons possessed by demons is carefully regulated by canon law in the Roman Catholic church.

The Poltergeist

From the German *polter,* meaning a noise or racket, and *geist,* meaning spirit, the poltergeist is believed to be a disembodied spirit or supernatural force and is credited with a wide variety of disturbing and usually malicious phenomena. If they're ignored or unsatisfied with their situation, poltergeists have a tendency to escalate their actions, resorting to violent activities like throwing stones and even setting fire to clothing, furniture, or hair.

Whether minor or dangerous, poltergeist activity has some common traits. The actions are usually repetitive. Rapping sounds, for example, often repeat a particular tempo or pattern endlessly. Most activity is sporadic and unpredictable, but becomes more and more regular as the danger involved rises.

According to popular belief, a poltergeist's activity appears to concentrate on a particular member of a family, often an adolescent. When strangers are present, the unusual phenomena often cease. A large portion of those reported to be victimized suffer from hysteria.

Easy Stuff: Give yourself 1 point for each correct answer.

1. What did the child chase on his dash across the railroad track?
2. What sort of vehicle did the Calusari drive?
3. What dead animals were discovered in the grandmother's bedroom?
4. Where in the Old Country had the family come from?
5. What was the grandmother's name?

Getting Tougher: Give yourself 2 points for each correct answer.

6. How did the boys' father die?
7. What was the grandmother's apparent cause of death?
8. What startling experience did Scully and the boys' mother share?
9. Name all *three* of the Holvey children.
10. What happened to the paint in the hospital room as the Calusari began their ritual?

ANSWERS

1. A balloon.
2. A woody wagon.
3. Roosters.
4. Romania.
5. Golda.
6. His tie became entangled in a garage door mechanism and he was strangled.
7. It seemed she had been pecked to death by chickens.
8. Both found themselves thrown against a wall by unseen hands that continued to pin them there in defiance of gravity.
9. Teddy, the toddler, and Michael and Charlie, the twins.
10. It melted off the walls.

YOUR SCORE: _15_

Skeptics point out that in many instances, the activities attributed to poltergeists have been explained as natural phenomenon such as the normal creaking of boards in an old house.

Some incidents, however, defy explanation.

- Civil engineers in St. Petersburg spent six months in an office building trying and failing to identify the source of a knocking sound. They also missed the cause of a sudden downpour of water that soaked an entire department—in a building that didn't have a sprinkler system.
- A government building in Salt Lake City had desks with drawers that had a habit of sliding open and gashing the knees of employees, and also had a case of repetitive knocking. Rearranging the desks didn't solve the problem.
- A recently renovated hotel had an elevator many people claimed was occupied by a poltergeist. From time to time, for no apparent reason, the hands pointing to floor numbers would run backward or indicate the wrong floor altogether. Hardly unusual for a sixty-year-old building, except that problems with the floor indicator were typically accompanied by giggling from *beneath* the elevator.

SWASTIKAS

Many fans may have been startled by the appearance of a swastika in this episode, especially in the hands of the good guys instead of the screaming, demon-possessed child writhing on the bed and trying to sink its teeth into whoever was handy. That's because most of us associate the swastika with the Nazi Reich. The symbol, however, is neither exclusively evil nor exclusively modern.

Among the many places it has appeared is on blankets and decorative objects produced by Native American artists in the southwestern United States. Even farther south, it was a common design element on Caribe cloth paintings and Guatemalan baskets. At the extreme southern end of the New World, the design, and variations on it, were woven into cloth. In Southeast Asia, some Buddhist and Taoist religious groups have adorned temples with a reversed swastika. The direction of the arms in the design was irrelevant in the New World crafts, and both left- and right-armed forms appeared.

Sharp-eyed viewers will notice that the symbol used on *The X-Files* rotated in a direction opposite to the Nazi swastika. Prior to its notoriety during World War II, the swastika, or Broken Cross, with its roots in the same tradition as the contemporary peace symbol and the Egyptian ankh, represented the four winds, four seasons, and four compass points. Its arms, turning clockwise, indicated harmony with nature.

Munchausen Syndrome by Proxy: The infliction of fictitious illness on children by parents who use constant visits to the doctor as a form of abuse.

UNDER FIRE

Code Name: "F. Emasculata"

CASE SUMMARY

Mulder and Scully are sent in to support the federal marshal's office in a manhunt for two inmates who have escaped from a prison where a highly contagious disease has broken out. The only problem? They aren't told of the outbreak until they're inside. Whether it's an outright attempt to eliminate the agents, or just an effort to discredit them, remains to be seen.

DEEP BACKGROUND

A Modern Plague

While there's little evidence that American prisons are being used as testing grounds for experimentation in disease control, the crowded conditions in most prisons make them, unavoidably, prime hosts for modern plagues like the "F. Emasculata" disease—and the Ebola virus that's been so much in the public awareness of late.

Ebola is one of a whole group of diseases known as viral hemorrhagic fevers. Like the fictional disease in "F. Emasculata," all four families of virus (filoviruses, arenaviruses, flaviviruses, and bunyaviruses) are easily carried by insects.

One of the most frightening things about Ebola is that there's still no firm knowledge of its natural host. If the disease in "F. Emasculata" had been studied using standard procedures, as Ebola was, a swarm of scientists should have been chasing vultures through the rain forest for a closer look. Fortunately, though its origins remain unknown, the progression and symptoms of Ebola have been well documented, a first step to early detection. All forms of viral hemorrhagic fever begin with an ele-

EYEWITNESS STATEMENT

Don't believe—for a second—this is an isolated incident!

—Dr. Osbourne, "F. Emasculata"

vated temperature and aching muscles, much like the common flu. Depending on the particular virus, the disease quickly progresses until the patient develops respiratory problems, severe bleeding, kidney problems, and shock—none of which can be confused with symptoms of the viral flu. The severity of viral hemorrhagic fever can range from a relatively mild illness to death.

Discovered in Zaire in 1976, Ebola was named for a major river in the area. Until mid-1995, only three outbreaks of the disease had ever been reported among humans. The first two outbreaks occurred in 1976: one in Zaire and one in western Sudan. With the third outbreak, in Kikwit, Zaire, a concentrated effort was made to identify the carrier. Investigators unsuccessfully tested thousands of specimens from animals captured near the outbreak areas. They did, however, discover that AIDS isn't the only disease contractable by both humans and monkeys. Several local monkeys were found to have been infected, but the failure of the disease to blossom into an epidemic was related to the insular nature of monkey bands, not to their natural ability to throw it off quickly.

The disgusting bugs shown on the warthog in the opening sequence were cockroaches, assassin beetles, and mealworms, none of which belong to the *F. emasculata* group of bugs the episode was named for.

The 1995 outbreak supports the theory that Ebola is most deadly in crowded conditions like prisons and hospitals. The first patient (patient zero) appears to have been a surgical patient at a local hospital, and it was hospital staff who first developed the symptoms. The virus then spread among other patients, to the families helping care for them, and then into the community at large.

The assassin beetle (a kind of cockroach) that carried the disease in "F. Emasculata." Would you let this sit on your arm for half an hour? Scully did!

Once diagnosed, medical teams from other areas of Zaire, the Centers for Disease Control and Prevention, and the World Health Organization were parachuted in and a full quarantine was declared. Less than a month later the disease had been largely contained. The response time to an acknowledged contamination? Less than forty-eight hours.

Would you trust your life to a simple surgical mask in a Hazmat 4 situation? Scully did.

As in "F. Emasculata," the most important part of the containment process is obtaining a confirmed diagnosis and isolating all infected, or possibly infected, individuals. While Scully had to sit with a cockroach taped to her arm for half an hour, Ebola requires much less exotic tests. Diagnosis is by detection of Ebola antigens, antibodies, or genetic material, or by culture of the virus from these sources. No burrowing larvae are involved.

Diagnosis is becoming easier all the time, but a cure for Ebola, or any modern plague, is far from a reality. The continuing research on Ebola and all its variants is limited to those facilities capable of providing a high-containment lab.

John Edgar Hoover

J. Edgar Hoover

Born in our nation's capital, J. Edgar Hoover (January 1, 1895–May 2, 1972) seldom left his hometown. But, as director of the Federal Bureau of Investigation, his influence stretched from coast to coast. The legacy of the Hoover FBI years is perhaps the most contradictory in the history of American law enforcement, as quixotic as the man himself. For nearly fifty years, Hoover, as politically savvy a creature as found anywhere, *was* the FBI.

From the beginning, Hoover understood the Capitol city and its people. Politicians came and went, but civil servants stayed forever —and civil servants with legal or accounting degrees rose to higher office than other civil servants. While working days at the Library of Congress, Hoover attended night school at George Washington University until he received the law degree he hoped would mark the beginning of a glorious career. He entered the Department of Justice as a file reviewer in 1917. (Some would later comment on the convenient timing that allowed Hoover, a healthy young man, to avoid World War I under the civil service clause, a clause that wouldn't have covered him in his more prestigious position at the Library of Congress.)

Two years later he'd made himself indispensable to Attorney General A. Mitchell Palmer, who named Hoover his special assistant. He spent the remainder of the war rounding up and deporting anyone suspected of being a Bolshevik (Communist precursors). His ambition took him to the top of the Bureau of Investigation. He was named acting director in mid-1924 and, at the age of thirty, became director in 1925.

The FBI would never be the same again.

Though Hoover had desperately campaigned for his position, it wasn't all that he'd hoped for. Rocked by scandals, subjected to hatchet jobs in the press, and loathed by criminals and law-abiding citizens alike, the Bureau's reputation was, for a man who'd changed his signature and his name on discovering that a John Hoover had been passing bad checks around town, intolerable. Hoover was determined that, like his own name, his FBI would be above reproach.

Under Hoover, the training academy for agents came into being. The selection process was so stringent that acceptance into the FBI ranks had real meaning again. The agents Hoover recruited weren't thugs, but the cream of the country's universities as well as highly skilled technicians. Hoover co-opted the fingerprint files, opened one of the most sophisticated criminology labs in the world, and actively sought out high-profile cases that would bring the new FBI into the public eye. True, none of his agents were women, only a handful were any race but white, and some of his methods were a little . . . unusual, but the public and the government seemed willing to overlook all that as long as he got results.

Ever the publicist, Hoover spent the early 1930s taking on the colorful gangsters who were on the verge of becoming American folk heroes. He tended to direct his efforts against whichever crook was currently looming large in the public eye. The names on the FBI's Most Wanted List often appeared to have little to do with the severity of their crimes. Headlines piled up; Hoover was permitted larger and larger staffs; the FBI was given sweeping new responsibilities and powers. By the end of the 1930s, Roosevelt had handed Hoover the right to investigate foreign espionage on American soil and the activities of anyone even *suspected* of being a Communist or a Fascist. The definition of "suspicion" consisted of nothing more than Hoover's thought that it might be a good idea to look into so-and-so's background. That such practices were clear violations of American civil rights didn't slow either Hoover or the FBI one bit.

The chill of the Cold War set in, and Hoover's FBI not only investigated the background of suspicious individuals, but began to watch them actively. Hoover's distrust of radicals included the Black Panthers, hippies, Martin Luther King, and the Ku Klux Klan, and he appeared to see himself as America's last bastion of defense against *itself*.

Information was Hoover's Holy Grail and, despite the distances involved, every regional director was expected to send him daily reports. Criminal activity was dealt with accordingly, but material that might prove personally damaging to politicians, celebrities, community leaders—anyone who might someday prove influential—was

TRIVIA BUSTER 46

Easy Stuff: Give yourself 1 point for each correct answer.

1. How did the two inmates escape?
2. What happened to the bodies?
3. Where did the disease originate?
4. How was the disease spread?
5. Where was the last escapee when Mulder boarded the bus?

Getting Tougher: Give yourself 2 points for each correct answer.

6. What's Mulder's badge number?
7. What was the name of the project that sent the biologist in search of the bug and its enzyme?
8. The prisoner attempted to escape by bus. To where?
9. What unusual tool did Dr. Osbourne use to determine if Scully was infected or not?
10. What was the last convict's cause of death?

carefully collected into "Mr. Hoover's private papers." With those files, Hoover survived both friendly and unfriendly administrations.

As the country continued to define the civil rights of its citizens and place limits on its policing bodies, Hoover came under criticism for his dictatorial vision of the FBI, his groundless persecution of radicals, and his use of FBI resources for personal purposes. Regardless, he held on to his post until his death at seventy-seven. He'd outlasted eight presidents and eighteen attorneys general.

Though Hoover lived with his mother through his adult life until her death, though his sexual orientation was often questioned, though his personal politics were often murky and his administration of the FBI always controversial, one aspect of his life was undeniable and self-evident: He'd created a law enforcement agency whose technical expertise was unchallenged, whose record of successful cases exceeded any other force of its time, and whose agents were perhaps the best trained in the world. He'd laid the groundwork for what is now among the world's premier policing agencies.

Code Name: "Soft Light"

CASE SUMMARY

When people start disappearing—leaving nothing behind but a black smudge on the floor—Scully is asked to assist a former student in finding a solution. Her partner's theories become more and more unwelcome as bodies continue to disappear. Mulder appears less than willing to share his theories of new physics and dark matter with the skeptical Scully, or, especially, with her even more skeptical protegé.

Dark Matter: The Kindergarten Physics

DEEP BACKGROUND

If you've ever had the unsettling experience of reaching out in the dark and having your hand make contact with an unfamiliar object, you've some idea of how physicists feel about the universe right now. For example, at one time, they thought it would be easy to extrapolate the weight of the galaxy. But then some scientists began to notice some disturbing discrepancies in their measurements. You see, in order for gravity to hold something together (like our sun and its planets), there has to be a certain amount of *stuff* there to create the gravitational pull. Even between all the planets in our solar system, there's just not enough mass to create a strong enough pull to keep us together. Without the huge gravity of our sun to keep us in place, the planets would quickly spin off into the space outside our system.

Scientists then further discovered that *most* visible galaxies don't have enough mass to stick together, yet seem perfectly stable. Obviously, despite all our newfangled technology for looking at the sky, there's stuff out there that we can't see!

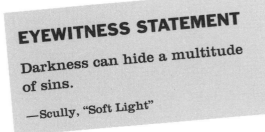

EYEWITNESS STATEMENT

Darkness can hide a multitude of sins.

—Scully, "Soft Light"

In fact, the things we can see account for only 10 percent of what *should* be out there. Ninety percent of anything is a lot, and physicists are now theorizing about what makes up this mysterious mass, or "dark matter."

What humans can't see directly, we can usually discern by watching for its effect on other things. Scientists managed to figure out the speed of light a full 200 years before they had any of the necessary tools to confirm their answer. With that in mind, it's not surprising that early speculation about the nature of dark matter has been a little exotic. If we can't see it in the usual ways, then it *must* be unusual. It's certainly very good at hiding itself.

Of the many dark matter theories floating about, no single idea accounts for all the missing mass or suggests what purpose it might have. To further complicate things, physicists, for all their sworn adherence to studying just the facts, seem to share a wish that everything be symmetrical—for every action, an equal and opposite reaction. . . . Applying that framework to the universe can lead to some exotic suppositions. For example, if the 10 percent of the mass that we can see is all formed of positive elements, a physicist might suggest that at least 10 percent of dark matter should be formed of negative elements.

Essentially, that's the theory put forward by Dr. Banton in "Soft Light," and, while it's certainly symmetrical, it's a practical nightmare. Suppose, just for a moment, that the universe *does* consist of two opposite types of matter. What happens when you bring them into contact with one another? Well, traditional physics would give us an either/or response: Either they'd cancel one another out, probably in a pretty spectacular fashion, or they'd weld themselves together like two opposite ends of a powerful magnet. If you were writing a television series, which possibility would you pick?

"Soft Light" couldn't propose that *everything* Banton's shadow touched would disintegrate, otherwise large sections of the city would disappear everytime he twitched. So, once again using the notion of symmetry, it was more practical for the writers to suggest that a human being could only disintegrate other human beings. If you accept that Banton's shadow really was composed of millions of tiny, negative specks of dark matter and if you're also willing to accept that dark matter and normal matter can't exist in proximity to one another, well, you've got all the raw ingredients of this episode.

Could it really happen? Is there some location somewhere deep in the black pockets of space where dark matter and normal matter are running into and annihilating one another? Possibly, but there's another theory that's equally likely: If dark matter is "dark" simply because we can't see it, we could be actually wading obliviously through heaps of the stuff every day.

Alphabet Soup

ACIC:	Army Criminal Investigative Command.
AFOSI:	The Air Force Office of Special Investigations, nominally responsible in the case of a confirmed UFO downing.
ASAC:	Assistant Special Agent in Charge (see SAC), reporting directly to the SAC and frequently responsible for the activities of a distinct group of agents within a division.
BATF:	Bureau of Alcohol, Tobacco, and Firearms.
CDC:	The Centers for Disease Control and Prevention, headquartered in Atlanta, Georgia.
DEA:	Drug Enforcement Agency, a sister organization to the DOJ.
DOJ:	Department of Justice, the parent department of the FBI.
INS:	Immigration and Naturalization Service.
INTERPOL:	International Criminal Police Organization.
NCIC:	National Crime Information Computer. A countrywide resource begun by the FBI, NCIC consists of a comprehensive set of databases. Information ranges from criminal records to missing persons information to fingerprint collections.
NIS:	Naval Intelligence Service.
SAC:	Special Agent in Charge, usually overseeing one of the more than fifty geographic divisions of the Federal Bureau of Investigation.

Easy Stuff: Give yourself 1 point for each correct answer.

1. What did Mulder shoot in this episode?
2. What did Dr. Chester A. Banton's company produce?
3. What was Scully's relationship to Detective Ryan?
4. Where did Banton hang out to avoid making a shadow?
5. What was Mulder's original theory about the burn marks?

Getting Tougher: Give yourself 2 points for each correct answer.

6. What was the name of Doctor Banton's company?
7. Who was Banton's first victim?
8. From what facility was Banton abducted?
9. What was the room number of the victim in the hotel?
10. How many people did Dr. Banton deliberately kill?

Code Name: "Our Town"

When a federal employee suddenly disappears in the chicken capital of Arkansas, and his rare, noncontagious disease crops up in a statistically impossible number of his neighbors, Scully begins to wonder if he hasn't been turned into chicken feed. The discovery of dozens of oddly mutilated skeletons, however, has Mulder on a different trail that leads to the chicken plant owner's odd eating habits.

CASE SUMMARY

Cannibals

Though New Guinea—where Chaco the Chicken King crashed his plane—is the second largest island in the world, it's one of the most sparsely populated—a fact some attribute to its history of cannibalism. Cannibalism has been acknowledged by all three of the island's large tribal groups: the Papuans, the Melanesians, and the Pygmies. Contrary to early theories, however, cannibalism was more likely to be associated with war than with religion or dietary preferences.

DEEP BACKGROUND

War in New Guinea was a highly ritualistic practice, tied to the supernatural world of spirits. Guerrilla tactics were never used until formal notification of the intent to make war was delivered. Attacks on women and children were strictly taboo among most tribes. Holy men and women were required to be present for any major skirmish to ensure that none of the rules of engagement were broken. And, perhaps most important, when an enemy was killed, his soul had to be accounted for immediately. To leave even an enemy wandering the supernatural world was unconscionable. It was this last rule, and the Papuans' method of ensuring that the spirit didn't wander, that led to cannibalism.

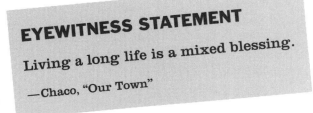

EYEWITNESS STATEMENT

Living a long life is a mixed blessing.

—Chaco, "Our Town"

The spirit was considered a material object, part of which permeated the body, another part of which was tied to the material soul but not tied to the real world until the material soul was destroyed. As might be expected, the destruction of the material soul was tied to the destruction of the body. The Papuans believed there was a limited amount of material soul, that their people would die out if the soul were liberated and unavailable to the next generation. So the soul must be returned to the tribe in some way. That way, at least in the case of war casualties, which were considered unnatural deaths, was by ingestion—cannibalism.

Much more esoteric, and more likely to have been encountered by Mr. Chaco, was the cargo cult, a fairly modern belief that, in the fullness of time, the white man's treasures would be delivered into the hands of the Papuans by ships and planes loaded down with goods. The advent of World War II, when scores of planes and ships sought shelter, crashed, or sank in the area, provided more immediate wealth than the island had ever seen. Were Chaco to have actually crashed on New Guinea in 1944, it was more likely he would have been robbed than eaten. Why eat something as awful tasting as a testosterone-filled adult male when he didn't even have a material soul to reclaim?

However, it's possible Chaco would have been adopted into whatever tribe claimed the contents of his plane. He would have been initiated as an adult, thereby learning of the cannibalistic rites.

Sound FX

Though sound is perhaps the most ephemeral aspect of any television project, it's the one pervasive element that can join disparate images and action. In series TV, it can link similar themes across episodes, as was the case with Mark Snow's use of the same score for the scenes Mulder shared with Sophie the gorilla and the Jersey Devil. It isn't until you see a scene being shot, however, that you realize how much sound work is done away from the set and from the actors. As little as a quarter of the soundtrack may be laid down during original filming. Each section of the track, from dialogue to special effects, is recorded separately and not combined until the final rerecording session.

DIALOGUE

While microphone placement on the tight confines of a television set is more stable than on the larger soundstages favored by films, nothing can change the fact that David Duchovny is a foot taller, and thus a foot closer to the microphones, than Gillian Anderson. Canadian production crews eventually adopted ADR, automatic dialogue replacement, which uses digitization to smooth out these differences.

SOUND EFFECTS

Every sound heard by the audience, even subliminally, with the exception of speech, music, and natural movements, is considered a sound effect. In the case of explosions, gunshots, or knocking sounds, it's not unusual for actors to have to react to noises they're not actually hearing. The click of Flukeman's "teeth" against the glass in "The Host" was a happy coincidence of action and resulting sound. The production schedule for *The X-Files* has often been so tight that sounds in the final cut can come as a surprise to those who were there when the episode was made.

MUSIC

Music falls into two types for filming purposes. Background music, which is meant to emphasize on-screen action—crests for dramatic points and mellows for tender moments. Source music is intended to be heard by the characters as well as the audience. An example of source music is Bobby Darin's "Beyond the Sea" in the episode of the same name, or the music playing on the car radio when Duane Barry is stopped by the police officer. While source and background music have different purposes, neither is likely to be recorded during initial shooting. Besides possibly drowning out the dialogue, it would be nearly impossible to create smooth joins from shot to shot or scene to scene.

The Music of Mark Snow

It's rare for a musician's work to be noticed on television. While film soundtracks are often sold commercially, television scores seldom gain notoriety as anything except background noise. Luckily for 'Philes, Mr. Snow's music will shortly be released on his own CD.

The Work of Mark Snow

A Brief Filmography

Caroline at Midnight, 1994
Moment of Truth: Caught in the Crossfire, 1994
Oldest Living Confederate Widow Tells All, 1994
The Substitute Wife, 1994
Witness to the Execution, 1994
The Man with Three Wives, 1993
In the Line of Duty: A Cop for the Killing, 1990
Disaster at Silo 7, 1988
Blood & Orchids, 1986

Code Name: "Anasazi"

CASE SUMMARY

Mulder's being drawn deeper than ever before into the dangerous world of conspiracies—and his career, his family, and his very life could be at stake. Trying to find answers, both partners are in for a shock when Scully takes him to the one man who can decode sensitive documents recording the government's involvement in alien contact.

What's in a Name?

DEEP BACKGROUND

One of the fun parts of creating a piece of fiction is the freedom to play with character and place names. Take Crowley High and Mrs. Paddock in "Die Hand Die Verletzt," for example. The former is a reference to the founder of the modern Wicca religion mentioned in that episode, Alistair Crowley. The latter is much older, harking back to Shakespeare's time when the word meant *toad,* not corral.

Unlike print writers who can slip in the occasional acknowledgment, film and television writers have limited options for thanking those who have supported their efforts. In "Die Hand Die Verletzt," there is a subtle tribute to an on-line fan whose name, Ausbury, was used as the surname of a family central to the episode. In "Little Green Men," the flight manifest contained not only George Hale, Mulder's alias, but also the names of more than a dozen real-world fans.

Several members of the crew have been immortalized on film without ever appearing before the camera. "Val Stefoff," a tribute to Vladamir Stefoff, first assistant director, was Scully's alias in "E.B.E." when The Lone Gun-

EYEWITNESS STATEMENT

Gentlemen, that was the phone call I never wanted to get.

—The Smoking Man, "Anasazi"

men issued passes to get the agents into a secure facility. The name of Tom Braidwood, first assistant director, and also Frohike of The Lone Gunmen, replaced that of Howard Graves on Graves's parking space in "Shadows."

The names of The Lone Gunmen should spark an X-Phile's curiosity. Frohike isn't the most common of names, but coincidentally one Robert F. Frohike was once assistant secretary of defense and a close acquaintance of Hoover's. Byers may have drawn his name from the real-life Billy Byers, a Texas oilman and another close friend of Hoover's. And, while none of Hoover's inner circle was named Langly, a suspicious fan might ponder the tie between The Lone Gunman's name and the CIA headquarters and training facility in Langley, Virginia.

Regulation U.S. government ammunition.

Literary allusions haven't been in short supply either, as seen in the "Colony" and "End Game" two-parter when a mysterious CIA agent who called himself Ambrose Chapel appeared on the scene. As was the case in the Hitchcock film *The Man Who Knew Too Much,* when the phrase "Ambrose Chapel," referring to a church, was assumed to belong to a nonexistent person, *The X-Files'* Ambrose Chapel wasn't a real person either, or, if he was, it was just a convenient alias adopted for the moment by a shapeshifter. Other literary references go way back in time, as with Gird Thomas in "Red Museum," a clear allusion to the Peeping Tom of Coventry fame.

Finally, it should come as no surprise that the names of "Fox Mulder" and "Dana Scully" were given thorough consideration before the characters came to life on screen. While it's been speculated that "Fox" was a nod to the Fox network, according to Chris Carter it was the name of a childhood friend. "Mulder" has an even closer connection for Carter; it's his mother's maiden name. A more light-hearted approach led to "Scully"—a tribute to Vincent Scully, voice of the L.A. Dodgers for many seasons.

Personnel Dossier
#118-366-047

Name:	**Fox Mulder**
Position:	Special Agent, DOJ
	Federal Bureau of Investigation
Currently Assigned:	The X-Files

Personal Information

DOB: October 11, 1960
Height: 6'0"   Hair: Medium Brown   Eyes: Hazel
Marital Status: Single/Never Married/No Dependents
Parents: Separated
Siblings: One sister, Samantha T. Mulder, disappeared from the family home November 27, 1973. Whereabouts remain unknown.
In Case of Emergency: Agent Dana Scully, Washington Bureau
Religious Affiliation—Unknown

Educational Information

Agent Mulder graduated Oxford with a degree in psychology. Graduated high in his class, FBI Training Academy, Quantico.

Work History (chronological)

Completed Psychology Residency
Assigned Violent Crimes Section, Behavioral Science
Assigned X-Files, Field Agent
Assigned Intelligence Division, Communications
Reassigned X-Files, Field Agent

Supervisory Notes (chronological)

1. On the recommendation of his instructors, and in keeping with his graduate training, Agent Mulder has been assigned to the Behavioral Sciences Unit of the Violent Crimes Section.
2. An inquiry into the death of his former partner determined that Agent Mulder acted properly and was in no way responsible for Agent Lamana's death.
3. A notation of exemplary service in the Props case has been added to this file.

Easy Stuff: Give yourself 1 point for each correct answer.

1. What computer system did the Thinker penetrate?
2. Where did Mulder meet the Thinker?
3. What was exposed in the quarry by the earthquake?
4. Who shot Mulder?
5. What does *Anasazi* mean?

Getting Tougher: Give yourself 2 points for each correct answer.

6. What did Mulder call the original UFO documents?
7. What language was used to encrypt the documents?
8. Where did Mulder's father work before his retirement?
9. Other than Bill Mulder and Dana Scully, what familiar name appears in the encoded documents?
10. What did Scully find in the basement of Mulder's building?

1. The Defense Department's.
2. At the National Botanical Gardens in Washington, D.C.
3. A refrigerated boxcar filled with bodies.
4. Scully.
5. The ancient aliens.
6. The Holy Grail.
7. Navajo.
8. The State Department.
9. Duane Barry.
10. A dialysis filter in his water tank, which probably delivered some sort of hallucinogenic drug.

YOUR SCORE: 15

As in the Season One finale, an unusual message appeared in the credits for "Anasazi"— ÉÍ 'AANEÍÍGÓÓ 'ÁHOOT'É: "The Truth Is Out There" in Navajo.

Did you see "do-re-mi-fa-so-la-ti-do" in Navajo code?

4. At his own request, and with the consent of his superiors, Agent Mulder has undertaken the task of investigating some previously unsolved cases. It is anticipated that this is a temporary reassignment to help clear a backlog, and that Agent Mulder will soon be returning to VCS.

5. As Agent Mulder shows no indication of returning to his previous assignment in the near future, an informal inquiry into the value of his present assignment will be instituted to determine if his skills might be better employed outside the X-Files.

6. Agent Dana Scully has been assigned to the X-Files and will be reporting directly to the administration.

7. Following some unorthodox investigations, it has been determined that Agent Mulder will be reassigned to a regular field position. (Transfer to Intelligence, Communications, and Surveillance.)

8. Under the direction of Assistant Director Skinner, both agents Mulder and Scully have returned to the X-Files. Duration of this assignment has yet to be specified.

In Our Own Backyard

The truth is out there, all right, and it's often stranger than fiction. When students found this skull in Chaco Valley (the valley that inspired the name of the Chicken King in "Our Town") they were understandably shocked. Found on the ancestral land of Anasazi

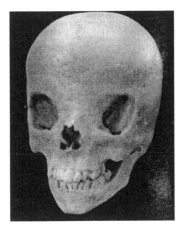

Indians, it, like the skulls in the buried boxcar in "Anasazi," exhibited the huge eye sockets, almost indiscernible nasal cavities, and diminutive mouth that appears in the vast majority of drawings of aliens made by abductees.

Is it proof that aliens exist? That the Anasazi really did have, as their name ("Ancient Aliens" in Navajo) suggests, a deep connection to an alien species friendly to humans? Maybe, but medical records show that it's more likely to have come from a child suffering from an unusual congenital bone defect called oxycephalia.

Still . . .

Trivia Buster Scoresheet

This is it. You've answered all the questions; you've kept track of all your scores. Now let's see what sort of X-Phile material you are.

1-100   Boy, are you out of the loop! The guy selling coffee and doughnuts outside knows more than you. Perhaps you should invest in a VCR, take a two-week vacation, and catch up on the important things in life.

101-200   I hear they're still hiring at the CIA. . . .

201-300   Better luck next time. You've got a good grasp of the basics, but those advanced questions stumped you. Either watch reruns or pay closer attention when real X-Philes ramble on.

301-400   Talk about a squeaker! I suppose we could give you wire-tap duty for a couple of years.

401-500   Couldn't promise you a plum assignment at the Bureau, but, if you can type, there's a guy named Danny who's been working some long hours. Seems like he never leaves the building—he could probably use a gofer.

501-600   Well, finally! You wouldn't believe how much trouble it is to find real FBI potential—especially since they upped the passing grade from 50 percent to 70 percent.

601-700   With a memory like yours, I think we may have the perfect position for you. Just take this hallway, turn left, and take the stairs all the way to the basement.

620

701-735   Wait a minute . . . weren't you seen in the company of a man known to be exceptionally fond of Morley cigarettes?

If You'd Like to Know More . . .

Ackerknecht, Erwin H. *A Short History of Medicine.* Baltimore: The Johns Hopkins University Press, 1982.

Asimov, Isaac. *Asimov On Numbers.* New York: Doubleday & Company, Inc., 1977.

Bailey, C. A. *Advanced Cryogenics.* London: Plenum Press, 1971.

Bernstein, Carl and Bob Woodward. *All the President's Men.* New York: Simon & Schuster, 1974.

Bishop, Peter. *Fifth Generation Computers: Concepts, Implementations, and Uses.* New York: Ellis Horwood Limited, 1986.

Block, Eugene B. *Science vs. Crime: The Evolution of the Police Lab.* San Francisco: Cragmont Publications, 1979.

Brennan, Richard P. *Levitating Trains and Kamikaze Genes.* Toronto: John Wiley & Sons, Inc., 1990.

Budge, Sir Ernest Wallis. *Herb-Doctors and Physicians in the Ancient World.* Chicago: Ares Publishers Inc., 1927.

Cone, Joseph. *Fire Under the Sea.* New York: William Morrow and Company Inc., 1991.

Corliss, William R. *Tornados, Dark Days, Anomalous Precipitation, and Related Weather Phenomena.* Glen Arm, Md.: The Sourcebook Project, 1983.

Culpeper, Nicolas. *The Compleat Herbal.* 1597.

Dawson, George Gordon. *Healing: Pagan and Christian.* London: Society for Promoting Christian Knowledge, 1977.

Dawson, Warren R. *The Bridle of Pegasus*. London: Methuen & Company, Ltd., 1930.

Dethlefsen, Thorwalk. *Voices from Other Lives*. New York: M. Evans and Company, Inc., 1976.

Dyson, James L. *The World of Ice*. New York: Alfred A. Knopf, 1963

Freedland, Nat. *The Occult Explosion*. New York: G. P. Putnam's Sons, 1972.

Gentry, Curt. *J. Edgar Hoover: The Man and the Secrets*. New York: W. W. Norton, 1991.

Glushkov, Viktor M. *Introduction to Cybernetics*. New York: Academic Press, 1966.

Huxley, Francis. *The Invisibles: Voodoo Gods in Haiti*. New York: McGraw-Hill Book Company, 1966.

Jacob, Dorothy. *Cures and Curses: A Witch's Guide to Gardening*. New York: Taplinger Publishing Company, 1967.

Jameson, Eric. *The Natural History of Quackery*. Michael Joseph Inc., 1961.

Kee, Howard Clark. *Medicine, Miracle, and Magic in New Testament Times*. London: Cambridge University Press, 1986.

Kelsey, Morton T. *The Christian and the Supernatural*. Minneapolis, Minn.: Sugsburg Publishing House, 1976.

McKinnel, Robert Gillmore. *Cloning: Of Frogs, Mice, and Other Animals*. Minneapolis: University of Minnesota Press, 1979.

Maeterlinck, Maurice. *Light Beyond*. Freeport, N.Y.: Books for Libraries Press, 1972.

Malcolm, James F. *Christianity and Psychic Facts*. Stirling, Scotland: Observer Press.

Messick, Hank. *John Edgar Hoover*. New York: David McKay Company Inc., 1972.

Moore, E. Garth. *Try the Spirits*. New York: Oxford University Press, 1977.

Morgan, Jim. *Secret Agenda: Watergate, Deep Throat, and the CIA*. New York: Random House, 1984.

Oberg, James E. *UFOs & Outer Space Mysteries: A Sympathetic*